Does It Matter
If God Exists?

Does It Matter If God Exists?

Understanding Who God Is and What He Does for Us

Millard J. Erickson

**Study Guides and
Teaching Suggestions
by Roger and Phyllis Hedberg**

Baker Books

A Division of Baker Book House Co
Grand Rapids, Michigan 49516

Published by Baker Books
a division of Baker Book House Company
PO Box 6287, Grand Rapids, Michigan 49516-6287

Printed in the United States of America

Library of Congress Cataloging-in-Publication Data

Erickson, Millard J.
    Does it matter if God exists? : understanding who God is and what he does for us / Millard J. Erickson ; study guides and teaching suggestions by Roger and Phyllis Hedberg.
        p.   cm.
    Chapters 2–5 were presented previously as lectures during the Midwest Bible Conference at Hannibal-LaGrange College, Hannibal, Missouri, March 16–18, 1992 and chapters 6, 8 and 9 were delivered as the Staley Lectures at Southern College of Seventh-Day Adventists, Collegedale, Tennessee, March 11–12, 1993.
    ISBN 08010-5477-X (pbk.)
    1. God. 2. Christian life. 3. Pastoral theology. I. Hedlund, Roger and Phyllis. II. Title.
BT102.E74   1996
231'.044—dc20   95-50283

To my brother,
Stanley O. Erickson

Contents

Preface   9

1. A Question Worth Asking   11
2. Here Comes the Future   21
3. Somebody Knows Your Name   39
4. Is Anyone in Charge?   57
5. Something Does Not Move   75
6. The Universe Right Side Up   93
7. Have You Checked Your I.D. Lately?   111
8. Is That All There Is?   127
9. Strength Out of Weakness   145
10. Will Evil Finally Win?   161
11. Give Me Liberty or Give Me Death!   179
12. Getting Out the Spot   197
13. So What?   215

Teaching Suggestions   223

Preface

It has struck me as I reflect upon American society and to a considerable extent, all western societies, that God is perhaps like Rodney Dangerfield, who says, "I don't get no respect." Or perhaps he is treated the same way the comic strip character, Ziggy, is when he complains to his psychiatrist that no one listens to him, and the psychiatrist calls out to the waiting room, "Next!" Within American society, large numbers of persons seem to live without any conscious relationship to God. Either they have no belief in him or, if they do, he is not really part of their lives in a way that makes any significant difference to them. While God is generally believed in by more than 90 percent of Americans and treated deferentially, he is not a vital force in the lives of most of them. Consciously or unconsciously, many persons do not think of God as making any real difference.

It is the contention of this book that the question of God's existence is of crucial importance, for the existence of the Christian God has far-reaching implications for our life and experience. Our very living out of our own existence involves us in numerous questions, some of which are sensed only dimly at the edges of our experience. However, these questions are basic in nature, and God is vastly important to them. The exploration of these questions and the exhibition of the relationship of God to them is the special purpose of this book.

Two contrasting approaches to the question of the starting point for Christianity can currently be found within the church. One approach begins with the needs of humans and seeks to show how Christianity can meet those needs. The other emphasizes the importance of God and the truth and authority of his revelation. The former faces the danger of being merely wish fulfillment, the latter the danger of seeming harsh and unattractive. If, however, God has created humans in his own image and has placed within them a need and a hunger for fellowship with him, then he is indeed the satisfaction of the deepest needs of the human heart, although not always in ways that would be immediately and consciously evident to the human, such as the transformation of personal thoughts and values. This book is built upon this conviction and seeks to show unbeliever and believer alike that true fulfillment in life can only be found through giving oneself fully to God through Jesus Christ.

I wish to thank those who have given me the opportunity to test these ideas and have assisted me in thinking through them. Some portions of this volume were presented at two institutions: chapters 2–5 were presented previously as lectures during the Midwest Bible Conference at Hannibal-LaGrange College, Hannibal, Missouri, March 16–18, 1992 and chapters 6, 8, and 9 were delivered as the Staley Lectures at Southern College of Seventh-Day Adventists, Collegedale, Tennessee, March 11–12, 1993, a series cut short by the "snow storm of the century." I appreciate the hospitality of both institutions and especially Dr. Barry Morgan and Dr. Robert Bergen of Hannibal-LaGrange College and Dr. Jack Blanco of Southern College for inviting me. The questions and comments of those in attendance at the lectures helped me immensely in sharpening my thinking. Mr. Jim Weaver of Baker Book House was of great help in shepherding this project through the publication process. I especially appreciate the work of Roger and Phyllis Hedberg, who wrote the supplementary material. Roger is a seminary graduate with many years of pastoral experience, and Phyllis is a seminary Christian education graduate, former local church director of Christian education and denominational director of children's work. Their experience and skills did much to make this a more usable volume.

It is my wish and my prayer that the questions and observations in this small volume may be used by God to draw the reader closer to him.

1

A Question
Worth Asking

In the mid–1960s, the headlines screamed out the news: "God is dead!" Even such secular news magazines as *Time* magazine carried stories regarding a new theology (or perhaps, more correctly, atheology), known as the "death of God" movement. That particular theology was of rather short duration, so that some soon after spoke of the death of the death of God. Yet the question which this movement turned into an answer is still very much with us. Sometimes I manufacture a headline that says, "God Is Dead," and hold it up before a church audience or a seminary class. After reading from an article purportedly in that paper, I ask them these questions, or perhaps more correctly, ask them to ask themselves the questions, "What if you became convinced that God really was dead? What difference would it make in your life?"

These are important questions which I would like you to think about with me for a moment. What if there really is no God? What difference would that make in your life, your understanding of things, the way you approach life and other persons? Or perhaps, for you the questions may need to be stated the other way around. Perhaps you do not really believe. Perhaps you are, in practice or in theory, a person who does not really believe there is a God. What difference would it make in your understanding of things and your way of living if you became convinced that there really is a God, an active, powerful being who has created us and everything else that exists, and who is in control of what goes on within our world? Or, what does it mean logically if you are right that there is no God? Perhaps you have been living on borrowed capital, as it were, living in part upon the basis of things that are only true if there is a God, in whom you do not believe. What should life be like if you were consistent with your beliefs? Or, if you are a believer, what should the fact of God mean if you really thought it out consistently? How should you be living in light of this belief which you hold?

These questions are posing a thought-experiment. If there is a God, then there is nothing you or I can do to put him to death, objectively. Conversely, if there is no God, none of us can bring him into existence by any effort of our own. Thus, we cannot conduct an actual experiment to try out life with and without God. We can, however, create a hypothetical situation, imagining what it would be like if there were (or were not) a God. This is done by thinking out the logical implications of each of those positions. Something similar is sometimes done in investing, where persons create a hypothetical portfolio of stocks without actually buying and selling them. The portfolio exists only "on paper," or in the "investor's" imagination. This is one way to test a theory of investing without actually risking any money. The same thing can be done with gambling. My wife and I once attended a greyhound race track in Corpus Christi, Texas. We each placed imaginary bets, announced to each other our choice before the beginning of each race, then compared our results. My wife, who subscribed to the double-or-nothing approach, "won" considerably more than I did.

Before we proceed too far with this thought–experiment, however, we should ask ourselves what it is that we are actually talking about. For the death of God meant several different things to different theologians in the Death of God movement and may have several different meanings today. Depending upon which of these conditions may apply to you, the solution may be quite different. To some of these persons, the death of God meant the death of the experience of God. He had been, but was no longer, a meaningful element in their experience of life. Whereas previously they had experienced him in worship, now they had a profound lack of sense of his presence. Going to worship was like going to someone's house and finding that there was no one at home. Many of these were persons whose religious experience was related to the idea of God meeting them in an encounter in which they were absolutely sure of his presence, but which had to be initiated by him since they were unable to do anything to induce that presence. Now, however, God did not seem to initiate such an encounter.

Beyond the absence of an experience of God, there was for many an experience of the absence of God. Certain features of their personal experience, or of their experience of the whole of reality, seemed to argue that God must not be there. In particular, the problem of evil seemed to constitute a real obstacle to belief in an all-powerful God. The presence of evil in nature, such as earthquakes, tornadoes, hurricanes, and volcanic eruptions, as well as such dread diseases as cancer, multiple sclerosis, leukemia, and cystic fibrosis, seems to argue that God either is absent, indifferent, malevolent, or does not exist at all. Perhaps most disturbing of all, however, are the so-called "moral evils," the cruelty to and exploitation of persons by other persons. How the highest of God's creatures could treat fellow human beings this way is a continuing cause of amazement, to say the very least.

A second variety of those who believed God was dead actually seemed to hold that God was inconceivable. There was no longer any way to think of God. Part of this was a result of the dominance of empirical science, with its treatment of those things which can be experienced as being the most truly real. Science could demonstrate its beliefs by pointing to sense data. Beyond that, the application of its findings in technology gave powerful practical confirmation of those claims. Theology, on the other hand, had nothing to match the technological wonders of television, fax transmissions, space launches, and heart transplants.

Part of this is due to the fact that the acts which formerly were considered to be performed by God are now adequately completed by other means. For example, God was the solver of problems. In biblical times, if one was seriously ill, one prayed to God, who healed and restored. If one's wife were barren, one prayed to God, he answered the prayer, and, in biblical terminology, he "opened her womb." If there was a drought, one prayed for rain, and God sent it. Now, however, God is no longer needed to perform these functions. In a case of infertility, one visits the gynecologist, preferably a specialist in infertility, who prescribes a fertility pill, and an entire litter of children is born. If there is drought, a cloud with a little bit of moisture is found, a plane is flown over it, the cloud is seeded with silver iodide or some similar substance, and down comes the rain. God is displaced as the solver of problems.

The other function God previously performed was as the answer to mysteries. Where did the universe come from? How did life originate? How did human beings, with the complexity of their minds and spirits, come into existence? Certainly, said the conventional argument, there must be a God, an almighty creator and designer, who stands behind all of this. Numerous other puzzles similarly called for an answer which seemed best given by the idea of God. Today, however, this is not necessarily the case. Science offers answers in terms of natural forces. For example, the universe is believed to have originated in a "big bang," when all matter was concentrated in one spot and then exploded outward, bringing into existence the entire universe with all its stars, planets, and other entities. Life began through chance happenings, the combination of atoms, motion, chance, and time. Then, through a process known as survival of the fittest, more complex forms arose by chance (mutations). Since these mutations were better able to survive in a competitive context, they persisted and other life forms died out. So eventually, through this process of evolution, humans finally arrived on the earth. Given these alternatives, the role of God as answer to the mysteries of the universe and life also disappeared.

Thirdly, there was the sense by some that the death of God meant simply the loss of the reality of God. He was somehow obsolete, an appropriate member of another period in time, but not someone who fit in the modern world. He belonged in an earlier, simpler world, but not in our modern, scientific world. It is as if one went into an ultra-modern house. This house contains all of the most recent technology. Climate control is automatic; the owner simply sets the desired temperature and humidity, and the climate control system automatically adjusts by heating or cooling and humidifying or dehumidifying as needed. An electronic air cleaner purifies the air. A central vacuum system with outlets in each wall enables one to clean the house by carrying only the hose around, with the mechanism remaining centrally located in the basement. Being located in the colder part of the country, this house has automatic heating units on the gutters to assure that they do not become frozen. Heating coils are imbedded in the driveway so that when snow falls, it melts and runs off rather than collecting. There is an entertainment center with a television, high fidelity stereophonic

DOES IT MATTER IF GOD EXISTS?

radio and CD, telephone answering machine, perhaps even a fax machine. The latest model washer, dryer, and dishwasher are found in the utility room. But then, in the corner of the kitchen where the refrigerator-freezer would ordinarily be found, there is an old style icebox, which cools and preserves food by the melting of ice. Periodically, a new block of ice must be inserted, and the drain emptied. Such an appliance would seem strangely out of place in a modern home such as that, generations behind time.

Yet that, says this way of thinking, is what God is like in our day. Believers live in two worlds. For one hour on Sundays, from eleven A.M. to noon, people come to church and live in a world in which axeheads float and donkeys speak, food is miraculously multiplied, and people are raised from the dead. Then they leave church, get into their air-conditioned automobiles with automatic transmission, power brakes, power steering, power seats, power door locks, power windows, anti-lock brakes, traction control, and cruise control. They live in a different world for that one hour than they do during the rest of the week. The fact of the matter is that God is out of place in the modern world in which most of us reside and do our actual living. The death of God, for such people, means that God has ceased to be a part of the world in which we live.

Finally, for some of the death of God people, this idea meant that God as a separate being, outside the world, had ceased to be. This was not through his actual expiration, but rather through his transformation into an existence totally within this creation. God does not now reside outside the world as "a being" but rather is part of the being of every person, dwelling immanently within the human race. He is to be found within every one of us.

Perhaps for some of my readers one or more of these phenomena describes your experience. Possibly for you there is no experience of God. You may go to church and the great songs which stir others, or perhaps once stirred you, have no real effect upon you. The idea of relating to God seems unreal. Prayer does not appear to take hold upon anyone, seeming rather to be a conversation with yourself. Or perhaps your experience is of the absence of God. Personal tragedy, such as the death of a loved one or a great deal of suffering from disease or injury, may cause you to ask, "Where was God when this happened?" Or possibly your awareness of the massive suffering and injustice in the world poses continually the question, "Doesn't God care about these people?"

Perhaps you simply find the idea of God too difficult to conceive. In a world in which reality is increasingly identified with what can be seen and touched, to relate to an unseen God is difficult. God may seem to be unnecessary, since we have found ways to deal with most of the problems in our world and understand the things for which God previously had to be posited as an answer. Or perhaps he appears to be an outmoded carryover from a day when people believed in spirits and thought that diseases were a result of demon possession, rather than being caused by microorganisms. Or, possibly, the traditional God who is great, mighty, and far removed has been displaced by the idea of a god who is within everyone and everything. Thus, in a sense, we are God, and have no need of anything external to ourselves collectively. Prayer has been replaced by turning inward or by meditation.

Suppose that these things are true, in whatever form. Suppose that there is no one who has created us. We are rather simply the product of chance occurrences among physical particles. Further, there is no intelligent, powerful being who is in charge of our world, directing it to his preplanned goals and ends. There is no one outside of us to answer prayer. It must be done by each of us or by our combined, cooperative effort. When we come to the end of our resources, there is no one to take over and supply the strength and the wisdom we need. We must, by the best of our insight and planning, attempt to understand the world and the future. No superhuman force is at work, combatting evil. If we are merely part of the faceless mob within society, there is no one in charge who knows each of us as unique individuals and cares about us. There is no one able to forgive us, not merely of the individual wrongs we do to individuals, but of those wrongs done against persons unable to forgive us, or against society in a larger sense. And there is nothing beyond life. Death is the end, not only of life as we know it, but of everything.

Suppose, however, on the other hand, that there really is an all-powerful, all-knowing, and good God. Such a God has created all that is, including us human beings. Such a God is in control of all that happens within this creation. He not only watches over each of us individually, but he guides the whole process of history. He is able to take what is evil or intended for evil, and use it to accomplish his good purposes. He also gives life beyond death, a life in which there will be a judgment that guarantees that justice is done and that future rewards and punishments correspond to the state of the persons concerned.

DOES IT MATTER IF GOD EXISTS?

For some time, Christians have been concerned with the question of whether there is a God, and have sought to show nonbelievers that this is indeed the case. Yet, in recent years it has become increasingly apparent that for many people the question of whether there is a God has become secondary to the question of what difference it makes. Indeed, skepticism about the latter question has in some cases precluded even asking the former question. I would contend, however, that even in the experience of the most secular individual there are certain questions implied, if not asked overtly. Some of these are: *Does anyone know and care about me as an individual? Am I truly free? Is life really going anywhere? Is there help available to me when I come to the end of my strength?* I would further argue that God, the Christian God as revealed in the Bible, constitutes an answer to these deeply felt questions, and a better answer than the alternatives. Thus, he is enormously important. While that importance does not render it certain that he exists, it does make the posing of the question of his existence extremely important.

Noting the questions to which God is the answer also gives us a greater understanding of who God is, for the question frequently sheds a great deal of light upon the answer. Indeed, failure to recognize the question may result in considerable misunderstanding of the answer. This is seen in the game show, "Jeopardy," as well as the Great Karnack skits in which Johnny Carson used to engage periodically on the Tonight Show. One of my favorite such jokes is this. Answer: Four score and seven years ago. Question: What happens when a bases-loaded home run is hit, and when was the last one hit in a major-league all-star game? The meaning of those five words is quite different when understood in relationship to this question than if the question is believed to be, "What are the opening words of the Gettysburg Address?"

These questions pose for us the question of what God really means. Does the existence of God make any difference, or is the world and our experience simply the same regardless of whether he is? These are the issues we will be pursuing together in the chapters which follow. Whether you are a believer wondering what real difference your faith in God really makes, an unbeliever wondering what you may be missing, or a person uncertain about whether there is a God or not but also uncertain what difference it would make, I invite you to explore with me something of what God means in our world of experience today.

Study Guide

Key Questions

1. How would you answer the question: "What if I became convinced that God really was dead?" Take time to write your answers. Use the questions of the second paragraph of the chapter to help you think through your answers. Or, if you do not believe in the existence of God, write your answer to the question "What difference would it make in my understanding of things and my way of living if I became convinced that there really is an active, powerful being who has created us and everything else that exists and who is in control of what goes on within our world?"

2. Describe the four views of the **death of God** adherents. Have you, or do you now look at the subject of God and hold to one of these views? Why? What led you to think this way?

3. If you are a believer, spend time with the questions "What should the fact of God mean if I really think it out consistently?" and "How should I be living in light of this belief I hold?"

Bible Investigation

1. Read the story of the life of Saul recorded in 1 Samuel 9–11, 13, 15, 18, 19, 23, 28, and 31. Ask the same questions of Saul that you asked yourself in **Key Questions** #1 above. What led him to regard God, or not regard him, as he did?

2. Read the story of the life of the Apostle Paul as recorded in Acts 26:12–20. How would he answer the same questions?

Personal Application

Do you feel you live consistently with your beliefs about God? How does believing that God exists, or not believing, make you different from others who believe differently? How does what you believe about the existence of God affect how you live today? What will you do to witness to the fact that you believe in the existence of God? Or, if you do not believe, are there some things you do that counter your lack of belief because they are essentially assumptions based on the existence of God?

For Further Thought

1. Read John 18:37–38 where Pilate asks, "What is truth?" and from Acts 17:16–34 where Paul confronts the Athenians and foreigners gathered at the Areopagus. Do you agree that pursuit of truth is a universal human trait?
2. Study Scriptures that identify Christ with God. Include John 1:1–3; 10:30, 38; 1 Corinthians 1:24; Colossians 1:15–17, 19; 2:2–3, 9–10; 1 John 5:20.
3. Think about it. These are among the questions you'll be considering in your study of *Does It Matter If God Exists?*
   (1) What is the basis for your confidence and security?
   (2) Where do you receive comfort in sorrow and peace in times of disappointment and frustration?
   (3) What do you do when your strength is weak? Where do you go to renew your strength?
   (4) What is your attitude toward death? Do you fear it? If so, how do you deal with that fear?
   (5) Do you feel free? Do you know what real freedom is?
   (6) Do you know how to handle guilt feelings?

2

Here Comes the Future

"The times, they are a-changing," said the words of a popular song of a few years ago. That was a reminder of the constant fact of change, which makes itself so apparent to us daily. Yet that truth was not something just discovered recently. Several centuries before the time of Christ, the ancient Greek philosopher, Heraclitus, said, "No man can step into the same stream twice." With the passing of even an instant, different molecules of water are flowing by, and even a man is not quite the same person he was a moment earlier. In the midst of the discussion which those early pre-Socratic philosophers had about the nature of ultimate reality, Heraclitus was convinced that change was the most characteristic feature of reality. To be real is to be in process. Erickson's seventeenth law of education says that whenever there is a teacher who says "yea," there will be a student who says, "nay." True to this law, Heraclitus had a student named Zeno, who contended that there is no change, no motion. "No man can step into the same stream once," was Zeno's maxim. All motion is illusory. It only seems to take place; it does not really happen. Zeno worked out his famous paradox, to demonstrate this. One cannot get from A to B, he argued, because to do so one must first go to C, which is halfway, but to get to C, one must first go to D, which is halfway, and so on. Thus, one can never get there. It is a sort of infinite regress.

Time, however, has shown that in at least this case the teacher rather than the student was right. In our day we have read of "future shock," which was Alvin Toffler's label for our reaction as we strive to cope with the rapid change taking place around us, and, for that matter, within us. One of the most popular formal philosophies of our day is process philosophy, which emphasizes that the basic element of reality is not substance but event, that change and development are characteristic of all reality, including (in process theology) God himself. Not only is change occurring, but it is accelerating, and we struggle to keep up. The term "rapidation," was coined as a label for this accelerating change. All of us, in one way or another, feel this tendency, and we experience a certain amount of tension or uneasiness as a result.

In view of this fact and this type of experience, one aspect of God's nature is especially appropriate and helpful. It is the future dimension of God, the fact that he is not a being who lives only in the past or in the present, but also in the future. This is emphasized within this text. There are two ways of translating the Hebrew name of God in Exodus 3:14. It can either be translated, "I am," and "I am who I am," or it can be translated "I will be," and "I will be who I will be." It is in the Hebrew imperfect, which stresses the uncompleted or ongoing nature of the action. Although most translators have chosen to render it as "I am," I believe "I will be" to be the preferable translation, primarily because of the context. For in the next verse, Jehovah says, "This is my name forever, the name by which I am to be remembered from generation to generation." The reference is not merely backward-looking—"the God of Abraham, Isaac, and Jacob"—but also forward looking—"forever," and "from generation to generation."

As we face a world of change, in which the future is increasingly difficult to predict or even to anticipate, there is encouragement in this aspect of God's nature. For this God who revealed himself to Moses as the God of his future is also the God of our future. This is shown in three phases in Moses' experience, which is also instructive to us.

The first is that God understands the change that is taking place. Sometimes from our earthbound and time-bound perspective, we find it difficult to keep pace with change, both in terms of understanding and of living. We may then project those same limitations upon God, wondering whether he can fully appreciate either the rapid and radical nature of change, or the stress we feel in light of it. Yet, not only does God know and understand that change, but he is the very cause of it.

The appearance of Jehovah to Moses was a sudden and dramatic matter. It came without warning. There was no advance notice, no countdown as we observe with rocket firings, "T minus two, T minus 1," and so on. One moment, so far as we can determine from the text, nothing unusual was occurring and the next moment the bush was aglow. There were no real antecedents to the event. Further, there was a considerable disparity with the environment or setting. This took place in the desert, a place which by definition and the very meaning of its name, was an isolated and uninhabited place. The very word in many languages means literally, "nobody there," or "deserted." Into this tranquillity came this dramatic event, striking in nature, and thus capable of arousing the interest and curiosity of Moses, or of anyone else who might observe it. It also was unusual in terms of its incongruence relative to usual experience. Quite possibly Moses had seen fires in trees or bushes before, perhaps as a result of a lightning strike. This fire, however, was unlike any he had ever seen. For the fire burned, and burned, and burned, but it did not burn out. It did not consume the tree. The tree was like the fiberglass logs in a modern gas fireplace. It was not consumed. This aroused Moses' curiosity, so he went over to see the fire, to attempt to determine why the tree was not burned up. The form of the revelation was in this case especially appropriate to its substance or content. It was as incongruous to the setting as the thrust of the message was dramatic and radically different from what had preceded it. Radical change was signaled by a radical style of revelation.

Jehovah then gave Moses a message of a future for Israel radically different from its present situation. Instead of their sojourn in Egypt, they would return to the Promised Land, which was so significantly associated with the covenant. Instead of slavery and bondage, they would now be free to worship Jehovah as they wished. Instead of being obliterated or perhaps absorbed into Egyptian culture, they would survive as God's chosen people.

Moses must have been excited as he listened to what God had to say. With Moses' identification with the people of Israel and the opportunity he had experienced of observing firsthand their suffering, this was in many ways the fulfillment of a dream. God's dramatic action was a wonderful thing, with wonderful consequences.

Then, however, the revelation took a different direction. Instead of simply dwelling upon what he planned to do with respect to Israel, God personalized the message. "So now, go, I am sending you to Pharaoh to bring my people the Israelites out of Egypt" (v. 10). Suddenly the beads of perspiration inspired by excitement were changed into a cold sweat. Eagerness turned to virtual panic. Moses had not reckoned with such a possibility. He was excited about the end, but not about the means to that end, for this would require a radical change in his own life and lifestyle as well.

The radical change meant for Moses a radical change of location. He would leave this quiet, peaceful place where there was no one and nothing occurring and go back to the halls of Egypt, the center of commerce and of culture for virtually that entire region. It meant a change from leading a group of relatively agreeable, compliant, cooperative sheep to leading what in effect was the world's first congregation, which he was soon to call a "stiff-necked people": independent, rebellious, complaining, a group that would frequently turn to constructing and worshipping idols, (despite their lack of ability to help them) and would desire to return to Egypt, talking about how good they had it in what was actually the place of slavery. If Israel's future was to be radically different from her past, that was all the more true of Moses' future. His reaction, "Who am I, that I should go?" (v. 11), as well as the remaining steps in his response, indicate that he saw how different his own future was to be.

This radical change will be experienced by all of us as well. Our world is changing rapidly. We can see it politically. Think back upon the change that took place in the world geopolitically in the late 1980s and early 1990s. In 1989, my wife and I traveled to Europe to attend a conference in Yugoslavia. Our youngest daughter, who lived in Germany at the time, traveled with us and we spent a week vacationing at a seaside resort in Slovenia and then attended the sessions in Croatia. Those were then states within Yugoslavia, but are now independent nations. We took a few days as well to drive to Berlin and visited East Berlin for the first time in thirteen years. We passed through the famous wall by train this time, and then went back out by midnight on the "Cinderella pass." We also walked a considerable distance along the wall on the west side and peered over it at the Brandenburg Gate. That was July. By the following Father's Day, our daughter was home permanently from Germany, and one of her Father's Day gifts to me was a piece of that wall. I am glad we had an opportunity to visit that part of the world one more time, because that world no longer exists. Who would have believed that the political changes which took place in about two years in Eastern Europe could have happened? The same is true, economically. We are gradually coming to realize that probably the most important power in our world is not primarily military power, but rather economic power. The rapid rise of Japan to become such a powerful economy has changed the balance of power in the world, and other countries are in their own way challenging even Japan, among them countries like Korea. "Made in Japan" once represented cheap, poor quality merchandise, but electronics products, watches, cameras, and automobiles from Japan now dominate world markets. Some unemployed persons will never go back to the same type of job they once did, for those jobs are gone forever. Robots or computers now perform those jobs, or else the products once produced by those workers are now obsolete. Textbooks in fields like physics and chemistry quickly become outdated as new discoveries alter the knowledge of those subjects.

The same is true in the life and ministry of the church. Compare the church worship services you attended ten years ago with those of today. How different they are. If your church is basically worshipping as it did ten years ago, attend a service at one of the "new look" churches that is supposed to be on the cutting edge of worship and see how different things are there. Notice how different are the praise choruses being sung from the hymns and gospel songs of a generation ago, and then notice the new songs that are coming forth, including contemporary hymns. Think of the strategies and tactics of ministry employed by churches. At one time, coffee houses were the "in" thing that every church had as a means of outreach. Then came the great bus ministries of churches, and the market in used school buses boomed, only to crash when the bus ministry craze faded. In the early 1990s "seeker services" and "user-friendly churches" became "hot."

Yes, church has changed a great deal in any recent ten year period, and it will continue to change. I had a call on one occasion from the search committee of a church that was engaged in a seeker service ministry. Their pastor had left to plant another church of that kind, and they were looking for someone with experience in that type of ministry to call to their pastorate, and the committee chairman was asking me for suggestions. I told him I would need to take some time, and I spent about five hours of research before being able to submit some names to him. When I called him back I told him, "I think what you want, and what I have tried to give you, are the names of resourceful, creative pastors. These are the type of persons who, when times change so that the seeker service type of ministry is no longer effective, will have the ability to devise new forms of ministry which will then work." I think I took him completely aback by that statement. My impression was that he thought that "seeker service" was the final form of ministry, the way ministry would be done until the Lord comes back again. But just as times have been changing, they will also continue to change, and ministry will have to change to fit those changed times.

The problems to which the church ministers change also. I do not refer simply to the problems of divorce and marriage breakup, of alienation between children and parent, of drug abuse. I think of the complexity of issues and activities that confront us, even among Christians. One summer I received a telephone call from a church I had once served. They were calling me because their pastor was out of the country and they were facing a problem with which they did not know how to deal. A couple in the church had divorced earlier. That in itself is not a particularly unique situation in our churches, by any means. One member of the couple had continued to attend the church and the other had not, but now had returned to a worship service recently, announcing his desire to resume attending there. Even that phenomenon, of both members of the former marriage attending the same service, is also no longer rare. With many of their friends still in the congregation, it is understandable that they would want to continue their involvement there. At churches with multiple services, they often arrange to attend different services, so that they never see each other. I have noticed that old habits die hard, so that even the pew formerly used continues to be occupied. That meant that in one church I served, the man sat at one end of the third row and his former wife at the other, one sitting alone and the other, whichever had the children that weekend, sitting at the other end with the children. The problem, the people calling me said, was that the presence of her former husband was upsetting to the former wife, and that I can understand as well. It could certainly call to mind countless memories, some pleasant and some unpleasant. What I was told next was what

DOES IT MATTER IF GOD EXISTS?

was somewhat startling, however. The person on the telephone said to me, "The difficulty is that the former husband, Robert (not his real name), is now Roberta. He has had a sex-change operation and this is very disturbing to his (her?) former wife." The church wanted to bar this person, whether male or female, from attending church services, and wanted my advice as to what to do. I said, "First have your attorney check on the court case in Oklahoma in which the congregation excluded a woman for adultery, the woman sued for defamation of character, and when the judgment went against the church, they lost their church property."

I was never taught in seminary how to deal with problems like this because we did not encounter open transsexuals in those days, or at least not in church. And that church had also excluded one member for having an extramarital affair; another wife had loudly accused her husband in the church auditorium in the hearing of scores of fellow-worshippers of having an affair; an associate pastor had been sued for sexual harassment, a charge which made the local newspapers. I really was not prepared for that type of ministry when I was in seminary. I was not taught how the church should relate to and minister to AIDS patients. It probably would not have been possible to anticipate those problems and thus to prepare clergy persons to deal with them. Similarly, it is not possible to prepare students in seminary now for the problems to which they will be called to minister during the span of their careers. There simply is no way to predict those. The world is changing, and the church's ministry will have to change to adapt to those as well. If change has been great in the past ten years, then I predict that it will accelerate so that it will be greater in the next ten. In some areas such as geopolitics, that is not likely, for we have just seen megachanges, epoch-altering changes. But overall, the rate of change will increase. The rate of growth of knowledge is increasing. The change in communication is such that new developments reach other people, and thus have their effect, even more quickly than ever before.

The point to bear in mind here is that this change, radical as it was, did not catch God unawares. He was fully aware of the new so that he could, if he wished, have told Moses not only what was to happen in the immediate future, but also in the more remote future. He could have told him everything that would have happened in the whole march from Egypt to the Jordan River, and everything else that was to follow as well. He knows the future from beginning to end, for he not only knows the future, he is in control of it. As we have pointed out elsewhere in this volume, God is actively involved in all that happens. It is not, in every case, a matter of direct or causative action. Sometimes it is merely a matter of agreeing to allow something to happen, of acquiescing in something that might not be his preference, or his desire. In retrospect, we often can see God's work in everything that has occurred. What this passage says to us is that he will also work—indeed, is also already working—in what will come to pass. Today's future is tomorrow's present, and the day after tomorrow's past. When tomorrow becomes yesterday, we will be able to see God working there as well.

God himself works differently in different periods of time. This is not to say that his basic purposes or values change. That will never happen. The actual tactics by which he accomplishes these and the specific things he does at a given time change, however. We can see that simply by tracing out the history of divine working through the pages of Scripture. This is a development. There are two testaments or two covenants. We therefore should not be shocked or disturbed at the fact of change. This is not to say that all change is good, or that God is pleased with all change that occurs, but it is part of life, part of the world and its history that are moving onward.

At the same time, God's permanence is stressed in this. As Jehovah called Moses to remember that he was the God of Abraham, Isaac, and Jacob, he was pointing out, of course, that he was dealing differently with those people at varying times and places. He also, however, was emphasizing his constancy and faithfulness through all of this variation. Just as he had kept his word and covenant to Abraham, so had he done with Isaac and Jacob as well. We can count on him to be what he has always been, and to be that forever.

The philosophy known as process philosophy argues that change is not simply a characteristic of reality, an alteration or exchange of one quality or substance for another. Rather, change is reality, and reality is change. And it argues that God also participates in this change, so that he is growing and developing, becoming God as it were. That is not true of Jehovah, the God who has revealed himself in Scripture. That God is the same, "yesterday, and today, and forever" (Heb. 13:8). What he is now, he has always been, and always will be. Thus, we can rely upon the God who made himself known to Abraham, Isaac, Jacob—and Moses.

We may find encouragement, secondly, in the fact that God understands our sense of inadequacy when facing the future. Because of the radical change which the future represents from what has been experienced to this point, it is not surprising that we feel a sort of incommensurability between our capability and the demands made of us. This comes out in Moses' question, given as a response to Jehovah's call, "Who am I, that I should go to Pharaoh and bring the Israelites out of Egypt?" That sounds like an innocent, rhetorical question, doesn't it? When you think about it, however, who was Moses? What was he really saying by this response?

Moses was actually the adopted grandson of Pharaoh, king of Egypt. He had come to that position through a remarkable set of circumstances in which his life was spared and the king's daughter took him into her home. His own mother became his nursemaid, so that while he was trained in the Egyptians' learning, he was also given the religious heritage of the Hebrews. Thus, he was Egyptian on the outside, but Hebrew on the inside. All of his loyalties, his allegiances, were with the Hebrew people and their God. One day he saw one of the Egyptian slave drivers beating a Hebrew slave, and his heart went out to the Hebrew. He killed the Egyptian and hid his body in the sand, thinking no one had seen him and he would not be discovered. The next day, however, when he tried to mediate a dispute between two Hebrews, he discovered that they knew what he had done, and presumably, so did everyone else. He therefore decided he must flee for his life. When Moses said to Jehovah, "Who am I, that I should go?" he was really saying, "Don't you remember me, Lord? I'm Moses, the failure. I tried once on a small scale to help my people, and I bungled it. How can you expect me to undertake a task of this magnitude?" Behind that was an even more general statement, however. He was saying something like this: "I do well as a shepherd, Lord. I know how to handle that. But to go and try to deliver the people of Israel? That's too much, Lord. Please just leave me where I am comfortable."

Moses was probably one of the first persons to experience the "Peter principle": he was being pushed to the level of his incompetence. Actually, it probably should be named the "Moses principle" instead, since Moses probably discovered it or at least experienced it long before it was labeled. He was being pushed outside his comfort zone, and it was unpleasant and threatening. He knew how to lead sheep. They basically were obedient, following where they were led. The people of Israel, on the other hand, were rebellious, fickle, difficult to lead, and they would first have to be released by a king who would not be eager to lose a large slave force. Moses wanted to stay with the present situation, not to move into God's future for him.

We probably all can identify with that, unless we have an unrealistically high self-image. We have done a certain thing for so long that it has become familiar, second nature, comfortable. Then we are called upon to assume a new set of responsibilities at a different stage of life, and it is challenging and demanding for us.

We hear a lot about "the good old days," although perhaps not as much as we used to. What was good about the good old days was actually the fact that they were old. We knew and understood them, so we knew how to cope with them. The new is unfamiliar, so we have to learn it all over again. Part of the tension with the new is therefore simply the fact that it is new. When I moved from the pastorate of an inner city Chicago church to a semisuburban Minneapolis congregation, I found that I had a major learning task before me. It seemed as if on that first Sunday morning 500 people came by at the door and said, "My name is Johnson." The secretary had drawn for me a chart of the relationships, and it revealed that Willis Johnston and Richard Johnson were brothers, and that William Johnson was not related to either of them. Beyond not knowing the names, however, was my problem with not knowing and understanding the structure and governance of the church. In my previous congregation, administration was like touch-typing. For Christian education I pushed this button, for finances, that key. Now it was as if I sat down at the typewriter, and someone had completely changed the keyboard. I had to type by hunt-and-peck. And, as everyone who has worked long with a church knows, the official labels were not always the really accurate indication of the true structure of the church. The chairperson is not always the true power center of a committee. Consequently, it was a matter of trial and error to find out how to get things accomplished. There were times when I yearned to be back in Chicago, where I understood how things worked. That experience has been an encouragement to me ever since to pray especially for those who are making transitions into new places of responsibility. Even when the new situation is not more complex, it is more difficult simply because it is unfamiliar.

Beyond that, however, the new will be more demanding, more difficult. Not only did Moses not know how to lead the Israelites the way he led the sheep, but leading the former was a much more difficult undertaking than leading the latter. The future would require more of him than had the past.

We find this on every hand, don't we? If you have ever served on a church nominating committee, you have had a chance to see just how humble Christians can be. It is not just that they are being falsely modest or trying to avoid the office, or practicing the new hypocrisy—pretending to be worse, rather than better, than they are. They feel genuinely inadequate for what is coming. A person may have served well as an usher, but now is asked to work with finances. Or a trustee has handled well the property issues of the church, but now is asked to be one of those entrusted with the spiritual welfare of the congregation. Perhaps a woman has taught primary girls in Sunday school, but now is asked to teach an adult women's Bible class. Adult women? They study their Bibles. They ask hard questions! Or a man has taught a men's class and now is asked to take responsibility for a class of junior high boys. Junior high boys! Even the biggest, strongest, most macho man can experience terror at the prospect of dealing with a room full of junior high boys.

It is not surprising if, in the face of either real or possible experiences like this, we feel a desire to go back to or remain at the simpler days. Sometimes it is simply a wish to divest ourselves of some of the manifold responsibilities. I recall the experience of a former colleague of mine who had done his doctoral studies the hard way as I had done: going to graduate school while pastoring a church full time. He found the multiple demands very stressful, and reached the point where he felt he must get away for a vacation. He went hunting for a week in Montana, and thoroughly enjoyed himself. As he headed back home by train, however, he felt the burden of his responsibilities beginning to build again. He thought of the pile of mail that had probably accumulated on his desk, and must be dealt with. The train stopped in a peaceful small town in Montana, and he saw a little white church with a steeple, and thought, "I wonder if that church needs a pastor."

I can identify with that. Not long after he told me that anecdote I had an interesting week myself. I taught my weekly Monday morning class, then flew to Seattle, where I spoke five times on Tuesday through Thursday at a pastors' conference, arriving home in Minneapolis at 11 o'clock Thursday evening. I taught my Wednesday and Friday classes on Friday morning and picked up the examinations which they had taken on Wednesday. I then flew to San Francisco on Saturday afternoon. On the way from the San Francisco airport to Palo Alto, I was briefed on what I was to say at the alumni meeting. After the meeting, we drove to Santa Rosa, an hour and a half north of the Golden Gate Bridge, arriving at 1:30 A.M., which was 3:30 A.M. in the time on which I had arisen. I preached there the next morning, then traveled down to the Berkeley area to preach on Sunday evening. On Monday morning we drove out to Tracy for the pastors' conference at which I was to speak. It was a peaceful little town of about 7,000 population, just about sixty miles east of Oakland in the San Joaquin Valley. The church had about 200 members. My colleague and I were walking back to the motel the next morning, a beautiful sunny November day with a temperature of about seventy degrees, and I said, "In ten years, Cliff, if this church is without a pastor, I'm applying for the job." We finished our sessions and were rushing back to catch the 5 P.M. flight out of San Francisco so we could teach our 8 A.M. classes the next day. I was sitting in the back seat and in the front seat our director of church relations was speaking enthusiastically about how well the conference had gone and he said, "Next year we are going to have twice as many of these, and we need to have a theologian at each of them." I poked my colleague and said, "Five years, Cliff; five!"

I find myself thinking that way and I say to myself, "Erickson, you're getting old. You don't respond to challenges the way you used to." But it is not only those of us who are elderly or pre-elderly who feel this stress. It was not long after that experience that we were sitting at dinner and our youngest daughter, who then was six, looked out the kitchen window and saw her friend, Tammy, playing in her back yard. Her comment was, "Tammy's lucky. She's in kindergarten. Kindergarten is easy. First grade is hard." She was right, of course. First grade is a lot more difficult than kindergarten, and second grade is harder than first grade, and third grade is harder than second grade. It never gets any easier. And shortly thereafter our oldest daughter, then eleven, said in the midst of a difficult experience: "I wish Mommy could take me and rock me in the rocker, like she used to." It was still physically possible, of course. But one reaches the stage where the problems of life cannot be solved by rocking or by kissing the "owie." Life moves on, and it gets more demanding.

God understands, however. There are different ways in which he might have responded to Moses. He might have become impatient with him and told him simply to get out there and do it. He could have related to him in a coercive fashion. He did not, however. He understood the sense of inadequacy Moses was experiencing, and he identified empathetically. He sought to respond to the concerns which Moses expressed. He dealt with him where he was. And so he does with us also. Although he himself does not experience future shock, he realizes that we do, and there is comfort in recognizing his understanding approach to our concerns.

Third, we find comfort here in God's presence in the future. God's response was a simple one: I will be with you. God had been with Moses in the past, when he had been spared and had become part of the king's household. He had been with him when he fled to Midian, became a shepherd, and married into Jethro's family. He definitely was with him now, speaking from the burning bush in an unmistakable demonstration of his presence. There was no fear for the present. What God was promising, however, was that he would certainly also be present with Moses in the future. He therefore need not be afraid of the future, either.

Note that God gave no argument regarding the problems. He did not dispute Moses' self-assessment, telling him that he was the most eloquent speaker of all time. And if he did not contest the internal problems, he also did not question the reality of the external problems, saying that Pharaoh would quickly and readily let these slaves go, and that the people of Israel would simply be waiting for him to lead them out, and would unquestioningly go wherever Moses asked them to go. Those problems were genuine and serious. What God did offer, however, was simply his presence. That is his promise to us as well.

I believe what sometimes happens to us is that we tend to think of God as identified with the past. The incidents in which he revealed himself were in the past, so that is where he fits and belongs. So we find it hard to conceive of him as being present and active in the future. What is happening here, I believe, is that our unofficial theology is overwhelming our official theology. Our official theology is what we believe in theory, what we say we subscribe to. In this case, our official theology is that God is eternal, living in past, present, and future. He is omniscient, knowing everything. He is omnipresent, existing everywhere. Our unofficial theology is what we actually believe in practice, the belief that underlies what we do, and is revealed in our actions. Once in a while, we can get a glimpse of this, as if we could turn around really fast and see the back of our head, although much of the time it is hidden from us. Here is one of those places where we can catch just a glimpse of our unofficial theology. We may believe that God was present in and understood a society where people rode on donkeys and camels, but not the world of high speed freeway travel and air travel and even space travel by rocket ships. Our image of him is of an old man in a flowing white robe with a long white beard. Such a God does not fit into our present, so we tend to exclude him in favor of modern science as the means of dealing with contemporary complex issues, and we certainly tend not to expect him in the future in a post-Christian or postmodern or posttheistic time.

J. B. Phillips, in his delightful and insightful little book, *Your God Is Too Small,* tells of a psychological test given to a mixed group of older adolescents during World War II. They were asked "Does God understand radar?" In nearly every case they answered, "No," then laughed when they realized what they had said. The idea of God living, really living, in their modern world was foreign to them. Their unconscious idea of God was of the "Grand Old Man." God, of course, has always understood radar. He is the one who designed and created the creation with the characteristics which scientists then study and formulate into what they call the laws of physics upon which radar is based. He has been waiting in what was then the future for people to invent radar. He is waiting out there in the future, which as yet is unknown and unexperienced by us, waiting for us to arrive there. I like to think of God as living in the future and (anthropomorphically speaking) looking at his watch and his calendar and saying, "It's—. In just a few days, humans will discover or invent such and such." Better yet, I hear him saying, "It's—. If those Christians only knew the blessings that I have in store for them this year." For to God, even the future is just like the present.

DOES IT MATTER IF GOD EXISTS?

We are accustomed to thinking of God moving history by pushing, as it were, causing it from the past. But another way of thinking of him is as the God who moves it by pulling from the future where he already is. This is the major contribution the theology of hope has made to our understanding of God: that he lives in the future as well as the past. Just as he led Abraham from Ur of the Chaldees to Palestine and was there in the future when he got there, so he led Jacob as he fled to another country and was there when he arrived. Just as he was with Moses when he went back to Egypt and was there in what was then the future as well, so he will be with us in the unknown future, when it comes.

This means that we will not have to face alone the new, different, and demanding dimensions which change will bring about. He will be there, supplying us with the strength to live and fulfill our responsibilities. That little six year old who thought that kindergarten was easy and first grade was hard? She did not know at that age that one evening when she was twenty-four she would stand for a half hour on a railway station platform in Koblenz, Germany, held at knifepoint by a crazed man who was convinced that she was the girlfriend who had rejected him. A six year old could not deal with a problem like that, but God was present in her life and with her on that platform that night giving her peace and presence of mind and effective use of the German language. Nor could a six year old deal with the Ph.D. program in which she later enrolled, which was much more difficult than first grade, but God was there with her, as well. And that eleven year old who wanted to be rocked by her mommy in the rocker? She could not know that some day she would be leading an educational tour group and would be in Nicaragua with a group of twenty persons when the airline that had flown them into the country announced that it was no longer providing service to and from that country. But God was with her there, giving her the calmness and presence of mind to do what needed to be done. And she could not know, as an eleven year old, that on January 24, 1991, she would give birth to a beautiful little baby girl that would be the joy of her and her husband's lives, and that on October 13 of that year they would rush that wonderful little girl to the emergency room of the hospital where meningitis would be diagnosed, and that by the next evening they would have to make the decision to give her back to God. But God was with them in that intensive care room as they watched their daughter lose the battle for life, and in the conference room when they had to make the decision. No eleven year old could deal with that sort of problem, but God was present when it was necessary.

God is the God of the future. He is not only the God who was and who is, but also the God who will be. We can trust ourselves to him, for he is there in the future, waiting for us. We need not fear that future, for he is there, building us, revealing himself to us, and beckoning us to join him in that future. It is thus that the psalmist could write: "Lord, you have been our dwelling place throughout all generations. Before the mountains were born or you brought forth the earth and the world, from everlasting to everlasting you are God" (Ps. 90:1–2). And we can join with the songwriter in singing: "Oh God, our help in ages past, our hope for years to come. Be thou our help while life shall last, and our eternal home." For he is the God who will be.

Study Guide

Key Questions

1. What is your view of the future? Do you fear it, ignore it, look forward to it with anticipation? Why? Why not?
2. This study emphasizes the fact that "God understands the change that is taking place." In relation to this the author writes "Not only does God know and understand that change, but is the very cause of it." How can this realization contribute to your understanding of change as it affects you? Beyond that, you are being taught that God is already working in your future. It is easy to accept this in relation to the "good things" that will come your way, but what of the difficult and sorrowful things?
3. How can knowing that God understands your sense of inadequacy about facing the future be an encouragement to you? You are asked to commune with Him and make your requests known to Him. Why can't you expect protection from the bad and have only good things happen to you? What encouragement should you be looking for?
4. Reread the discussion on your "unofficial theology" and your "official theology." Do you understand the difference between these? Which of your beliefs are those you say you subscribe to and which ones are revealed in your actions?

Bible Investigation

1. Glean, from the author's comment, three phases in Moses' experience. Have these in front of you as you read Exodus chapters 3 and 4. In what ways is Moses' attitude toward the future like yours? How does God want to encourage and comfort you as he did Moses?
2. Find other Scriptures that promise God's understanding, encouragement, and comfort with regard to the future. Here we suggest a few: Psalms 91:11; 121; 138:7–8; Philippians 1:6; 2 Thessalonians 3:3; and Hebrews 13:6.

Personal Application

1. Memorize Hebrews 13:8. How does the fact that God never changes counter the teaching of **process theology**? If God was

"growing and developing, becoming God" as the proponents of process theology teach, would you be comforted and helped to face an uncertain future?
2. What help do you find in the meaning of the name of God, "**I am**" found in Exodus 3:14?
3. Think about Psalm 90:1–2. Offer a prayer of praise to the God of your future. Sing the hymn "Oh God, our help in ages past, our hope for years to come."

For Further Thought

Reread the section of the chapter dealing with change in the church. Examine the history of your church. How has change affected it and you? Are you involved in these changes? Are you understanding and helpful toward others who find change difficult?

3

Somebody Knows
Your Name

The words of the theme song of a popular television program in the late 1980s and early 1990s said, "You want to go where everybody knows your name." That expresses well a feeling which most of us have at one time or another. We need that human warmth and recognition. At other times, however, we have exactly the opposite feeling. We want to go where nobody knows our name. That is a logical feeling when we have done something embarrassing, or when we just want to have some seclusion. At times I go to a library where I am not recognized, where I can go about my work without someone asking me a question about something.

Quite often, however, that is not what we desire. We want to go, not where everyone knows our name or nobody knows our name, but where someone knows our name, where we are regarded as a person, a real human being. We want to be an individual rather than just a nameless, faceless, statistic. It is disconcerting to be treated this latter way, to be called, "Hey, buddy" or "Hey, mister." It is, of course, similarly disconcerting to be treated with familiarity by people who have not earned that familiarity and have not proved that they care for us, such as the stranger who calls us on the telephone and addresses us by first name. For such a person, the name is really not a name, not a representation of the unique personhood. It is just a label, more like a number than a name.

We see many indications of this trend toward depersonalization in our society. One is the use of numbers rather than names. In many settings, one's identification number is more significant and more widely used than is the person's name. Do you know who I am? I am XXX-XX-XXXX. That is who I am to the federal government: the Social Security Administration, the Internal Revenue Service, and the Federal Aviation Administration. That, for all practical purposes, is who I am. But there is nothing distinctive about that number, no dimension of personality, of uniqueness. It is really not much different from YYY-YY-YYYY.

Years ago, an outstanding English major in the Christian liberal arts college where I was teaching at the time applied to graduate school. One very prestigious university in the east responded to his letter by saying, "Here is your identification number. Please use it in any further correspondence with us. Henceforth, it will not be necessary to mention your name." He applied instead to Princeton University, which still believed in the use of proper names, and eventually completed his Ph.D. degree there.

At one time I served on a faculty which had a faculty-staff parking lot with assigned spaces. The spaces were not marked with the names of the persons to whom they were assigned, but only with numbers. I knew that space number eight was my space, and so I faithfully parked in that spot. After a time, however, the faculty became dissatisfied with this arrangement and wanted their names on their spaces instead. Part of the problem was that outsiders were parking in the reserved lot, and the reasoning of the faculty was that persons would be less inclined to do this if they knew that they were taking the place of some specific person rather than simply any one of twenty-five or so spaces. We petitioned the administration to affix nameplates to the spaces, offering even to bear the cost ourselves. The reply, however, was that the president did not want names, feeling that numbers had a greater esthetic quality. Finally, we asked the president to meet with us to discuss the matter. I suggested that perhaps in the conversation we could refer to and address one another by our numbers rather than our names, saying, "Thank you, six," or "I think nine's idea is a good one," instead of "Bill" and "Fred." For the real issue for many of the faculty was not someone else violating a sacred reserved spot, but the depersonalization.

We see this in other ways, as well. One is the use of statistics. Because of sheer numbers, we become callous to deaths, casualties, etc. We read that only 140 casualties were suffered by an army, and we tend to be rather unmoved by that number, for it is *only* 140.

DOES IT MATTER IF GOD EXISTS?

Yet each one of those 140 is a real individual person, precious to someone. There is a personal dimension to tragedy which the statistics tend to obscure. It may be our society's way of protecting itself against the sense of loss and pain, but there is a greater loss to our humanity in the desensitizing effect which we undergo.

Probably you have had an experience of hearing stories of either fortunate or unfortunate experiences that have happened to someone, but being unmoved by those because you did not really know that person at all. It was just a "someone" out there. I think, for example, of watching the ten o'clock news one night and hearing of the hunting death of a Bill Shodeen. The name struck me immediately, because I had a student at that time with that name, who also was attending the church of which I was then the interim pastor. I wondered, "Could that be the Bill I know?" I did not want to call his home at that hour of the evening and in effect ask, "Is Bill dead?" I found an indirect way to get the same information. When I learned that Bill was indeed still alive and well, I relaxed and dismissed the matter from my mind. I did not know this Bill, so this was no concern of mine. About three years later, however, I attended a luncheon honoring a friend of mine and found myself seated next to a woman, a friend of my friend's wife, who was the widow of the man regarding whom I had heard that news account. Now I felt the pain of that man's death as this woman told me, with pain that still was very evident in her life, of the death of her Bill. Now the story had become personalized, for Bill had become a person and not just a faceless name.

What is saddest about this story is that it reveals my own real lack of care and attention to a truly sad story, a tragedy. Because I did not know this man, and therefore did not treat him in my thinking as a real person, I felt nothing for him or for his loved ones. If an individual is not a person that we know, he or she becomes for us a thing, and most of us have been socialized to care about things less than we care about persons. Of course, we cannot begin to feel deeply about every person in the world who undergoes some sad experience. If we did, we would probably be overwhelmed with grief. Somewhere between massive grief and gross indifference, however, there ought to be some intermediate ground, the empathy for persons whom we do not know simply because they are persons and we recognize them as such.

Part of what we are facing here is what I call the baggage approach to personhood. Have you ever watched baggage handlers throwing bags onto the conveyor belt? Each bag is the same to these persons, who have no special interest in any of them. Bags are simply objects to be loaded, and the workers basically treat them all alike as part of doing their job. When passengers come to claim their bags, however, it is different. Each person's bag is special to him or her. They want their bags treated with a care which may not be accorded to other persons' bags. I am afraid that in the depersonalized, crowded world in which we live, we feel like just another bag at the hands of most other people. This is of course part of our modern society. In an earlier period, when most people lived in small towns, most people knew most other people in their community. Transactions were often handled with a verbal agreement, or at most, a handshake. Legal contracts, with their impersonal language, were unnecessary. When someone had a problem or a need, this was known to the rest of the community, who frequently pitched in to help out. What was done by individuals for individuals in that setting, however, soon came to be handled by committees, agencies, and administrations. There has been the gain of anonymity, in which privacy is preserved, but again there is the feeling that the loss may have been greater than the gain occasioned by the depersonalization.

Part of the problem here is losing track of things. Two things with different numbers are not as easily distinguishable in our thinking as are two objects with different names. Perhaps that is why we have made a practice in our family for several years of naming our automobiles. They then took on a personal character and received a type of affection that they might not otherwise have had.

How many of us have had problems with errors being made on our charge accounts or other numerically-oriented areas of personal concern? Sometimes a credit does not get properly entered, or a computer error continues to recur. I think, for example, of a credit purchase which I once made on a large item. It was offered on a special credit arrangement, under which no payments would be due until six months later, and interest charges would not even begin until that time. Since the interest could then accumulate in my money market fund, the interest rate on which was then nearly ten percent, I calculated that this would in effect be a five percent discount on the purchase price, so I readily opted to make the purchase under that arrangement, rather than paying cash. Unfortunately,

DOES IT MATTER IF GOD EXISTS?

however, the dealer used the incorrect forms in submitting the charge to the company's credit office. Soon my first monthly bill came, demanding an installment payment, and indicating the new balance, which included one month's interest on the entire amount of the principal. I called the credit office which referred me back to the dealer from whom I had made the purchase. He then sent in the paperwork necessary to correct the error. Each month, however, the bill came, showing an accumulating amount of interest (including interest on the unpaid interest) and a past due amount. Finally, after repeated calls to the dealer, I received a bill with the correct amount. I quickly paid the bill, glad to be rid of the aggravation. I had been dealing either with an unknowing computer or an unresponsive bureaucracy, neither of which treated me as a person and neither of which consequently appeared to me to have the characteristics of a person, either.

Other aggravating experiences come to mind. One of the bank card companies whose credit card we hold decided to upgrade the five-digit zip code numbers of all of their accounts to nine-digit numbers, which were correctly looked up and applied (at least in my case). Then, however, after a month, the computer (or some person) lopped off the first four digits to make a new five-digit number. Now, instead of the correct five-digit number, 55112, I had a new, incorrect number, 25431, which, it happens, is a small town in West Virginia. My next month's bill was then promptly sent to that zip code. By the time the post office realized that this was an addressing error, I had received a notice from the credit card company that my payment (on a bill that I had not received) was overdue, a notice that my credit was being suspended, and even that my account was canceled and revoked. When I finally received the bill, I wrote the company, explaining that I did not live in that town in West Virginia, had never lived there, probably would never live there, and could not be responsible for paying bills that went there rather than to me. The error was corrected, my account reinstated, and there was no further difficulty. The root of the problem, however, was probably that my name, street name and number, and the city and state in which I live, had been ignored, so that attention was only paid to the incorrect zip code number.

Numbers are terribly dull, aren't they? There is no character, no charm, no romance, to most numbers, with the only exceptions being unusual numbers like 9,999 or 10,000. Perhaps that is why there was such resistance some years ago to the conversion of telephone exchanges from names to numbers (and incidentally, the demise of the concept of a telephone exchange). A number like 742-8559 is all right, but it can't begin to compare for color with RIverside 2-8559, nor is there the same ring to the sound of 889-3176 that TUxedo 9-3176 has. That inspired the formation of an organization known as the Anti-Digital Dialing League, which engaged in a sort of low grade guerrilla warfare against the telephone company, bending, stapling and mutilating their computer billing cards and overpaying their bills by two or three cents each month. "Give me back my ALbany, or my NAtional, or my JUniper," was their cry. They felt they were being robbed of something vital and precious.

Part of the cause of the difficulty is that no one out there knows us, or cares about us. The same works in reverse, as we noted earlier. We don't know, or care about, very many people. It is only the people closest to us that we really know or who really know us that we care about. And the sheer number of people precludes our getting very well acquainted. Then people lose their identity. Instead of Jim or Mary, it is at best the person in apartment 301, or the tall blond woman in accounting.

This can happen to us when we have a large number of persons to deal with in rapid sequence. They begin to blur into one another, becoming virtually indistinguishable in our minds. As a pastor, I tried to call on hospital patients on an average of twice a week, more frequently if their need was urgent. On one occasion I had been out of town all week. Returning on Saturday morning, I resolved to call on all my hospitalized patients that afternoon. I made calls on all seven of them, in seven different hospitals, ranging all the way from the western suburbs of Minneapolis to the east side of St. Paul, and even the far south of Minneapolis, near the airport. I resolved, however, that I would not again do my hospital calling in that way, if it was at all possible to avoid doing so. The problem was that all the patients began to blur together, as if they were on an assembly line. I was unable to treat the last ones uniquely. I was beginning to relate to them as just another patient with a set of symptoms. They did not receive a call from a pastor, but rather from a pastoral-calling machine, who went through a routine. I had become depersonalized by the same process that had depersonalized them for me.

When large numbers of persons are involved combined with a computer glitch, then the difficulty becomes compounded. One Christian ministry which operates a popular nationwide radio program moved its headquarters to another state, crossing the mountains in the process. Somehow the main computer was damaged in the move so that it had to be replaced, at a cost of approximately three quarters of a million dollars. The damage was discovered when the computer malfunctioned, rendering inaccessible the names and addresses of everyone whose letter had been received in a three–day period. They were lost, irretrievably. The only recourse was to mention this fact on the radio program, hoping that those people would write again. Lost, unknown! What a fate. That happens to us sometimes, doesn't it, although it seems that the record of our indebtedness is for some reason (perhaps Murphy's Law?) less likely to be lost than is the record of our payment. And it never seems to be the case that the Internal Revenue Service completely loses track of us, does it?

It is relatively easy to understand how machines or other devices can lose track of someone, but how can persons, human individuals, ignore other individuals? Part of the problem is that we get so preoccupied that we don't listen to other people, or even really see them. A man who had worked as a bank teller mentioned to me that once, while he was entering a customer's deposit, the customer continued telling him some small-talk item, to which the teller replied in his customary fashion, "That's nice." When the customer had left the window, the next teller asked my friend, "Did you hear what she said?" "No," replied the first man. "She said, 'My mother just died.'"

It also happens that people do not listen to others because they are preoccupied with themselves and what they want to say. I once knew a man like that. He would respond to what the other person said with something unrelated, or at least that did not respond to the other person's statement. Or he would respond before the person had finished what he or she was talking about, because he really was not listening to the other person. Instead, that time was a waiting period until he could talk again. It was used to think about what he planned to say next, not about what the conversation partner was talking about. On one occasion, at a coffee break, a woman was telling about a problem which one of her family members had. When she paused momentarily, obviously not finished, this man proceeded to tell an anecdote from his experience that had been recalled because of what she said. As soon as I could get him aside, I gently pointed out what he had done. It was all the more serious because he was this woman's supervisor. When we treat people as listening machines, or some sort of recorder into which we talk, we have robbed them of their personhood.

All of this is sad, regrettable. Unfortunately, this very depersonalization also occurs in Christian settings and in situations of ministry. One form that it takes is institutionalization of the ministry. What had been a means to an end now becomes the end in itself and what had been the end becomes the means. An organization is created to minister to the needs of people. It may be a church, a school, or a social agency. Then, however, the organization has need for more of these persons as clients or recipients in some sense of its ministry. So, for example, a Christian college needs more students to pay tuition, which will in turn help to pay the bills. Or a church needs more members to give and to work to sustain the church. Of course, the reason usually given is that these people are needed so that the organization involved can minister more effectively to more people, but somehow the purpose has become obscured or reversed. It is the institution that must be ministered to, rather than the reverse.

What has happened in these situations is that we have come to treat people as objects whom we control and manipulate rather than as subjects with value in and of themselves. They are things to be counted and used. A generation ago, Sunday school contests were very popular, and still may be in some settings. I have a great appreciation for Sunday school contests, properly done. I have seen them bring a church to life, creating a real sense of ministry that had been lacking. There is, however, a subtle danger, that people will come to be regarded as things, to be sought and brought into the church building. The argument goes something like this. "We have two hundred things that sit on chairs from 9:45 to 10:45 on Sunday morning. Some sit on small chairs, some on medium-sized chairs, some on large chairs. Let's go out and find another thirty or forty things to come and sit on these chairs on Sunday morning." The goal, originally worthy, has become corrupted. Whereas formerly the emphasis was upon what could be done for these persons when they came within the church, now it is instead an emphasis simply upon the objects.

This takes different forms in different times and settings. Sunday school contests may be passé, but megachurches are not. Big is beautiful with these "full-service" churches. Success is measured by size. Quantity is regarded as the measure of quality, but the question may be neglected, "quality at what?" It may come in connection with the financial needs of the congregation. I sat in a business meeting of a church of which I was a member as the chairman of the building committee introduced the plans for the new unit that was to be constructed. I shuddered when he said in connection with the mortgage payments, "To handle the debt service on this construction will require the addition of twenty-four more giving units to the congregation." Giving units? I wondered whether Jesus ever looked at persons as giving units. The terminology almost produces the imagery of robots that write checks, or mechanically reach into their back pockets, pull out their wallets, extract some currency, and place it in the offering plate. This is depersonalization, dehumanization in ministry. It does not matter what the person is like, what his or her needs, hopes, fears, or joys are, as long as the body is warm and the check is good. Any giver will do so long as he or she has the money, for that is where our interest in them lies. Even more repulsive is the situation of the ministry which is in financial need, and which has been placed in the will of a now seriously ill person for a large sum ("deferred giving" is the euphemism for this type of donation). Do the persons at the potential recipient ministry pray for the healing of that person? The executive of one such ministry said, semi-tongue-in-cheek, in commenting on the year's financial report: "We are fortunate; a larger than usual number of our deferred givers passed away (another euphemism) this past year."

We have talked about the tendency to lose individual caring regarding persons in this sort of depersonalized society. There also occurs a loss of the sense of value of human lives in this sort of context. For example, the calculation that takes place regarding human lives reveals this sort of callous approach. Whenever the risk of a certain action or substance is measured by the cost in human lives, we are experiencing something of this phenomenon. When the propriety of a particular military objective is evaluated in this fashion, we are in effect placing a certain value upon those human lives. It is estimated that capturing a certain town or hill is going to result in the loss of a certain number of lives. It is then decided whether the attainment of that objective is worthwhile or not.

Where does this leave us? Are we important? Does anyone know who we are, if we are ordinary people? And does anyone care, other than our immediate family? At times it does not seem to be the case. We are just another member of the human race, just another specimen, another statistic. Yet deep within us is a craving for recognition. It was this which caused the existentialists to cry out in protest, to insist upon individuality, uniqueness, and freedom. It was this which caused the student at the University of California at Berkeley during the student protests in the late 1960s to carry a sign which said, "I am a human being. Do not fold, spindle, or staple."

There is a dimension of the doctrine of God which speaks directly to this concern. It is found in the tenth chapter of Matthew, verses 29 and 30. Here Jesus spoke of the Father, and of his knowledge and care for humanity. He used as the basis of his argument the Father's knowledge and care of birds of the air. They were so cheap, so numerous, so dispensable that two of them were sold for a tiny coin. Certainly, today we tend to feel much the same way toward the sparrows. They are so numerous that we tend to be indifferent to the loss of one. "There's plenty more where that one came from," is often our thought. Unless we are persons with an exceptional concern about nature, we probably do not fret or get disturbed over the death of one of them. They seem so abundant, so prolific, so dispensable. Any sparrow is the same as any other. Any one will do. There is no value in any individual bird per se. It is only when a species is in danger of extinction that we begin to think about their value, and certainly the sparrow is far from extinct. Here, however, is the amazing thing: "Yet not one of them will fall to the ground apart from the will of your Father." Think of it! He is aware of and concerned about the fate of each individual sparrow. Now Jesus goes on to make the point that God knows all about us, even the very number of the hairs of our heads. That is a very minute point of information seemingly trivial in nature and certainly unknown about us by any other human being and no doubt even by ourselves. Yet God knows it. I do not think that Jesus was saying that this type of information is especially important to God. It was a vivid way of saying that he knows all about us—not just our circumstances—but *everything* about us. If there is one malignant cell within my body at this moment, God knows it. It does not escape him. In other words, no harm can come upon us or even threaten to come upon us that God is not aware of. Nothing, absolutely nothing, escapes him.

DOES IT MATTER IF GOD EXISTS?

Jesus then applies the logic of his argument. Directing us back to the point he has just made about God's knowledge and care about the birds, he says, "Do not be afraid. You are of more value than many sparrows." The thrust of the statement is this: if God knows and cares 5 y about a bird, then he must know and care 5,000 y or something similar about us, for we are of much more value than such a bird. This is seen in the value he conferred upon us in the creation since he made human beings in his own image and likeness.

This knowledge is not merely information for its own sake. It is knowledge for the sake of divine control of what occurs. Nothing ill can happen without the Father's will. The events that happen are not unknown to him. They are also not something which occurs contrary to his will or decision, or something that he is unable to control once they happen. All matters are part of his will.

This is not to say, however, that he is the cause of all that occurs. There are at least two senses of the word "will" here. One is the initiating or causative will, in which God actively decides that something shall happen and then acts in such a way as to bring it about. In this sense he can be said to be the cause of what occurs. There also is the permissive will of God. This refers to situations that he does not actively choose to have happen, or act to bring about. They are things which he may actually be opposed to, or wish would not eventuate. Yet he wills to let them happen, often as a concession to the insistence of sinful or evil persons. One example given in Jesus' ministry was the Old Testament practice of divorce. Moses had permitted this by issuing a "bill of divorcement." Yet Jesus said that this was not God's original intention. It was not, as he said, "this way from the beginning." It was permitted because of the hardness of heart of the people (Matt. 19:8–9). God did not wish, did not want, did not desire for this to be the case. He did not approve of it, but he decided to permit it as a concession to the weakness and perversity of the people. If someone says that since God could have prevented it and did not, he is therefore responsible and is the cause, this would be a very unusual sense of the idea of cause. We cannot lay the blame upon God as the cause of this.

Another important factor is at work here, as well. Jesus told his hearers not to be afraid of those who can destroy the body but cannot destroy both soul and body in hell (Matt. 10:28). Jesus is pointing to what is really important in life. As significant as is physical or earthly life, or the health and welfare of the body, it is still secondary in nature. Those who can destroy only that need not be feared. The one with the capability to destroy not only soul and body in hell must be feared. We sometimes act as if we think that the former is what is ultimately important. We would like to have someone know about our situation, care about us and care for these temporal needs. In so doing, our decisions, prayers, and expectations may not be the wisest, in the light of eternity. That is because we cannot see the future and see the possible consequences of those other occurrences, in addition to the rather obviously good ones that we desire and seek.

A rather vivid illustration of this is the short story, "The Monkey's Paw." A couple receive a monkey's paw and are told that whoever owns the paw may make three wishes. They decide to wish for a certain sum of money. Shortly thereafter, a representative of their employer comes to their home, with the sad news that their son has been killed in an accident at work, and presents them with a check as a compensation from the company for the death of their son. The amount of the check is the exact sum that they had wished for.

The parents of course grieve over their son. They long to have him back. An idea comes to the wife. Could they not use one of the remaining wishes of the paw to bring their son back to life? Her husband disagrees, however. Had they not learned from the experience of the first wish? Yet that idea continues to agitate her. Then one night she takes the paw in her hand and wishes her son back. There is a knocking at the door, and she rushes to open it. Just before she reaches the door, however, her husband seizes the paw in his hand and wishes that whatever is outside the door should be gone, and the knocking ceases.

Sometimes our praying is of that nature. We pray for what we think is important, something that we think would make us happy, would produce our welfare. Yet, not possessing more than the normal limited human knowledge, we often pray for relatively unimportant, or perhaps even harmful, matters. One point of the reference to the Father's knowledge of the number of hairs on our heads is that none of us has that information. In other words, God knows us and our needs better than we know ourselves. He not only knows the things that we know we need, he knows the needs we have of which we are not aware. He not only knows our past and present needs, but also our future needs. We can especially trust him, and we need to pray that his will be done.

Some Christians think that this praying that God's will should be done is a sort of irresponsible praying, an unwillingness to take responsibility for our requests and insist upon them. It may even be a lack of faith according to this way of thinking, for then we can always rationalize the absence of a positive answer to our prayer on the grounds that "It wasn't God's will." This passage would suggest, however, that properly understood, it is the correct way to pray.

When in October of 1991 our little eight-and-a-half-month-old granddaughter lay desperately ill of meningitis, we prayed for God to heal and restore her. I laid my hand on her little head, where the infection raged most severely, and where the most serious damage was being done, and prayed for God to destroy the terrible pneumococcus. But I prayed that God would do this if it was his will. None of us knew what lay ahead for little Siri, whether if she survived this illness she might have a serious impairment, or might someday suffer far more in some physical way that would be even more painful for her parents than would be her death now. We could not know that she might grow up to commit some horrible crime, or to reject Jesus Christ. As fervently as we wished and prayed for her complete healing, we were willing to let her go if that was what God wanted to do, and she is safe with him now.

The one who knows us and protects us knows what concerns are really most important, what things are of eternal duration. Jesus' ministry frequently emphasized this dimension of the value of the eternal versus the merely temporal. This is seen, for example, in his instructions not to store up for ourselves treasures on earth, where moth and rust destroy, and thieves break in and steal, but rather to store them up in heaven, where they are not subject to such losses (Matt. 6:19–21). His whole ministry was based upon the assumption of the superiority of the eternal over the temporal. It is also seen not only in his teaching to believers but to those who were weighing the issues and decisions of loyalty to him or not. What should it profit a man, he asked, if he were to gain the whole world and lose his own soul? What would he give in return for his soul (Matt. 16:24–26)?

We can therefore trust God, for he is not only aware of our needs such as the physical comfort and health that is so apparent to us, but also of the much more significant dimensions of life. He can control even the things over which no one else has any influence.

To see the meaning of Matthew 10:29–31 we must see that Jesus was not saying that nothing bad will ever happen to us. Rather, he is saying that nothing ultimately bad can happen to those who are God's children. He will not always spare us from temporal adversity, loss, suffering, disappointment, or even death. There are whole segments of Christianity which are based upon such an assumption. Yet it is not supported by this passage. What Jesus is saying in this passage is that nothing ultimately bad can happen to those who are God's children.

The other major point of the passage is the value of each individual human being to God. Not only does God not overlook us in the sense of not seeing what happens to us, he does not overlook us in the sense of failing to care about what happens. We are never just a statistic to God. He never thinks, "What is one more or less?" Just as he cares about each sparrow of the air, insignificant though they may seem to be, so he cares about each one of us as well. He knows us and cares for us personally.

This is seen in other places in Jesus' teaching. One was the parable of the lost sheep, where the Father is compared to a shepherd. The shepherd had one hundred sheep, of which ninety-nine were safely with him. One, however, was lost. The shepherd might have thought, "ninety-nine percent is not a bad average. What does that one matter? Let him be. If I go looking for him, something might happen to one or more of the other ninety-nine." That is not how the Father reasons according to Jesus. Leaving those ninety-nine, he goes looking for the missing sheep, searching until he finds it. When he does find it, he joyfully puts it on his shoulder and returns home. He calls together his friends and neighbors, saying, "Rejoice with me, I have found my sheep." Jesus then makes very clear the point that he is emphasizing: "I tell you that in the same way there will be more rejoicing in heaven over one sinner who repents than over ninety-nine righteous persons who do not need to repent." There is nothing in the parable to indicate that this was an extraordinary sheep, the prize sheep of the flock. It is described simply as a sheep. Since in a parable the teller can insert any details he wishes or considers significant, the argument from silence is significant in such a passage. It was not because this sheep had special qualities that distinguished it from the others or that made it especially valuable or desirable to the shepherd that he went and retrieved it. It was simply because it was a sheep. The shepherd would, in other words, have done the same for any of his sheep.

This should be an encouragement to us. Most of us are not very "important people," or "beautiful people," as the world measures such things. Paul reminds us that not many "wise by human standards, influential, or of noble birth" were called (1 Cor. 1:26). We are not the kind of people who cause heads to turn when we pass by, or to whom people rush when we enter a room. It is not surprising, for God simply has not called many of this kind. We may think that because we do not get much attention, nobody knows or cares. With the famous people, every detail of their lives, every development, is a source of interest or at least curiosity to many people. The fans of famous athletes or entertainers devour magazine articles which divulge information about them. Some of these people know details about their idols which those persons themselves may by this time have forgotten. The point of this teaching of Jesus, however, is that everyone is of concern and interest to God. Each of us is an object of his love and care. He knows us, all of us, in a much more thorough and intimate way that those fans know their heroes and heroines.

There is one more passage which we should look at before we conclude this subject. It is Jesus' use of the imagery of the Good Shepherd in John 10. Jesus used it of himself, but it also by implication applies to the Father who sent Jesus. He spoke of the knowledge which the shepherd has of his sheep, calling them by name (v. 3). Conversely, the sheep follow the shepherd, for they know his voice and recognize when he, rather than someone else, is calling and leading them (vv. 4–5). We can place our trust in a God who knows each of us and knows our name when perhaps no one else around us does. And we can trust him that in the situations of life there is a distinctive quality to his voice. Those who know him, who are trained by experience to recognize his voice, are able to follow him. When we do that, we are assured that the shepherd will lead us only into that which is ultimately good. He will lead into life, and abundant life (vv. 7–10). The thief may come to bring harm to the sheep (v. 10a). That is never true of the Good Shepherd. We can trust him. We can trust the one who knows our name.

Study Guide

Key Questions

1. The author introduces this chapter with a statement about the need of people for "human warmth and recognition." Why is this a need? Why is it that people cannot feel complete without relationships that affirm and encourage?
2. How does the fact that God knows what happens to the little sparrow help you understand his love and watchcare over you? It is pleasant to realize that he knows the good things about us, but what about the bad? Doesn't that make you fearful? How do you respond to the fact that God knows everything about you and what is happening to you?
3. In chapter two we discussed the fact that God not only understands change but is the very cause of it. Think through the statement in this study that says God is not the cause of all that occurs. How does the author distinguish between the **initiating or causative will of God** and the **permissive will of God**?
4. What can you learn about prayer from the fact that "nothing ill can happen without the Father's will"? Does this make you more trusting and thankful to the God who knows your name?

Bible Investigation

Study Matthew 10:29–30. Reread the section of the study that deals with these verses. Use a Bible commentary to add to your understanding of it. The author writes: "Think about it." Take time to think through what they can mean for your life. God knows all about us. "Absolutely nothing escapes him."

Personal Application

1. Examine the way you have responded to others in this past week. Have you **depersonalized** someone or used the **baggage** approach to their personhood? Resolve to know their name and to show love and care for them. (1) Seek to **listen**—to **really see them**. (2) Seek not to be preoccupied about self and what you want to say.

DOES IT MATTER IF GOD EXISTS?

2. Thinking of your own relationship to Christ, rewrite the parable of the Lost Sheep (Luke 15:3–7). Address Jesus as your Good Shepherd and express His watchcare over you and your response to Him. Use the John 10:1–18 passage to help you with this.

For Further Thought

Look at the ministry programs of your church. Do you see any of them that depend upon those to whom they minister to keep them alive? Pray for your church and be a part of the focus that strives to minister to the needs of people.

4

Is Anyone in Charge?

For most of us, a lot of good things happen in our lives: friendship, families, health, a degree of material prosperity. When these things occur we feel good about the events, and thank God, tending to give him the credit for our "good fortune." We may see this as the answer to our prayers, and may testify to his goodness. It is easy to see God's hand in the "good" events of life.

Not all of life is that way however, either for us individually or for the world as a whole. There are times of disappointment, when we fail at something we had hoped to accomplish, or when the opportunity we had hoped for does not come our way. Sometimes life brings pain or even death. We lose loved ones, or we see them suffering. On the larger scale, bad things happen. Disease claims human lives. Tornadoes, hurricanes, earthquakes, volcanic eruptions, and floods all cause great human distress. Beyond natural disasters there is also human cruelty, manifested in crime and war. When we read the morning newspaper or watch the evening news, there seems to be more bad news than good news reported. Probably this is partly because of the nature of news editorial policies, but it is profoundly indicative of the problems that seem to plague the world in which we live. And then we ask, "Where was God when this happened?" It is as if he was not doing his job, for the assumption with which most of us operate is that God's goal and task in life is to so guide the events of the world that good things happen and bad things do not. We may feel like Shakespeare's Macbeth, that life "is a tale told by an idiot, full of sound and fury, signifying nothing."

It is not our purpose to attempt to solve this entire problem, generally referred to as the problem of evil. That puzzle has been with us for many years and has tested the faith of many persons while also challenging the intellects of the greatest theologians who have lived. We do, however, want to wrestle with the simple problem of whether there is any meaningful way to think of God as being at work in the unpleasant and seemingly undesirable events of life. It seems that this question could be answered rather simply for Christians, because Romans 8:28 says, "in all things God works for the good of those who love him." That particular way of putting it points to part of the problem: that there is no apparent correlation between the moral and spiritual state of the person and the fortunes of his or her life. It is not just, "why do bad things happen to good people?" That is the most obvious form of the question. It is also, however, "why do good things happen to bad people?" That was the question which the psalmist posed many years ago, as he envied the prosperity of the wicked (Ps. 73:3). It was difficult for him to understand why such persons should fare so well, apparently undeservedly so.

Yet, somehow Paul could speak of giving thanks in all circumstances, since this is God's will for his readers (1 Thess. 5:18). He himself could write, "Rejoice in the Lord always" (Phil. 4:4), and add, "I have learned to be content, whatever the circumstances" (v. 12) from a prison cell. He could say in connection with his "thorn in the flesh," "I delight in weaknesses, in insults, in hardship, in persecutions, in difficulties" (2 Cor. 12:10). Somehow he had learned that God is at work, even when the external circumstances seem to indicate otherwise. Note that this was something which he had *learned.* It apparently is possible to acquire this sort of understanding that God is at work both in the obviously pleasant and the seemingly unpleasant circumstances of life. If he could learn this, perhaps we can as well, and thus obtain the sort of peace and tranquillity which he displayed. The thrust of this dimension of biblical truth is that God is a God who works to accomplish his purposes in and through all of the events of life. Are there places in Scripture where we may especially observe this unusual fact?

One of the most remarkable people in the entire Bible is Joseph. He is remarkable for a number of reasons, not the least of which is that we are never told of any major failure in his life, any point of disobedience or indifference to God in some notable matter. More than that, however, is his remarkable sense of providence. Joseph went through a remarkable series of "misfortunes," yet he was able to look back upon these and see God's hand at work in and through all that had transpired. It seems extremely likely, too, that he approached those very events and lived in the midst of them with this same sense of God's working, for we detect no bitterness at the time or after. Somehow he understood that God is not limited to the use of good means, or of those things which he directly causes or sends in the accomplishment of his good ends.

Let's rehearse for a moment the major events of Joseph's life which are relevant to us here. He had been born as the eleventh son of Jacob and was Jacob's first son by his favorite wife, Rachel. As such, he was the favorite of Jacob, as of course he must have been of Rachel. His father, perhaps rather unwisely, distinguished Joseph from the others by giving him a conspicuous garment. The usual version which we have learned in Sunday school is that it was a coat of many colors, but it seems likelier that it had long sleeves, for the Hebrew word here means literally, "long in the extremities." When he wore it, it was apparent that he was especially preferred by his father. This became a source of irritation to his brothers. The irritation and jealousy was exacerbated, however, when Joseph had a dream in which he and his brothers were binding sheaves of grain out in the field. His sheaf stood upright, while those of his brothers bowed down before his. When he told this dream to his brothers, they saw this as an indication of his intention to rule over them, and they hated him more than ever. There was yet another dream, however, and this time the sun and moon and eleven stars were bowing down to him. His brothers were jealous of him, and even Jacob rebuked him for the idea that his mother and father, as well as his brothers, were to bow down to the ground before him.

Soon this jealousy and hatred spilled over into overt action. On one occasion his father sent him to his brothers, who were grazing the flocks. When they saw him coming, they wanted to kill him, but the oldest brother, Reuben, persuaded the other brothers not to kill him but instead to cast him into a dry cistern, so that he could rescue Joseph later. When a group of traders came by on their way to Egypt, the brothers, in Reuben's absence, sold Joseph to the traders, who in turn sold him into slavery.

Slavery was bad enough, but things were about to go from bad to worse. Joseph had been sold to Potiphar, an official of the king of Egypt, a captain of the guard. Under God's blessing, Potiphar prospered because of Joseph, and entrusted all of his affairs to him. His wife, however, had a romantic attraction to Joseph, who was a handsome young man, and tried to seduce him. When Joseph continued to resist her advances, she accused him of attempting to rape her, and Joseph was thrown into prison.

Here again, however, God blessed Joseph and gave him favor with the warden. Just like Potiphar, the warden entrusted matters to Joseph's supervision and had no concern for them. There he met the king's chief cupbearer and chief baker, who had offended the king and consequently been imprisoned. Each had a dream which Joseph interpreted. Joseph asked the chief cupbearer, whose dream meant that he would be restored to his former position, to speak well of him to the king when he was restored, so that Joseph might also be released. When his good fortune came, however, he forgot Joseph, leaving him to languish in prison for another two years.

Then the king had two puzzling and disturbing dreams, which none of his magicians and wise men could interpret. At that point the chief cupbearer remembered Joseph and his failure to keep his promise. He told the king, who in turn summoned Joseph. Joseph was able to interpret the dreams correctly, meaning that there would now be seven years of good crops and prosperity, followed by seven years of famine. As a result of this display of wisdom, the king put Joseph in charge of managing the commodities. He did this wisely, conserving the resources for the time of need. Finally, great good for Joseph, for the nation of Egypt, the surrounding nations, and, when his brothers came to purchase grain, even Joseph's own family, issued from the very unpleasant experiences he had undergone.

There are a number of important truths for us in this sequence of events. The first is simply that God is at work in everything, both the pleasant or obviously good and the unpleasant or seemingly not good events. It most certainly did not seem pleasant when all these things happened to Joseph. It is neither necessary nor appropriate to assert that God caused these things to happen. Both the deeds and the motives behind them are clearly opposed to God's values and commands. Certainly God does not inspire or approve of the hatred, jealousy, opposition, and virtually attempted murder by Joseph's brothers. The adulterous lust that drove Potiphar's wife and then, when rejected, caused her to act spitefully as she did is clearly not of God. Further, the forgetfulness and lack of gratitude shown by the chief cupbearer was the very opposite of God's faithfulness and compassion. Yet, even when these things contrary to God's will were being perpetrated, God was at work. He had an ultimate goal toward which he was working.

Yes, God was at work even in these matters. Joseph saw that. He must have believed it all along. When he revealed himself to his brothers, they were "terrified at his presence" (Gen. 45:3). Then he responded by saying that they should not be distressed or angry with themselves for what they had done, because "it was to save lives that God sent me ahead of you" (v. 5). Again he says, "But God sent me ahead of you to preserve for you a remnant on earth and to save your lives by a great deliverance. So then, it was not you who sent me here, but God" (vv. 7–8). Even when it appeared that God had abandoned Joseph, he was there, working for good in all of these unpleasant experiences.

There is an important lesson to be learned here. We have a tendency to think of God as working only in the dramatic, the cataclysmic, or the miraculous. The rest of the time we are on our own, and so is the rest of the world. Things just "happen" in such a way of viewing life. God, however, takes no vacations. He does not even take breaks in his day's work. He is constantly and everywhere active. The secular view that sees natural causes as the whole explanation of what occurs is refuted by Joseph's life. So also is the dualistic view which attributes certain things to divine activity and others to chance.

Of course, some cautions must be observed here. One is that we cannot necessarily identify God's working within every specific circumstance. To interpret every possibility within life in terms of whether it will come to its usual result or to a complete reversal may border more on superstition than upon faith. We need simply trust that God is at work, whether we can identify that with specific details or not.

The other caution is to avoid a passive orientation. If one believes that God is constantly and everywhere at work, he or she might believe that it does not matter what he or she does. Note, however, that Joseph diligently applied the gifts which God had given him. He interpreted the dreams. He actively managed the crops. We dare not relax, thinking that since God will take care of things, we need not be wise and diligent.

A second major observation which needs to be made is that God is able even to use evil to accomplish good. Think of what an omnipotent God he is who can do this. A very powerful but not all-powerful God would not be able to allow anything wrong or evil to occur if he was to accomplish his purposes. If some sin contrary to his will and word intruded, he would lose the ability to control the outcome. Insecure in his power against evil, he would have to control everything closely. An all-powerful God, on the other hand, is able to allow some slack in the system and still accomplish his goals. God is the great counterpuncher, the master of the counterattack.

There were varying degrees of evil in the actions of several people. In the case of the chief cupbearer, it was simply neglect or forgetfulness. In the case of Potiphar's wife, it may have been a spur of the moment type of thing, a sort of retaliation for Joseph's lack of response to her overtures. With the brothers, however, there was a greater degree of premeditation. They had some time to think over what they were going to do, and although they modified the more extreme original intention of murdering Joseph, they nonetheless confirmed their decision by their action. In all these varieties of evil, God was at work.

We often tend to think of events as having a single cause and a single purpose. That is not the case, however. While the brothers intended the outcome of their action to be evil, God intended that it be good. Humans have rather limited foresight, both in terms of the distance ahead that they can see and the number of results they are able to observe. God, however, sees that while the most common and hence the most likely outcome of event *a* is *x*, it can also be *y* or *z* and he steers those events to a different and humanly unforeseen end.

Joseph had grasped this truth, too. When Jacob died, Joseph's brothers feared that he would now retaliate for what they had done. They assumed that he had withheld this punishment because he did not want to make Jacob unhappy. So they sent a message to Joseph, telling him that before his death Jacob had asked that Joseph forgive them. Joseph, however, without minimizing the seriousness of what his brothers had done, indicated that he understood this complex causation far better than they did. He said, "You intended to harm me, but God intended it for good, to accomplish what is now being done, the saving of many lives" (Gen. 50:20). The reason that b results in y rather than x is that God adds his factor to the equation, so it is not b leads to x, but bc leads to y.

What is especially impressive is how God completely reversed the brothers' intentions to bring about the very thing they were attempting to prevent. They were incensed at the idea that Joseph would rule over them and that he thought likewise. Yet by selling him off into slavery, they enabled him to rise to a position of power relative to that entire part of the world. Their action had helped bring about the very thing they feared, and to an even greater degree than they had ever imagined. He ruled over not only his brothers, his father, and mother, but virtually the entire region.

There are other examples of this type of divine countering activity in Scripture. Probably the most striking and certainly the most important is the crucifixion of Christ. That was an evil act, done by evil humans to the Son of God, and Peter made that clear in his message at Pentecost. It was "this Jesus, whom you crucified," but the full statement of what God had done was, "God has made this Jesus, whom you crucified, both Lord and Christ" (Acts 2:36). Once again God's counterattack had overcome the actions of sinful men, thus negating the results of those actions.

Note here also that, just as in the case of Joseph, God brought about not only what these sinful human beings were attempting to prevent, but much more than that. They may have thought that they were preventing a political ruler from gaining power, or perhaps a prophet or teacher from gaining a degree of influence. What they were helping him to become was a savior, the fulfillment of his mission as the incarnate Son of God.

A third important necessary observation is the difference between the short range and the long range results of certain events. When judged by the short range results, what happened to Joseph at each step in the process was very unfortunate. The result of his brothers' action was that Joseph was separated from his family, was taken out of his own country, and became a slave. The result of the actions of Potiphar's wife was that Joseph was thrown into prison and lost even a slave's liberty. The chief cupbearer's negligence resulted in Joseph having to remain in prison longer than he would have otherwise.

When we look at the long range effects of these actions, however, things appear quite different. Note how each of these occurrences fit within God's long range goal. Had the brothers not sold him off into slavery, it is unlikely that he would ever have come to be in Egypt, and even if he had, he probably would never have been in a position to come to the attention of the king. Once there, he would not have been moved beyond Potiphar's household for Joseph was, after all, a slave who had no mobility, no power or right to change employers and move upward. Unless, of course, he were thrown into prison where he would come into contact with one of the king's closest servants. And had the chief cupbearer remembered Joseph so that he was released from prison immediately, the timing would not have been right. He might have been somewhere else by the time of the king's dreams, or the chief cupbearer, without the underlying sense of guilt, might at the later point have forgotten about Joseph's ability to interpret dreams. Each of these injustices in its own way contributed to Joseph being able to manage the crops and commodities of Egypt when the important events occurred. The long range consequences turned out to be in some ways virtually the exact opposite of the short range effects.

There should be a word of guidance for us here not to judge circumstances too soon. We need to ask not only, "what are the results?" but also, "are they all in yet?" We see this phenomenon in other areas as well. Sometimes the first scattered election returns from a few unrepresentative precincts show a lead for the candidate who ultimately turns out to be the loser of the election. Similarly, scores from the early part of an athletic event often are misleading. Only the final scores really count. Not all the returns may be in when we try to evaluate the overall effect of certain actions.

There is a fourth valuable lesson here: the importance of not allowing oneself to become bitter. Joseph certainly would have had adequate basis for bitterness toward these persons. They had wronged him, engaging in largely unprovoked actions. He found himself in unpleasant circumstances which he did not deserve. Life is not fair, we often hear, and that is certainly true. But what we do about those injustices often determines the end result. If Joseph had allowed himself to become embittered, he would have been allowing his brothers to hurt him even more than they already had. It is true that quite frequently the person who displays the bitterness, rather than those against whom it is felt, is the loser, the one hurt most by that bitterness. Joseph no doubt had adequate opportunity for retaliation. When he became the ruler over the supplies of Egypt, he was in a position to take vengeance on anyone whom he chose, including Potiphar, Potiphar's wife, and the chief cupbearer. The most he did was to make his brothers squirm a bit, but that was not a spitefully done act.

It is in our own best interest to forget the wrongs. One Christian leader found himself in a situation in which many felt he had been the victim of an injustice. Although he had no intention of litigating, one person counseled him to sue, "to teach them that they can't treat people that way." A good and wise friend, a former student of his who had recently gone through a similar experience, offered him some good advice. He said, "Put it behind you as quickly and completely as you can. Don't do anything that might prolong your experience and your memory of it. Get on with the rest of your life." That was both good theology and good psychology.

There is yet another dimension to this refusal of bitterness, however. It is the importance of not becoming embittered toward God. It might have been easy for Joseph to resent God for these misfortunes, whether he saw God as the cause or as the one who could have prevented them but failed to do so. If so, he would probably have forfeited the right and the opportunity of these additional blessings. This frequently is what happens when unpleasant events come into the lives of people, even Christians. They blame God for allowing these things, apparently assuming that God owes it to them to allow only the best of things to occur. This is not what Joseph did, however. And as a result he passed these tests and thus was given even greater opportunities.

One Christian businessman rose within the executive ranks of a large corporation with several subsidiary companies. At one point, the position of president of one of those companies became vacant, and he believed he was next in line for that position. To his disappointment, however, someone else was instead appointed to the position. He could have sulked and perhaps left the corporation. Instead, he resolved to remain and do the best he could, waiting for another opportunity. Soon the presidency of one of the other larger and more influential subsidiaries became vacant, and he was appointed to the position. Then he discovered that this was the position which the board had already planned for him to fill, and had consequently passed over him for the earlier, lesser position. That is how it is with God and us, sometimes. If we continue to trust in his wisdom and goodness, even greater blessings are possible.

Now, however, we must ask further about the practical application of this. For we must ask ourselves, "If this was true in the case of Joseph, and in our own case as well, what are we to do in light of this?" How can we cooperate with what God is doing so that it will have the maximum benefit, or so that God can do most fully what he purposes to do in our lives and through us? What in Joseph's response made the results possible which, if he had not fulfilled it, would have made these results impossible? These will be clues to us as to how to respond to what God is doing.

One important directive is to be alert for opportunities for service. It is apparent that looking backward, Joseph saw that these situations gave him opportunities for usefulness to the Lord. Although the text does not say so, it seems likely from Joseph's conduct at the time and his lack of surprise at the outcome that he was alert to these possibilities at the time. This is not to say that Joseph knew the possibilities, but that he was conscious that such would and could present themselves, and he sought to capitalize upon them. If he had not been alert to such possibilities, they would simply have passed him by.

This was a matter of knowing that such opportunities may be found in the most unlikely places. From the standpoint of his point of origin, Egypt was not a place of opportunity, not the place where God was. He was not in the covenant land, the place to which God had led Abraham. Something of this consciousness persists in his requirement that when the people of Israel are led up out of Egypt they were to take his bones with them for burial in the Promised Land (Gen. 50:24–25). Yet, he did not exclude the possibility that the same God who had revealed himself to him through dreams would also be active in Egypt. Certainly, one would not expect to find God in slavery or in a prison, but Joseph was alert to what God was doing and consequently became a vessel of that divine working.

We may be inclined at times to think that God works only in ideal situations or at certain preferred times. When or where it is not those times and places, we may not think that he can or will do anything significant. We may attempt to control God's working, thinking we must plan and prepare for what is to happen, and in effect tell God how and when he is to work.

What we need to do is modify our thinking and broaden our outlook of what God can do. This is a matter not merely of thinking that God can work in spite of problematic situations, but that he could work much more effectively if it were not for these problems. Rather, we will need to see that it is because of these very factors and through them that God will work. We will therefore seek to exploit those factors.

I have known some Christians whose sensitivity to opportunity was developed to a very high degree. Somehow, they always seem to have more opportunities for effective service than do most people. One was a missionary, who looked upon every adversity as a prelude to witness. If he had a flat tire on his jeep while driving through the jungle, he would look around to see who the Lord was going to send to stop and help him with his flat so that he could witness. Another pastor whom I knew sought for opportunities in other persons' problems. He would frequently stop to help a motorist who was having difficulty, then when he left gave the person a card which said something like, "I am a Christian. It is because of Christ's love for me and my consequent love for people that I have sought to help you. If I can ever be of any additional help, please do not hesitate to call me." It included his telephone number.

One friend of mine discovered that those seemingly chance occurrences which are frequently disappointing in terms of one's original intention may not only open doors, but may open doors which could not be opened otherwise by any amount of human effort and force. On one occasion he was planning to go goose hunting with three of his friends. On the day before they were to leave, however, the man who was to be paired up with Don became too ill to go. That left them with an odd number and Don with no partner, but they decided to go hunting nonetheless. When they arrived at the place where they were to hunt, Don explained to the proprietor his situation and asked if there was anyone else who did not have a partner with whom he could be paired in a goose blind. The man replied that there was a Mr. B. who was hunting alone, and wondered if Don would want to be paired up with him. When Don replied affirmatively, the man added, "By the way, this is Mr. X. B., of XYZ," and named a large brewing company which bore the man's name. Now what would you do if you were paired up in a goose blind with the president of a brewery? Apparently the geese must have been on vacation, for it was a very slow day, and Don and his hunting partner began to talk. They talked about world conditions, and the other man said, "I'm certainly glad that our children are grown, for I'd hate to try to raise children in a world like this," and Don, who had two teenage sons and two teenage daughters at the time, saw his opportunity. He said, "I agree that this is a difficult time to raise children. My wife and I are Christians, however, and we have dedicated our children to the Lord, and we are trusting them to his care." The conversation progressed rapidly, and although Don did not lead that man to the Lord that day, the man said as they parted, "I've enjoyed our conversation. The next time you're coming here to hunt, please let me know. I'd like to hunt with you again."

Suppose you had felt led to witness to that man, to try to bring him to faith in Jesus Christ. How would you do so? It would not be possible to get into his home, past servants and possibly even bodyguards. It certainly would not be possible to make an appointment to talk to him at his office. Yet, without planning and preparation, Don had been given a chance to witness to this man while "off-duty," as it were. God had done the planning, and God had utilized the circumstances. Suppose, however, Don had said to himself, "This is not a scheduled witnessing time. I have not made an appointment to talk to this man. It is not Tuesday night, the time for evangelistic visitation in my church. This is relaxing time, not witnessing time." If that were his mode of thinking, he would not even have thought about sharing his testimony. He would not even have noticed the opening presented by the man's words about the difficulty of raising children in our society.

Not long after Don told me that story I found myself free on a Friday afternoon. I had completed my week's teaching, and I felt a need to unwind, so I decided to play a round of golf. I called one after another of my usual partners, all of whom were unavailable. One professor had promised his wife he would baby-sit that afternoon. A writers' conference, a department meeting, and a professional society each took its toll on other potential partners. Finally I decided that I would simply go out to the golf course alone and see who else was lacking a partner or simply play by myself. As I approached the first tee from one direction, another man came from the opposite direction. Virtually simultaneously, we asked, "Playing alone?" and off we went. He was a salesman who had achieved his quota early and was out to celebrate. The Bible says, "Do two walk together unless they have agreed to do so?" (Amos 3:3). We had not formally agreed to do so, but we both had the same type of problem with our golf games, so we spent a lot of time walking down the right side of the fairway looking for our golf balls. Consequently, there were abundant opportunities for conversation, and about the eighth hole, the conversation turned to what that salesman called "religion." I did not convert him that day, but as I left, I thought that perhaps I should not tell my golfing partners I was going out to play more often, choosing instead simply to go to the golf course and see whom the Lord might send out there to whom I could witness. I had learned, in other words, that there may even be wisdom and value in seeking out the situations which I might otherwise be inclined to consider an undesirable or unfortunate situation.

What we have described are situations the Lord provides us which constitute opportunities for us to do something for him, if that is ever an appropriate way of putting matters. There also, however, are situations which also are initially disappointing or seemingly unfavorable which he uses as opportunities to do something for us. I also had to learn that through what was initially a rather trying experience.

In the spring and summer of 1976, I went to Munich, Germany, for a sabbatical leave of absence. I had received an invitation to study at the University of Munich with Wolfhart Pannenberg, the world's leading scholar in my field, systematic theology. I and my two oldest daughters went at the end of April, with my wife and youngest daughter planning to follow in early June. We had been unable to arrange housing in advance, but having been to Munich three years earlier, I assumed that we could find housing when we arrived simply by consulting the classified advertisements, just as we would do in this country. Imagine my chagrin, however, upon arriving, to find that there was a newspaper strike in Munich! No classified advertisements were available. We took two rooms on a nightly basis from a woman with whom we had previously stayed in the vicinity of Dachau, about fifteen miles north of the university. That, however, would not serve our purposes for very long, and I realized that finding a furnished apartment for a short term would be very difficult.

On our first full weekend in Germany we decided to travel to Interlaken, Switzerland, a popular vacation spot we had visited three years earlier. When we arrived on a Friday afternoon, we drove along the road between the mountains and the lake, just outside of town, looking for a place to stay. We would pull our car out onto the shoulder of the narrow road, get out and inquire at each place, then get back into the car. At one point, as I got out of the car and the door clicked shut behind me, I realized that I had made a serious mistake. My keys were still hanging in the ignition. Ordinarily that would not present such a serious problem, but on this vehicle, a leased Renault, when the door was locked and was opened from the inside and then closed again, it was again locked. The only way to alter this situation was to get out, stick the key in the lock, and unlock the door. Because I was still unfamiliar with the idiosyncrasies of this foreign car, I had forgotten to take my keys, and they were now locked inside the car, as was the other set of keys, in my daughter's backpack. I knew I needed a locksmith, so I flagged down a passing motorcycle policeman. He listened sympathetically to my explanation of the problem in German, and said he would send a locksmith back from the next town to help me. Soon a dapper locksmith appeared. He carefully taped the door of the car so that he would not scratch it with his tool. Then he reached in and popped the lever open. The charge was twenty-five francs (at that time about ten dollars) and for some reason I asked for "eine Quittung" (a receipt). I was collecting receipts for every expenditure on this sabbatical trip, and just in case this expense was a tax deductible matter, I thought I ought to have one for this also. The mechanic said he did not have a receipt with him, but if I would come with him back to the shop, he would be glad to supply one. As we drove the three or four kilometers to town, we noticed a woman who waved at us from the second floor of a house, which had a sign, "Ferienwohnung" (vacation apartment) on it. I resolved that on the way back we would stop and inquire of her. We did, and found that we could rent very reasonably a furnished four room apartment with cooking facilities. We enjoyed that weekend, but in the midst of it I began to think. There were popular vacation spots not more than an hour's drive from Munich. Certainly they would also have Ferienwohnungen, and since my classes at the university met only on Monday and Thursday, an hour's commute would not be prohibitive.

The next Thursday we started out in search of our apartment. We drove down the east side of the Starnberger See (lake), then headed for Garmisch-Partenkirchen, a popular ski resort. We spent the night there after looking at some possibilities, then drove the few miles to Oberammergau. Since this was also a popular tourist

DOES IT MATTER IF GOD EXISTS?

spot in the foothills of the Alps and this was not a year when the Passion Play was being performed, I reasoned that there might be some excess tourist facilities. We found the Verkehrsamt (chamber of commerce), which had a list of available apartments. We picked out the likeliest appearing one, and rang the doorbell. A young woman carrying a baby met us at the door. Unlike the somewhat cool older women whom we sometimes met running these establishments, this woman spoke excellent English, having worked for a time as a "nanny" in Britain, and liked Americans. In fact, our only problem with her turned out to be getting her to speak German with us. We felt an immediate bond with her. She said, "If you are staying that long a time, I would want to reduce the rent, and of course I would not charge you for heat and electricity." We drove back to the Verkehrsamt, prayed about it in our car, and then went in to indicate that we would like to rent that apartment. "Did Frau Meyer talk to you about the price?" the man asked. While we drove back to the office, she had called and reduced the price even below what we had settled upon. We had a very nearly ideal situation, and very reasonably. But I would possibly never have thought of looking for a Ferienwohnung if we had not stayed in that one in Switzerland. And we might never have found that if we hadn't locked ourselves out of our car so that we drove by that woman's house. God had used our adversity to lead us to what he had in mind for us. That was only the first of a whole series of adversities, always coming on Friday, which the Lord used to bless us. In fact, one Friday my oldest daughter said, "Dad, it's Friday. What bad thing is going to happen that the Lord will use for good for us?" The opportunities are often there in the midst of the problem, if we think to look for them.

There is one other dimension to this matter of the Lord's blessing through adversity. The way in which the believer reacts to difficulty can often be a powerful testimony to God's grace. Think of what a testimony Joseph was to the people of his time, but beyond that, to the people of all time who have read that story. He is an excellent illustration of how God can use circumstances and give grace to a believer, not to fret and become distressed, but to remain at peace and thus capitalize upon the opportunity.

The same can be true of us. What we do with the trouble that comes to us speaks eloquently not only about us but, more than that, about the God whom we serve. Complaining is one way to react. Trusting God is not a natural way of responding to difficulty for most people, but it speaks very loudly.

Recently I had the privilege of conducting the funeral service of a great man of God. I had been his pastor many years before and had been given the privilege of leading this man to faith in the Lord. Within two weeks of making his own decision, he led another man, a customer of his, to the Lord. Now, however, this great hulk of a man had in his last days wasted away under the awful devastation of cancer. In those last months, however, as he knew he was dying, he had used the opportunity to let everyone at his place of work know about Jesus Christ. At his funeral, there was an opportunity to share what Harry had meant to them. His boss was there, and spoke with great respect and admiration of the type of person Harry had been, and the credibility of his testimony, given not only in his words but also in the way in which he handled the suffering he was experiencing. More than one Christian believer has borne eloquent witness to divine grace and mercy, before friends and acquaintances, medical personnel, and other patients, by handling the problem so courageously.

Yes, life will not always deal us the set of circumstances we would want, would have prayed for, or would believe to be the type of thing we think God would want for us as his children. It is not necessary to regard these as God's direct doing, his causation. If, however, we have the kind of understanding Joseph had, that God is at work in everything, then that will indeed be the case. For our belief or disbelief in this matter frequently makes the difference in whether he is able to work in all of these circumstances to accomplish his will.

Study Guide

Key Questions

1. Have you been able to see God at work in your life? In the bad experiences as well as the good? How did you know or why could you not tell?
2. List the **important truths** the author has gleaned from the story of the life of Joseph that outline the activity of God in the happenings of life. Carefully consider the illustrations that clarify the truths.
3. What are the three views regarding the working of God in the circumstances of life? Joseph's story refutes both the secular and the dualistic view. He emphasized that God is "constantly and everywhere active." The author, however, explains two cautions that must be considered: (1) "we cannot necessarily **identify** God's working within every specific circumstance" and (2) we need "to avoid a passive orientation." What does this mean?
4. "How can we cooperate with what God is doing so that it will have the maximum benefit, or so that God can do most fully what he purposes to do in our lives, and through us?" What are the two steps given in the text?

Bible Investigation

1. Compare Romans 8:28 and Psalm 73:3. Could one person express both thoughts? Why or why not? Think about what prompted the writers to pen these verses.
2. Read Genesis 37–50. Look for clues to indicate how Joseph's **attitude**, the way he had **learned** to deal with misfortune, gave him confidence that God was continually working. What was Joseph's attitude toward bitterness? Does it pay to be bitter?

Personal Application

1. Memorize Romans 8:28. Accept the first part of the statement and concentrate your focus on the second part.
2. Explore the meaning of Amos 3:3 with your activities. When chance meetings like the author's illustration (golfing) come your way, do you let them become opportunities to see God at work? Pray about such encounters.

3. Apply the two steps given in answer to the question "How can we cooperate with what God is doing . . . so that God can do most fully what he purposes to do in our lives, and through us?"
   (1) Be alert for opportunities to serve.
   (2) Broaden your outlook to what God can do.

For Further Thought

1. Review the life of Christ. Focus on how God throughout Jesus' life used every kind of "misfortune," "hardship," and planning of the evil one to "make Jesus . . . both Lord and Christ" (Acts 2:36). Share your thankful heart-thoughts in praise to God!
2. On every hand people are challenged to set goals and set them high. How did Joseph rise to such a high position without making political advancement his goal? Frame a statement that Joseph might have used for his goal in life.

5

Something Does Not Move

Perhaps you have had this experience, or one similar to it. You are sitting in a train, or perhaps in an airplane, waiting at a gate. Suddenly you have a sensation that you are moving. Yet, as you look more closely, you see that you are not. What is actually happening is that the train or plane next to you is moving, and you consequently get the feeling that you are moving. When our point of reference moves, we often cannot tell whether *we* are moving or *it* is moving. The only way to detect which is occurring is to find some neutral focal point that is not moving at all and measure against it. Sometimes the results are quite harmless, as the time recently when I was in a car wash. Thinking my car was rolling, I stepped down hard on the brakes only to discover that the car was stationary but that the wash mechanism, which was all that I could see through the spurting water, was moving. At other times it may have rather serious results. On one farm there was an old deteriorating silo. Each year before filling the silo, the farmers would inspect it. On one occasion, the farmer who was in the top of the silo looked up and, seeing the clouds moving by, thought the silo was falling. "There she goes," he shouted, and jumped to the ground, suffering injuries.

The point of these examples is that we can only judge and evaluate things by reference to some fixed or objective standard, and when that standard is moving, we have very little basis for evaluating our own situation. This is a popular form of the general problem of relativism. This appears in many different ways. It can be illustrated by the story of Joe and Moe, who were shipwrecked alone on an island in the Pacific Ocean during World War I. After many months, a Coca-Cola bottle washed up on shore. It was a new, larger bottle, which neither Joe nor Moe had ever seen. They knew only the old, smaller, bottles. Pulling the new bottle from the water and comparing himself to it, Joe called out to Moe in near panic: "Hey Moe, we've shrunk!" A more complex or sophisticated version of this same effect is found in the phenomenon of "Gs." We usually identify "down" by the direction in which gravity seems to pull us, and "up" as its opposite. When, however, we are placed in a situation such as an aircraft making a sharp change of direction, the same effect is felt. The direction in which centrifugal force pulls us would be perceived, all other things being equal, as "down."

All of what we have been discussing have been instances of relativity of perception, where what we feel or see is dependent upon other factors. In the twentieth century, however, there have been actual intellectual developments in which some of the most common sense absolutes have been shown not to be so absolute.

Newtonian physics was a physics of the absoluteness of time and space. Space simply was that which occupied area. Although something could grow or shrink, be stretched or compressed, its basic dimensions were relatively fixed. And in this scheme, because the speed of light was fixed, it was expected that there would be addition and subtraction of velocities of the speed of light. By this terminology was meant that when two motions were present, they would either be added or subtracted, depending upon the direction. So two cars approaching each other from opposite directions each moving at 60 miles per hour have a relative speed of closure of 120 miles per hour, and when they pass, they move apart at the same 120 mile per hour speed. When a car traveling 60 miles an hour approaches from behind another traveling 50 miles per hour, the speed at which the former overtakes the latter is 10 miles per hour, and after passing, it pulls away at 10 miles per hour. Similarly, consider a man walking on the deck of a ship, at the speed of three knots. The ship is moving at 12 knots. When the man walks forward on the deck, his speed relative to the shore is 15 knots. When he walks toward the rear of the deck, however, his speed is only 9 knots. This is common physics and mathematics, and is the type of thing that often is the subject of math and scholastic aptitude tests.

One would expect, then, that since the speed of light is constant at 186,284 miles per second, according to Newton's calculation, the law of addition and subtraction of velocities should also apply here. Suppose two stars are rotating around a common point at the speed of four miles per second. The light from the one moving toward us should be traveling at 186,288 miles per second and that from the one moving away from us should be traveling at 186,280 miles per second. Yet there is no such variation, a strange paradox which seemed insoluble until Albert Einstein proposed a unique solution. Suppose, said Einstein, that space and time are not absolute, but relative. Subsequent tests verified this hypothesis.

These results give rise to science fiction-like scenarios. An object moving at ninety percent of the speed of light is only one half the length, in the dimension of its movement, of what it would be if at rest. So, if you strapped a yardstick to the side of a rocket ship, accelerated that ship to ninety percent of the speed of light, and then flew it past an identical yardstick at rest, if you had a sufficiently fast camera to be able to capture the action, it would show that the moving yardstick measured only eighteen inches on the yardstick at rest. Similarly, if a thirty-year-old twin (or any other person, for that matter) took off in a spaceship, accelerated to ninety percent of the speed of light, flew for forty earth years and returned to earth, his watch would only have ticked and his heart would only have beaten half as many times as those of his earthbound twin brother, and he would have aged twenty years and would have a biological age of fifty, whereas his twin would have aged forty years and would now be seventy years of age. All of this is part of the theory of relativity in physics.

A parallel can be seen in mathematics. Those of us who studied plane geometry learned very early that the sum of the angles of a triangle is 180 degrees, whereas the sum of the angles of a rectangle is 360 degrees. This is a basic truth of Euclidean geometry. Yet in the twentieth century, alternative geometries were being developed, in which the sum of the angles was either more or less than 180 degrees, depending upon whether they were on curved surfaces of positive or negative curvature. The older Euclidean geometry was a geometry of flat surfaces, but flat surfaces are not the only type of surfaces which occur in reality.

All of this is interesting, you may or may not say. What, however, does this have to do with our topic? This deals with objective sciences, natural science, and mathematics. What is the relationship of issues like this to our Christian faith and practice, or to religion and ethics in general? What has happened in our generation is that this general understanding that so much is relative has carried over to other areas such as right and wrong. We are encountering relativism, the idea that "it all depends," in so much of life. One view is as true as another, according to this view. This quite definitely has an impact upon matters which as Christians we consider very important.

What we are facing, in other words, is a major confusion among people in American society about what is right and wrong, and what is true and false. This shows itself in a number of ways. One is the ethical view of relativism. On this view, there is nothing absolutely right or wrong. It all depends. What is right for one person may be wrong for another, or what is right at one time or situation may be wrong in another.

A very popular form of this thinking which has developed in the last twenty-five years is known as situation ethics. Although the term is seldom used anymore, the ethics involved is still very much alive, well, and influential. It took its classical expression in the thought of an Episcopalian clergyman and ethicist, Joseph Fletcher, who wrote in the middle 1960s.

Fletcher insisted that there are no absolute rules, and that nothing is absolutely good at all times, with one exception in each case. The only thing that is always good is love, and the only rule with no exceptions is "always do the most loving thing." He argued for this on several grounds. One is that there is conflict between the various things that we consider to be absolute, so that at most there could only be one absolute, one winner in the tournament of absolute rules, as it were. A further problem is our limited knowledge, so that we can never know all of the circumstances or considerations involved in a given decision. From this uncertainty about what is right there results a skepticism as to whether there actually is any one thing that is right.

Based upon this, Fletcher contended that nothing is inherently good or right or bad or wrong. In a given situation, good is the most loving course of action. Thus potentially anything can be good, depending upon the situation. Even murder or adultery are not necessarily always wrong. If murder is the most loving thing to do, then murder is good and right, and one should do it. He tells a story of "sacrificial adultery," involving a German woman, Mrs. Bergmeier, during World War II. She had been captured by the Soviets and knew that her family badly needed her. The only way she could be released was if she was pregnant. She found a friendly Volga camp guard willing to impregnate her and was released to be reunited with her family. The family loved little Dietrich most of all, because of what he had done for them. Fletcher maintains that what Mrs. Bergmeier did was not wrong or sinful. It was the most loving thing she could do for her family, including her husband, and therefore it was a good and right thing. Given this type of view, it is not surprising that there is confusion about what should be done.

Religious relativism exists as well. This comes in two forms. One is the sense that all religions either are the same at root, or that they are different, but equally true. Some have noted and emphasized parallels between Jesus' teachings and other religions. They have also noted the relative lack of success of Christian missions in relationship to other world religions as contrasted with its success with those of tribal religions. Coupled with this is a sense that it would be unfair for God to condemn large numbers of persons simply because they have had no opportunity to hear an explicit presentation of the Christian gospel. It must be, say some current religious leaders, that the various religions are alternate routes, different ways to get to the same God or to receive his favor and salvation.

The other form is that belief is not really important. Going back at least as far as Friedrich Schleiermacher at the dawning of the nineteenth century, there has been a growing contingent of people who hold that religion is not primarily a matter of belief but of feeling. Thus, different religious belief systems may embody equally valid religious experiences. What one believes is really relatively unimportant.

This may seem far removed from some of us. This, surely, is the way people outside the church think, but not people within the church, especially not evangelical or "born again" persons. Yet there is some startling indication that perhaps even this relativistic type of thinking has influenced true Christian believers. Rather than being "transformed by the renewing of their minds" (Rom. 12:2), some believers are apparently being "squeezed into the world's mold" (Philips translation). In 1991 the Barna organization, a Christian research organization in California, had published the results of its telephone polling on the religious beliefs of Americans. One statement posed to those called was, "There is no such thing as absolute truth; different people can define truth in conflicting ways and still be correct." The respondents were asked to respond with "agree strongly," "agree somewhat," "disagree somewhat," "disagree strongly," or "don't know." In the entire sample, twenty-eight percent agreed strongly and an additional thirty-nine percent agreed somewhat, while thirteen percent disagreed somewhat and sixteen percent disagreed strongly. But what of evangelicals? Among those who identified themselves as members of evangelical denominations, twenty-three percent agreed strongly, thirty percent agreed somewhat, seventeen percent disagreed somewhat, and twenty-five percent disagreed strongly. Among those who considered themselves born again, the percentages were respectively, twenty-three, twenty-nine, fifteen, and twenty-seven. In other words, over half of those who would be identified as evangelicals agreed somewhat or strongly with this statement of relativism. While one might wish that the question had been somewhat more clearly and explicitly stated so that the significance of the response could be more confidently interpreted, there is certainly enough evidence here to give pause to our belief that those who are conservative in religious belief and experience believe there is absolute truth.

This tendency to accept all views as equally acceptable is also part of a larger orientation which sociologist James Davison Hunter has called "evangelical civility." It is the tendency not to "rock the boat" or to appear too intolerant of others, perhaps because of the sometimes intolerant and even obnoxious image by which an earlier generation of fundamentalists was depicted. Hunter's survey of students in several evangelical colleges and seminaries revealed that there is among them a considerable amount of what he terms "hermeneutical subjectivism," or the tendency to understand portions of the Bible which had formerly been thought to represent historical events as merely symbolic representations of spiritual realities. Thus, the meaning of the statements was not their objective referent, but the inner subjective response or interpretation of the person reading the passages.

All of this is part of the general mood of our day, according to which truth is not something discovered but created. This came out in rather striking fashion in the confirmation hearings for Supreme Court Justice Clarence Thomas in October 1991. While most of the public interest focused upon the sexual harassment charges brought against Thomas by a former woman subordinate, I found much more interesting the interrogations of the nominee regarding natural law, a view he was believed to have acquired as a student in Roman Catholic parochial schools. This is the view that certain actions can be understood as right or wrong depending upon whether they can be seen to reflect some actual characteristic of nature. The chairman of the Senate committee doing the interrogation made very clear that these laws are not somehow based upon the reality of the universe, but that right and wrong is what Congress makes them to be by its legislation.

Here is a clear case of subjectivism and hence of relativism. I am reminded of the story of three baseball umpires, which I have used a number of times to illustrate different points. Three umpires were discussing their calling of balls and strikes. One said, "I call them as they are." That was the objectivist, or even the absolutist. The second said, "I call them as I see them." That was the relativist. But the third said, emphatically, "They ain't neither balls nor strikes, until I call them." That man was certainly the subjectivist in the group. That is the view that the chairman of the committee was espousing. Things are not really right or wrong until Congress decides which they are. Encouraged by existentialism and other voluntarist views of reality, subjectivism is very influential today. It gives to humans the power to create truth and goodness not by creating the facts but by deciding their character and value.

What all of these considerations do correctly point toward is that our understanding of the truth is limited by the fact that each of us is just one person with certain limited perspectives upon matters. How we perceive something is dependent upon that perspective. If four persons seated on a circle, ninety degrees from each other and each equidistant from a block in the middle, each side of which is a different color, look at that block and report what color they see, each will have a different version; the color of the whole block is reported as the color each individual sees. Unless each thinks and says, "the part of the block I can see is this color, but I cannot infer anything further about the color of the rest of the block," there is an apparent conflict in what they report. Each is correct, from his or her own perspective on the block. In this respect, they are like the five blind men, each of whom seized a different part of the elephant, and each of whom therefore perceived the elephant quite differently than the others. To have the complete truth, one would have to combine all the reports of these different perspectives. One should not conclude, however, that there is no absolute truth, or no truth that would be the truth for anyone looking at the block from a given perspective, or handling a given part of the elephant.

This can be seen with respect to the question, "What time is it?" It may be 12 noon in Chicago, but it is 1 P.M. in New York, 11 A.M. in Denver, 10 A.M. in Los Angeles, and so forth. It makes no sense to ask, "But what time is it, really?" There simply is no answer to that question. But while the answer to the question depends upon what time zone one is in, in that time zone there is a correct answer. It is not a question of 10:45 or 10:20 or 10:31. There is one correct time. In similar fashion from our earlier illustration, while time and space are relative, there is one absolute: the speed of light. Not everything is relative.

That is where the difficulty in deciding the right and the true comes in. What is needed is some standard by which to measure and evaluate the various options. If all we have are various opinions and claims about the right and the true, we have no way to judge among them. This can be seen clearly when listening to a political debate, which may involve several different candidates. Each makes his or her points, which may sound very plausible and even persuasive when we listen to them. As we then turn our attention to the next candidate, however, we may be equally impressed, so that we really do not know whom to believe. Ethical debates are similarly confusing, as each person claims to be presenting the truth. What is one really to believe?

The situation is like one we could imagine in which there were several rulers or yardsticks, no two of which agreed exactly with one another. What then are we to think? We must have some absolute measure against which to measure each of these claimants. Or imagine oneself at a race, run on an oval track and involving many laps, such as the Indianapolis 500 automobile race. As one looks out upon the track, it is difficult to determine who is in the lead. One car seems to be ahead of another, but it may actually be nearly a full length (or more) behind the other. The judgment of who is leading depends upon being able to identify the actual finish point, both in terms of the location on the track and the location of a given car's lap within the entire collection of laps which constitutes the race.

DOES IT MATTER IF GOD EXISTS?

To put the point more specifically: within all the viewpoints, all the claims of what is right and wrong, is there some ruling independent of all human opinions to which a judgment can be appealed, some measure outside the flux of the limited perspectives of human understanding? It is like persons watching a parade from different places along the route. Each would have a different opinion of what part of the parade is currently going by. But is there someone who has a viewpoint well above the ground and can see the whole of the parade at one time? In other words, is there a divine perspective upon the whole of reality?

We should not underestimate the importance of the question. For unless there is some such absolute or unqualified criterion, we are probably doomed to endless debate. There will be the attempts to persuade others of one's opinion, but eventually this becomes not an argument but a quarrel, with persons shouting at each other. For to each person, what is seen from his or her perspective seems so persuasive, but the other person quite literally cannot see it. And shouting matches may become fights of one type or another. That, in effect, is what politics and legislation are all about. Those in the minority are not convinced, as a rule. They are forced to conform to the viewpoint of the majority, who have the political power to pass legislation and compel the minority to submit. That is only a slightly more subtle form of coercion than that practiced by the physically stronger person who makes the weaker say "uncle." Or perhaps the power of rhetoric enables one to win the argument. In neither case, however, does this prove that the conclusion adopted is true or right. It merely establishes the superior political or rhetorical power of one party over the other.

What is needed, then, is some objective measure. This is something outside of humans and human opinion, something which does not in any sense derive from them. This is something which is what it is, regardless of what humans are or think. They then would be measured against it, rather than vice versa. It would be toward these human opinions the way all existent rulers would be toward the standard foot in the Bureau of Standards in Washington, D.C., when measured against it.

In the Old Testament book of Amos we find an interesting incident. There were prophets in the Israel of that time, but they did not take their message from God. Rather, they were prophesying according to what the king wanted prophesied. They sought to please him. As long as they were the official prophets and people had no other source to which to turn, what they said sounded quite impressive. Unfortunately, however, this was a case merely of one opinion being measured against another opinion. It was like measuring the ruler bought in one store against that bought in another store. The opinions measured were only like those found within a circle.

Many of the opinions we hear are like that. The opinion of a political commentator or an economist may sound profound and impressive, and we may be tempted to accept what he says. It is, however, when we discover that this person is not an independent scholar but a person retained by a particular officeholder or candidate that his opinions become considerably less impressive. A bias is present. It is not necessarily that the person involved consciously tailors his statements to the desires of the employer. In many cases, he or she has been hired because of sharing a common set of presuppositions or dispositions with that employer. There is, however a bias, nonetheless. This is not simply a completely objective opinion. It is colored by that prior commitment.

The same phenomenon can be seen in other areas of endeavor. The home field or home court advantage in sports is proverbial. Part of this seems to stem from the difference in officiating. I remember one Sunday morning talking with a basketball coach whose team had arrived home at two o'clock that morning after playing a game in a town some two hundred miles away. They had won that game, which was a very unusual occurrence on that other team's court, and we talked about how different the officiating tended to be when playing there. I asked him whether that was simply the conscious or unconscious influence of the crowd on the officials' judgment. "No," he said, "in this case it's more than that. That school gets officials from a city about fifty miles away, and there aren't many opportunities for those officials. They know that if the game they call does not please the coach of that team, they are not likely to get many engagements."

That is exactly the type of situation which Amos faced as recounted in the Old Testament book that bears his name. This was a time of great prosperity in Israel. Assyria had inflicted a severe defeat upon Israel's immediate neighbor to the north, Syria, and was now preoccupied elsewhere so that Israel had an unprecedented supremacy in the area. Israel's kings were now free again to appropriate new territory. All of the trade routes of the area were under their control and the merchants who traveled between Egypt and Mesopotamia met in the capital city of Samaria. This heightened commercial activity caused great amounts of wealth to flow into Israel. An affluent merchant class developed.

As so often is the case, the affluence of these merchants was not enough to satisfy their desires. As they built both winter and summer homes, they desired to increase their profits, often by whatever means they could. As the merchants became corrupt and unjust the peasants became poor, oppressed, and ill-treated. The rich became richer and the poor, poorer. Nor could the poor expect to obtain justice in the courts, for bribes were utilized to influence the judges in favor of the rich. Truth, in the justice system, was what someone could pay to have the judges say it was.

But what of the religious situation? Here there seemed to be encouraging activity. The worship of Baal had been suppressed by Jehu, who had succeeded Ahab, but although the form of such worship was gone, the spirit appears to have remained. There was proper worship, done in the right places, but religious faith and doctrine had been divorced from the ethical practice of daily life. The worship in the temple had no impact upon the practice of one's trade in the marketplace. It appeared that all was well, but Assyria would soon turn its attention to Israel. It would carry that nation into captivity, including its rulers and prosperous merchants.

Into this situation God sent Amos. He himself was from the south, but was sent to the north to prophesy. He was not of the well-to-do merchant class. He was not from a line of prophets, and was not a courtier like Isaiah or a priest like Jeremiah. He was a shepherd and a dresser of sycamore trees. He himself was part of the poor class which was oppressed by these rich, corrupt merchants and by the rulers of the land. He came speaking a word of prophecy against their practices and, in a sense, against the very structure of that society.

We need to notice carefully, however, what Amos was doing. He was not simply a shepherd, expressing a shepherd's opinion and objection over these who wielded economic and political power. If that had been the case, then it would only have been the opinion of one group against that of another group. There would not have been any real way to determine the ultimate right or wrong of either claim. Naturally, the poor would favor a view which supported their own desires and biases, just as would the richer people. One could only have expected that such persons would be biased in favor of their own welfare. The only means to determining the right would have been the courts, which as we noted previously, were controlled by those with the means to influence their judgment. The actions of the rulers were endorsed and justified by prophets whose living was provided by the king. There would be no way to determine what was really, ultimately, right. This was a case of "Might makes right," or the popular perversion of the golden rule: "He who has the gold makes the rule."

Amos, however, was not merely a spokesperson for the poor and oppressed class. If so, this would simply have been a case of class conflict, and there would not have been any way to determine rightness and wrongness, justice and injustice. What was needed was some independent standard, rooted not in the preferential judgment of one of the groups, but in something more basic and ultimate. And here it is important to see that Amos did not go to preach, but that he was sent. He was commissioned by God to speak God's word. And God's word is not merely God's opinion, placed alongside other opinions. God's word is truth, the expression of how things really are.

There was really no authority in Amos himself to give validity to what he had to say. He was certainly not drawn from the privileged or respected elements of the society. He was a shepherd, one of the lowliest positions within that society. Nor was he just any shepherd. The word used here for shepherd is a rare one, found only one other place in the Old Testament, in 2 Kings 3:4. It refers to the keeper of a peculiar breed of desert sheep, which had short legs and ugly faces but were highly valued for their wool. There is still an Arabian proverb of contempt, "Viler than a *naqqad*," referring to this word. There was, to say the least, no prestige in Amos's occupation.

Amos made abundantly clear that the very idea of prophesying had not originated with him. He indicated in his encounter with the priest Amaziah that he was not a prophet by occupation and that God had taken him from sheep herding and commanded him to declare this message (7:14–15). He had a sense of divine compulsion which led him to do what he did.

This message was almost exclusively one of divine judgment upon what was going on within that nation and society. With the exception of the closing verses of the book, in which there is a note of divine mercy in a restored Davidic kingdom, there is the message of imminent disaster. There was ease, comfort, confidence, whereas in actuality doom was very near. Soon the nation of Assyria would turn its attention to Israel, and affluence would be subsumed under captivity.

This judgment is expressed under rather vivid imagery. God is about to speak dramatically, as signified by the expression, "The Lord will roar" (1:2). The word used here for "roar" means the roar of a lion as he leaps upon his prey. It means that destruction is coming, and it will originate with God. Although the judgment is coming in the form of the Assyrians, it is God's judgment.

The prophecy came in the form of a series of visions. One of these was the vision in chapter 7 of the plumb line. God is measuring the entire nation of Israel, its religious, ethical, and political life. He is like a person laying a plumb line against a wall. Although the wall may, to the naked eye, appear to be perpendicular to the earth, the only way to evaluate this correctly is through the use of the plumb line. Because the force of gravity means that there is an attraction between two objects, the larger, the earth, attracts the weight of the plumb line, causing it to point toward the center of the earth. This is independent of various persons' opinions of the wall. It responds as it does because of gravity, which is found everywhere. It speaks the truth about the wall. While the persons who built the wall would have a reason to maintain that it is plumb, that is, perpendicular to the earth, the plumb line tells the truth quite apart from any of these speculations or arguments. Israel's worship, which appeared so pious, is seen to be warped and bent when compared to the truth of God's word. Similarly, the political and economic life, so easily justified by those who practice and benefit from it, is anything but straight. No matter what the eye of an individual may tell one, it is distorted.

The message of judgment brought by Amos was not welcomed, to say the very least. Immediately Amaziah the priest of Bethel objected, telling Amos not to prophesy there anymore. He reported to King Jeroboam what Amos was saying: prophesying against the king, declaring that Jeroboam would die by the sword and predicting Israel's captivity (7:10–11). And, as he told Jeroboam, the land could not "bear his words."

It is interesting to note what Amaziah then told Amos. He told him to go back to the land of Judah, to earn his living and do his prophesying there. His next words are significant: "Don't prophesy anymore at Bethel, because this is the king's sanctuary and the temple of the kingdom" (7:13). His response to the negative prophecy of judgment was to try to get rid of Amos. They did not want to hear the prophecy. There seemed to be the feeling that if the prophecy was not heard, there would be no difficulty. Quite possibly, Amaziah did not believe that Amos was a true prophet from the Lord. Perhaps years of prophesying untruth may have lead him to believe what he himself was prophesying. Or he may have realized that Amos was indeed prophesying truthfully on behalf of the Lord, but knew that it contradicted what he himself was saying. If the king were to believe Amos, he, Amaziah, would be out of a job. Or, rather, Jeroboam might be upset and emotionally disturbed by such a message. Whether protecting himself or his king, Amaziah was in effect stopping his ears or putting his head in the sand.

Amos did not accept this ultimatum, however. What he did was to measure Amaziah's words against the word of the Lord. He said, "You say, 'Do not prophesy against Israel, and stop preaching against the house of Isaac.'" He then pronounced God's judgment against Amaziah: "Therefore this is what the LORD says: 'Your wife will become a prostitute in the city, and your sons and daughters will fall by the sword. Your land will be measured and divided up, and you yourself will die in a pagan country. And Israel will certainly go into exile, away from their native land'" (7:17).

The point of this exchange was that when two human opinions clash, it does not matter how emphatically one opinion is put, or even how great the human authority arrayed behind one of the opinions. All that matters is which opinion is aligned with the word of God, the plumb line which measures all claimants to truth.

What God says and constitutes truth will prevail, no matter what humans may say about it. This is seen in the fact that despite rejection by Jeroboam, and the contrary prophecy of Amaziah, the threatened captivity occurred. It was the major criterion of an Old Testament prophet that if he was a true prophet, what he prophesied would come to pass. Failure of his prophecy, however, meant that he had not truly spoken from the Lord. In this case, the dispute would soon be settled when Amos's words of judgment were fulfilled while Amaziah's optimistic words failed to come to pass.

There is a lesson for us here. Truth will prevail, despite all contrary opinions and protestations, by no matter how many humans.

If a wall is crooked or not perpendicular, then no amount of extolling the wall by humans will have any effect. It is what it is, and the plumb line renders that certain. We can see that in other areas of life as well. When one is diagnosed as having a serious and especially a fatal condition, or when the death of a treasured loved one has occurred, there is the phenomenon of denial. The person simply cannot and will not accept the verdict of the medical personnel. Yet that does not affect the reality of the condition. If one proceeds as if nothing were wrong, which is frequently done, or avoids consulting medical personnel for fear of receiving such a diagnosis, that does not affect the progress of the disease. It is objectively present, and its presence and reality do not in any sense depend upon the patient's belief in the reality of the condition. If we ignore the economic conditions of a company in which we are investors because the truth would be painful, we only defer and perhaps exacerbate the final conditions.

This may not always be apparent because the effects of a condition may be slow in coming. In the case of this prophecy, the fall of Israel did not occur immediately. Peter records the comments of persons who mock the belief in the second coming of Christ, since the delay has been so great (2 Peter 3:3–4). Yet, he reminds his readers that the day of judgment and destruction is definitely coming (v. 7). Much in our society is contrary to God's will. Many do not care whether this is the case, or do not bother to inquire what God says on a given subject, or do not even believe that there is a God. Yet the consequences will inevitably occur. Our society is, as Francis Schaeffer used to say, like a person attached to a large rock by a very long rope. The rock is then pushed over the edge of a cliff. For a relatively long time, nothing happens, as the rope uncoils and the slack is taken up. During that period of time, there appear to be no effects of the rock's descent. Eventually, however, dramatic effects will occur. The truth will always have its effects, whether sooner or later.

We live in a society which has cut itself off, to a large extent, from belief in God and in any kind of absolute truth. Some consequences of this are being felt in our society, with the breakdown of much of the morality that we have been accustomed to expect in business and in government. Should we, however, really be surprised at these scandals? If there is no absolute truth or absolute right or wrong, what is inherently wrong about what these people have done? And, if the church itself and Christians have absorbed something of this same relativism, should we be surprised at the scandals that have surfaced in sexual morality and handling of finances of some large ministries? It seems likely to me that, rather than seeing the end of such political and business escapades, there may be much more ahead, with the only deterrent being the possible effect of discovery. It may well be that the breakdown of families, the increase in teenage suicides, the spread of AIDS, and other catastrophes in our society are the result of abandoning or ignoring God's truth and commands. And just as someone who tries to ignore or defy the law of gravity will nonetheless suffer the consequences, so it is true with all the rest of the divine pronouncements.

The Christian believer who takes seriously the objectivity of the word of the Lord, however, has real basis for confidence and security. For such a person, there is a basis for truth and for the right and wrong. God is the one measuring point that does not move, the one constant in a world of flux. Deep down, whether people admit it or not, there is a need for objectivity and order and the security which comes from it. To look complete relativism in the eye is a frightening and unsettling experience. I recently read a list of ideas on how to survive in a technologically oriented society. One of them was to hang onto things that give one's life some continuity, such as an article of clothing or something passed on from generation to generation, so that not everything is new in one's life. Another was to listen to music written before 1850. Since it was composed by people who believed in order, it has a calming and uplifting effect. If we are made in the image and likeness of God, intended for fellowship with him, then the presence of his guideline will be a source of comfort and peace to us. For the Christian, then, study and meditation upon the sure word of God will make the believer like the man described in Psalm 1, who, meditating on and delighting in the law of the Lord, finds the stability of a tree, planted by streams of water.

DOES IT MATTER IF GOD EXISTS?

Study Guide

Key Questions

1. Consider the statement "What we are facing is a major confusion among people in American society about what is right and wrong, and what is true and false." Do you agree? What is the cause of this?

2. Is it possible that "What is right for one person may be wrong for another, or what is right at one time or situation may be wrong in another"? The illustrations used by the author sound convincing. How does he help one see what is wrong with this view?

3. Examine your personal answer to the Barna research statement: "There is no such thing as absolute truth; different people can define truth in conflicting ways and still be correct."

   ___Agree Strongly,
   ___Agree Somewhat,
   ___Disagree Somewhat,
   ___Disagree Strongly,
   ___Don't Know.

   Why did you answer as you did?

4. What are some examples of decisions that are determined either by truth, by popular demand, or by personal gain? Think through the outcomes. Which contribute to the good of others, to personal fulfillment, and to honoring God?

Bible Investigation

1. Read the book of Amos. Find similarities between the beliefs and practices of the people of Israel and people today. How do you react to the arrival of Amos and to the message he would bring to you?

2. Reread the section of the text that discusses Amos and his message to the people of his day. Note the similarities in the political, economic, and social conditions of Amos's day and those in America today. Apply the message of the book to the conditions around you. How are you affected?

Personal Application

1. Memorize Romans 12:1. Think through your response. How will your life change if you fully apply the instruction of this verse?
2. Consider the statement: "God's Word is truth, the expression of how things really are." How does or how will accepting God's Word as your "independent standard" change your course in decision-making? Think about it. Act upon it.
3. Meditate on Psalm 1. Determine to "find the stability of a tree, planted by streams of water."

For Further Thought

1. Think of a time when you or a friend deliberately turned away from a Bible teaching. What was the outcome?
2. Apply the "plumb line" of Amos 7:7–9. Is there any **warping** or **bending** in your worship?
3. How do you react to the author's statement "It may be that the breakdown of families, the increase in teen suicides, the spread of AIDS, and other catastrophes in our societies are the result of abandonment or ignoring of God's truth and commands"? Do you agree or disagree? Why?
4. The author concludes "Truth will prevail, despite all contrary opinions and protestations, by no matter how many humans." Pray that through this study you may learn and desire to follow God's truth fully.

The Universe Right Side Up

I recall a comic strip I saw once. A man had fallen off the edge of a cliff and on the way down managed to grab a small tree that was growing out of the side of the cliff. Hanging there by his arms, he called up to whomever was above him, "What should I do?" The response came back, "Let go!" to which he replied, "Is there someone else up there who can give me a second opinion?"

I think our lives in relation to God may sometimes be like that. We want God's help, but we want it on our terms. We believe in God, but conditionally. I saw yet another poll recently regarding the religious beliefs of persons in the United States. Like all the other similar polls of the past twenty years or so, this one indicated that over ninety percent believed in a higher power, at least as they understood him. Whether "the man upstairs," "the force," or "the great whatever," they believed there was something higher and greater than they are, but were rather vague about what that might be.

This god is frequently someone we turn to for help. This is the typical place or role of God, as our American culture understands it. In most soap operas, the only religious references, other than weddings and funerals, are when someone is in desperate straits. Most praying by such characters is in hospitals, and especially in hospital chapels. In other words, they turn to God when they feel a need, rather than when they might offer something to God.

There is another dimension to this. When things go wrong, there is a tendency to blame God. Sometimes this seems to entail the idea that God is the cause of what has happened. That is what I call the insurance company view of God. In insurance policies, "acts of God" are disasters which could not be controlled or prevented humanly. If taken literally, since these acts of God are only negative or even catastrophic in nature, these references would suggest that insurance companies conceive of God as malevolent, as more like the devil than like God. More often, however, the idea is not that God caused the evil, but that he could have and therefore should have, prevented it. There is a feeling that he owes us only good, and therefore he should not have allowed this to occur.

The prophet Samuel had a great opportunity. For a period of some three hundred years, the word of the Lord had not come to anyone in Israel. Now, however, the Lord was appearing to him. He might have said, "I have a great opportunity here to get the ear of the Lord. I have so much to tell him, so many things to ask him for. And he might have proceeded to fill God's ears with a barrage of requests or even of demands. After all, why shouldn't he? He was the only one in that time who was open and tender to the Lord and his dealings. Yet he did not. His response was, "Speak, Lord, for your servant is listening." He understood that God was God and he was the servant. If he had instead said, "Listen, Lord, for your servant is speaking," he would have been reversing the order of things. He would have been treating God as the servant and asserting himself as the master.

Suppose that God is what we sometimes make him out to be, namely, someone who should grant what we want at all times, who in effect exists to serve us. The Westminster Confession, which says that the chief end of man is to glorify God and enjoy him forever, would then be transmuted to say that the chief end of God is to glorify humans and enjoy them forever. But what would that do?

It would mean, for one thing, that I must take on a much larger responsibility for myself and for my prayers. For if we take it upon ourselves to decide what is good and what God should do for us, we have in effect accepted his omnipotence, or his ability to do anything, but rejected his omniscience, or his ability to know everything.

What would I now have to know in order to be able to pray, under these circumstances? First of all, I would have to know all about myself. I would have to know just what I am, what I am like, what my strengths and weaknesses are. Yet, although in some ways we know ourselves better than does anyone else, in some ways we are the poorest judges of ourselves. Because we cannot stand outside ourselves, we do not see what others do. A whole school of psychology known as behaviorism has grown up around the idea that only observation of another's behavior, not introspection, is reliable as an indicator of the person's true condition. This has led to a joke about two behaviorist psychologists who met one another on a sidewalk. Looking at the other psychologist, the first one said, "You're feeling fine. How am I feeling?"

That joke is only a moderate exaggeration. Sometimes we greatly misunderstand ourselves. I was involved on one occasion in a seminar on social styles. Each of us had asked five different persons to complete a questionnaire on us, in which they checked those adjectives that they felt applied to us. The computer then tabulated the responses and assigned us a social style. There were two scales and the resulting chart was divided into four quadrants, each of which was in turn divided into four quadrants. We were asked to assess our own social style before we were given the results of the computer tabulations from our referees. Two men were six boxes off from the tabulation, seven being as far off as you could possibly be. One of the men was so devastated that he scarcely spoke a word during the time. The other dominated the discussion, trying to refute the validity of the test. The more he talked, the more he demonstrated that he was exactly the type of person that his referees had said he was. While the self-assessment of most of us probably would not be that divergent from how others who know us well would see us, it does point out that we may not be the best judges of ourselves and of our own personalities.

There are other significant facts about ourselves that we may not know. As part of a routine physical examination a few months ago, the tests showed a slightly higher than normal number of red cells in my urine. The doctor, being very thorough, ordered an IVP test. That showed a slight shadow on one kidney, which the doctor tentatively diagnosed as a benign cyst but, wanting to be absolutely sure, he ordered an ultrasound test. I was delighted to hear the results "It's definitely benign" (certainly one of the most beautiful words in the English language, in that context). There was no way, without those tests, however, that I could know what was going on within that part of my body. Even the doctor could not tell without the ultrasound what there was. None of us knows what abnormal cells may be within our bodies, what virus may have already breached our defenses without our knowledge. We do not know, then, just how to pray, or at least not in a specific way. Something that we may think is good for us may be just the opposite, and something that we desperately need may be quite hidden from us.

Yet to God nothing is hidden. He knows the inner recesses of our bodies and our minds with complete clarity. We are fully transparent to him. Jesus said, "Are not two sparrows sold for a penny? Yet not one of them will fall to the ground apart from the will of your Father. And even the very hairs of your head are all numbered" (Matt. 10:29–30). Jesus selected a seemingly trivial piece of information to illustrate how thoroughly God knows us and our situations. We do not know how many hairs we have on our heads, although most of us can tell by comparing our picture with those from a few years earlier that the count is probably less than it used to be. Yet God knows even these things in an up to the minute count. I don't think Jesus selected this specific issue as an illustration because it is somehow especially important. Rather, because it is such a minute matter and one which is for all practical purposes inaccessible to us, it demonstrates effectively the extent of God's knowledge.

To presume to tell God what he must do also requires that I have a detailed knowledge of the future. For if I pray about what God should do, that has implications extending into the future. The appropriateness of the particular favor which we seek from God depends upon what that future will be. Yet, we are limited in our knowledge of the present, let alone of the future. An incredible number of factors bear upon the future occurrences.

Not only is our knowledge limited, but it functions from our limited perspective. Sometimes we can see this in rather simple fashion. Reggie Jackson played for the Baltimore Orioles for a few years during Earl Weaver's tenure as manager. Weaver had a strict rule that no runner was to steal without a definite sign from the bench. On one occasion, Jackson was on first base and noticed that the pitcher's delivery was such that he was sure he could steal on him. Second base looked so inviting, and successfully stealing would put him in position to score on virtually any base hit out of the infield, so he decided to go on his own and safely slid into second base well ahead of the throw, then got up, dusted himself off and proudly smiled toward the dugout. Showing great restraint, Weaver waited until after the game and then explained to Jackson what had happened. With the Orioles' second best batter, Lee May, at bat, the other team decided to walk him to make a double play possible, and to bring to bat a hitter who in the past had done very poorly against this particular pitcher, a fact that Weaver knew. That forced him to use a pinch-hitter whom he had planned to save until later in the game. Jackson had thought only of himself, the pitcher, the catcher, and the vacant base. Weaver had to consider the entire span of the game. While the conventional wisdom among teachers is that a person changes when he becomes an administrator, I have observed that the type of faculty members who are conscripted into administration are usually not the typical professor. They are those who even as teachers are able to take in the big picture, see the woods rather than just their own particular tree.

We now must multiply this comparison by a much larger factor, however. Modern computer spreadsheets are able to work with tens of thousands of cells. All of these may be linked to one another in such a way that a change in the value of one of the cells results in changes in all of the other cells. To calculate the effect of one such change upon all of those cells might take a person working with a calculator hundreds of hours. Yet a modern home computer is capable of performing these computations in just a few seconds. All of the "what ifs" can be examined in just a brief time, whereas the human mind alone would be unable to think of all the implications of a simple numerical change of one value. I have a tax analyst program which is able to evaluate several different scenarios and tell me the impact upon my federal income tax of each of those. God is not merely an impersonal machine like a computer, which only recognizes a very literal spelling of our names. But he has, in terms of ability to foresee all of the possibilities and all of the implications of those, a mind with the capacity of an infinite computer. When we pray, God is able to anticipate all of the impact of each possibility.

Sometimes we may find ourselves or others complaining to or about God for things that happen that are less than ideal and may be downright painful. Yet we do not know what the future might have held had that event not occurred. From my years as a pastor, I knew that there are more painful and crushing experiences that can come later in life. God knows all of the possibilities. He acts in ways that are infinitely wise.

God, of course, is the heavenly Father of each one of us. His concern is not just with each of us as individuals but with all of us, or with the welfare of the whole. We may sometimes ask for things, or evaluate the circumstances of life, as if we were the only relevant persons in the world, as if our concerns were the only ones that mattered. From our perspective, comfort and even luxury may seem important. Perhaps, however, our comfort and affluence would result in not just discomfort and economic deprivation, but actually in the death of others. God does what he does from the perspective of the good of the whole.

If we choose to play God, to invert our theology and attempt to tell God what he really ought to do, we are taking on an even larger responsibility than we at first thought. For in changing what happens in our lives, we also affect the lives of numerous others. Our circumstances cannot be altered without changing those of everyone else. If we are at all responsible and are world citizens, then we must take on management of the entire world, not just the present population but also those who will follow.

But couldn't God work things in such a way that the best would always come to everyone? This might be accomplished by performing a series of miracles so that the good which comes to one person, which would ordinarily have evil or unpleasant consequences for another, would not have those results, and would instead have very favorable results. This, however, would produce a very different world from the one in which we now live. There would be no regularity of results flowing from consequences. In light of this, it would not be possible to calculate one's behavior, for everything would be apparently random from our perspective. One time a certain action would have one consequence, while another time it might have very different results. In that situation, our behavior would become random or chance, or at least unstructured, as well. And under those circumstances, character would be virtually impossible. While truly moral behavior at its higher levels involves doing what is right simply because it is right and not because of any intrinsic reward, at more rudimentary levels it is necessary for there to be punishments and rewards. In a world in which placing one's hand on a hot stove would not result in a burn,

DOES IT MATTER IF GOD EXISTS?

morality either would be a more problematic factor or would at least have to be quite different from what it is presently.

One football coach, when he took over the program of a new school, had his players and coaches wearing T-shirts which said, "WE is bigger than ME!" Even though its effectiveness was undercut when the coach left in less than two years to take a better job coaching a more prestigious football team, it is still a good slogan. We are part of the whole human race, and God takes the whole into account when he answers our prayers. He plays no favorites.

This might seem like something of a disadvantage at first glance. For surely the maximum satisfaction of our own wants would be most desirable to each of us. Would it, however? For part of what makes life worthwhile is the type of person we are. A notable radio preacher has said that life is one tenth what happens to us and nine tenths how we react to that. Whether the exact percentages are correct, the general idea certainly is, in my judgment. As we grow in altruistic concern, as we develop the ability to rejoice with the good fortune of others, we become better persons, persons who can take greater satisfaction in themselves and can admire their own best nature. The ability to rejoice with those who rejoice is a result of seeing the true nature of answered prayer: that it is not at the expense of others. For sometimes God answers not only the prayer that we utter, for something to be received, but also a more important prayer, a prayer for us to grow in our understanding of the needs of others and care for them. In the long run, satisfaction with what one is will considerably exceed satisfaction with what one has.

There is another dimension to this. God is not only wise, he is good. What if God simply gave us what we asked for, regardless of its possible effect long-term upon ourselves and others? If God were an indulgent God, more like the proverbial grandfather than like a father, he might simply let us have whatever we ask for, since turning us down might result in our displeasure with him. Even though he knew better, he might be so short-range in his concern for us that he gives just that which would bring us immediate satisfaction.

In Luke 11, Jesus tells us a story of a man who had an unexpected guest arrive at his home at midnight. Tired and hungry from the long trip, the guest needed to be fed, but the host had no provisions in the house and of course no market was open at that hour. What he did was to go to another friend of his who was already in bed, and ask him to lend him food to serve his guest. This was part of

Jesus' response to the request of his disciples to teach them to pray (v. 1). After giving them a short form of the model prayer known as the Lord's Prayer and this parable, he then added some seemingly puzzling words: "Which of you fathers, if your son asks for a fish, will give him a snake instead? Or if he asks for an egg, will he give him a scorpion? If you, then, though you are evil, know how to give good gifts to your children, how much more will your Father in heaven give the Holy Spirit to those who ask him!" (vv. 11–13). At first glance this looks rather puzzling. He seems, however, to be affirming both the knowledge and the goodness of God.

There are two reasons why a father might give the child a snake or a scorpion when the child instead asks for a fish or an egg. One might be that the father does not know the difference between the former and the latter, and the other is that he might not care. In this second case, it may be that the child asks for a fish, not realizing that it is actually a snake, or for an egg which is actually a scorpion. An indulgent father, not wanting to disappoint the child, might give what he asks for, even though it is not what he thinks it is. But a wise heavenly Father knows the difference between fish and snakes, and between eggs and scorpions, and a good father would not give a trusting but inexperienced child anything harmful.

Sometimes people scoff at Christians who pray that "God's will would be done." This appears to them to be a dishonest way to account for God's failure to supply the answers that they desire. In actuality, however, it is both a recognition of God's superiority to themselves and an expedient way of protecting themselves from their own shortcomings.

This principle which Samuel seemed to understand and practice is not restricted to the matter of prayer, however. It is considerably broader than that. It is found in the whole orientation of the human to God. For the essential issue here is that God is really God and we are his servants. We exist to love and serve and glorify him, not vice versa. And if that is how we were fashioned and created, then that is how we will find our greatest fulfillment and satisfaction in life.

Jesus expressed this in a number of ways. One was his statement regarding those who would come after him: "If anyone would come after me, he must deny himself and take up his cross daily and follow me" (Matt. 16:24). This was a challenge, for most persons who want to follow Jesus do not do so for the sake of the privilege of bearing a cross, which is the very emblem of suffering. They may think in terms of the benefits. Jesus said on the occasion of washing his disciples' feet that the servant is not greater than the master. Jesus would be crucified for his commitment to his calling, and they (we) should not expect anything better.

This statement has frequently, I fear, been misunderstood. We have spoken of this and thought of it as if it meant denying ourselves certain things. Thus, we would not engage in certain practices because they were wrong. In this, we have had a somewhat milder version of the Roman Catholic vows of poverty, chastity, and obedience, which priests must take. That is not really what Jesus was saying, however. The word here translated as "deny himself" is actually the same word which is used of Peter's denial of Jesus after his capture of the latter. What Peter did there was to disavow any acquaintance of or connection with Jesus. This is what Jesus is talking about here, as well. It is becoming sufficiently self-detached so that one does not feel powerfully one's own needs and desires. And that in itself is a wonderful, liberating experience.

Think what customarily happens when we hear either positive or negative things said about us. In the former case, we tend to feel pride; in the latter, defensiveness. This is natural. This is that tendency which Reinhold Niebuhr described when he asked whose picture we look for first in a group picture which includes us. When, however, we hear compliments or criticisms about someone whom we do not know, we are not so affected. Those comments simply roll off us. What Jesus was talking about was the state of self-detachment in which, when we hear either positive or negative things said about us, we can in effect say, "What is that to me? I don't know him."

Actually, this is the only way to find peace and satisfaction in life. Jesus said that he who would save his life will lose it, but he who loses his life for him (Jesus) will find it (Matt. 16:25). It is imbedded in the question, "what good will it do a man if he gains the whole world, yet forfeits his own soul?" It simply is counterproductive to attempt to find satisfaction by pursuing it directly. Peace and joy are found as a by-product of moving outside oneself to the service of Jesus and others.

Self, you see, is insatiable. Someone once asked John D. Rockefeller, "How much money does it take to satisfy a man?" His answer was, "Just a little bit more." If life is thought of as a fraction in which the numerator is what we have and the denominator is what we want, then there are two ways to balance the fraction to one. The way most people think of is by increasing what we have, so that it equals what we want. The second is by reducing what we want to what we have. The former does not really work because the denominator keeps increasing, thus keeping the fraction out of balance. Only the latter will adequately achieve balance and thus stability.

Part of the reason for this instability of the search for more is the inability for what is sought after to satisfy on any sort of permanent basis. Søren Kierkegaard observed this in his concept of stages on life's way. The first stage, the aesthetic, is the orientation to life that looks for immediate satisfaction of various kinds. The difficulty is that a given experience, substance, or person, eventually loses its powers of gratification. Then either boredom takes over or one must move to a different, less self-centered and self-gratifying approach.

Jesus also indicated in a number of ways that this satisfaction comes from submitting oneself or humbling oneself. He himself washed the feet of the disciples when none of them was willing to do so. He also indicated that he who would be leader should be the servant of all. He said that the first would be last, and the last first. Evidently, rewards in the kingdom of God go to those who do not seek them directly.

This is even seen in Jesus' depiction of the scene of the final judgment, in Matthew 25. There a separation will take place, between those on the right hand (the sheep) and those on the left (the goats). The basis given for granting eternal life to the righteous is that they have fed Jesus when he was hungry, given him a drink when thirsty, invited him in when a stranger, and visited him when sick and in prison (vv. 35–36). The unrighteous failed to do these things to him when they saw him in these situations (vv. 42–43). When Jesus tells the righteous this, however, they express surprise, stating that they had never done these things to him (vv. 37–38), and he responds that if they have done it for one of the least of these brethren, they have done it for him (v. 40).

There is another dimension to this. Jesus spoke of the importance of not laying up for oneself treasures on earth, but in heaven (Matt. 6:19–21). Here he emphasized the permanence of things laid up in heaven versus the transitoriness of things laid up on earth.

DOES IT MATTER IF GOD EXISTS?

On earth, moth and rust destroy and thieves break in and steal. These things cannot occur in heaven. Thus, the heavenly riches, which go to those who do not consciously seek their own advancement or benefit, are actually more beneficial to persons in the long run.

The reason these things work out in this paradoxical fashion is at least in part because of God's superior wisdom. When we seek our own good, we are dependent upon our own knowledge of what is really good for us. On the other hand, when we turn our lives over to God, we are entrusting ourselves to the wisdom of someone who knows and understands far more fully.

In every area of life we are now recognizing the benefit of expertise. Most of us would not think of trying to do our own medical treatment, for that has now become such a highly technical field that each aspect of one's health must be managed by a different kind of specialist. Similarly, we would not attempt to be our own attorney, even if we are by preparation an attorney ourselves. There is truth to the old adage, "he who is his own attorney has a fool for a client." Here again, each specialty is so technical that an attorney practicing in the field of marital law, for example, must turn a client over to a specialist in another field, such as real estate or tax law, when that is the topic of concern.

The problem with second-guessing God is that we make our judgments upon the basis of what is but never know what might have been. We assume that there would follow from what was in place the consequences which we think we can foresee from that, but such is not necessarily the case. For example, when something unfortunate happens, we think of the "if onlys" that would have prevented that. A friend of mine recently ran into a deer while driving his car, resulting in a certain amount of damage to the car. He said, "If I hadn't stopped to go to the bathroom before we left, or if I had been driving the speed I usually drive, rather than ten miles per hour more slowly, this wouldn't have happened." He realized, however, that there may have been any number of times when he avoided an accident such as this because of some delay, and because he was not there when the incident would have occurred, he never knew about that possibility that was never realized.

This was borne home to me one day when I was a pastor. I started out from home after lunch to make my hospital calls. I stopped at a red light of a major intersection, where the other street was a highway which came in from an oblique angle. The light turned green, and I was about to start out, but I turned and looked to the left, to make sure there was no traffic, no one trying to "run" a red light. It was fortunate that I did, for there, pumping his brakes and desperately but unsuccessfully trying to stop short, was the driver of a large fuel tanker truck. When he finally brought his rig to a stop he was completely across the intersection. Had I started out when the light changed, I would probably have been pinned against the traffic light, by a truck possibly full of highly combustible fuel. I pulled through the intersection and over to the curb, and prayed a brief, if somewhat trembling, prayer of thanksgiving to God for sparing my life. It was as if God allowed me to see what danger lurks around me at many times unknown to me. Whenever something unfortunate happens and I am tempted to think "but if only," I think back to that day and that incident.

Further, if we are to be God, we will have to be everywhere at once. There are an incredible number of factors at work in our world, and they are very much interrelated. One of the difficulties we face in dealing with social and environmental problems is that because of the interrelationship of these situations, we are able to solve or to improve one problem only by aggravating another. We are therefore constantly involved in tragic choices as to which of these we will prefer over the other(s). For example, in the northwest part of the United States there are disputes over logging of the forest lands. By continuing to cut forests without restriction, certain rare species of animals, particularly birds, are endangered. On the other hand, if these are protected, it is frequently at the economic cost of numerous jobs. One cannot improve one situation without jeopardizing the other. Economic and environmental issues are frequently in conflict.

God does not have the luxury of looking out for the welfare of only one person. He has billions of persons and trillions of situations to look after. He must deal with all of these, and do them simultaneously. If I take it upon myself to elevate my concerns to chief place among all of the things that could be given attention, then I assume responsibility for everyone else as well.

In one organization of which I am a member, the nominating committee had prepared a slate of candidates for the coming year. One segment of the membership, however, planned to nominate a separate ballot from the floor. When word got out that this was to be done, the official nominee for president withdrew, and with him the rest of the slate. In particular, the person who was to be nominated from the floor for president had a long list of complaints that he felt needed to be addressed, all of which concerned his interests and those of his group of supporters. I said to myself, "This man has a lot of experience as a griper. When he is elected, he will have an opportunity to find out what it is like to be a gripee." My expectations were soon realized. At the next meeting of the organization this president erupted with expressions of dismay at all the questions, suggestions, proposals, and complaints that had come to him from the membership. He was extremely defensive. He found out that it is easier to find fault with administration than to carry it out. He had discovered what one administrator called "psychological claustrophobia." Demands come from every direction, but the resources are few for meeting them. It probably would be a healthy thing for each of us (although perhaps tragic for everyone else during that time) if we each had the opportunity to be God for a day. The tasks of being omnipresent would prove quite challenging.

Trying to manage this whole world would probably prove to be like a game which a group of boys used to play. They would dig up a group of earthworms, divide them among themselves, and each would have a coffee can lid. Then at the word "Go!" each would take an earthworm, tie a knot in it, and lay it on his lid. The contestant who could keep the most worms knotted was the winner. I say "keep" for the worm would not simply lie there with a knot in its middle. It would twist and turn, untying the knot. That is what administration is like: the knots keep coming untied. And that is especially what it must be like to be in charge of the entire universe, including the whole human race.

At what point do we expect God to be God? Frequently, it is at the point of doing what we think he should do, or of not doing what we think he should not do. It appears that some of us sometimes think that God is responsible or answerable to us. When something goes wrong, we ask, "How could God have allowed this to happen?" or "Why did this happen to me?" Yet, we must ask ourselves exactly how much we involved God in our lives prior to that time. It is as if God is supposed to be there when we want him to, doing what we want him to do, but nothing beyond that. We must ask ourselves, however, what kind of a God this would be. If we make the decisions and we give the orders, who, then, is God, and who is the servant? Perhaps what we are looking for is not a God, but an almighty servant, one who is capable of doing everything we tell him to do. But if he is able to do what we cannot, is he not God? Why should he not be the one to do the deciding, rather than ourselves?

Careful students of the Bible have observed that there appears to be a tension between two types of emphases within it. On the one hand, there is an active or activistic motif. We are urged to strive, to labor, to fight, to run, etc. On the other hand, there is the passive dimension, the motif of surrender and rest. So, for example, we find the references to Jesus giving peace, to taking his yoke and burden upon ourselves because it is easy and light, to denying oneself, etc. How are we to reconcile these?

Perhaps part of the solution to this dilemma may be found in the distinction between direction and motion. Salvation is primarily what God does in us, rather than what we do. It is what he makes of us, rather than what we make of ourselves. At the same time, we cooperate or work together with God in this enterprise. We are urged to resist the devil, to emulate Christ, etc. This is the dimension of motion. On the other hand, we are to surrender to Christ the choice of what direction that motion is to take. If lordship means anything, it means that Christ selects the direction in which we are to march, but we still must do the marching.

In our activistic age, we tend to think more about having and doing than about being. If you ask a person who he is, the reply often is given in terms of what he does, i.e., his "occupation." Or it may be something else that one does, some role that he or she fulfills within society, or within a group (e.g., "I'm the treasurer"). Similarly, what we are is often defined, or at least measured, by what we have. This may be as obvious and external as an expensive car or a large home in an exclusive neighborhood. Or it may be something such as athletic ability or physical attractiveness. Thus, our prayers may be structured in terms of one or the other of these considerations. With God, however, the primary interest is in *being*. This relates to the fundamental character of the person. God does what he does because he is what he is. He speaks the truth and acts in genuine ways because he is genuine. So his primary concern for us is what he is making us to be, namely, likenesses of himself. This involves a rather different set of values than those which may inform our prayers otherwise.

Samuel could have seen God's approach to him as an opportunity to get God to do for him and to give to him the things that he wanted from God. If so, he probably would have become a frustrated and unfulfilled person. Instead, he chose to give God an opportunity not to listen to him, but to speak to him; not to validate Samuel's self-chosen direction in life, but to choose that direction. In short, he let God be God. The result was a life of usefulness, honor, and satisfaction.

Study Guide

Key Questions

1. What happens when a person reverses the order of things, making God the servant and himself or herself the one in charge? What then is God's role? The person's role?
2. List the three responsibilities that must be assumed when a person takes on the role of God for himself or herself.

Bible Investigation

1. Read and study 1 Samuel 1–3. After rereading the author's summary of the passage, review how Samuel responded. What made him respond this way? What was his attitude toward God?
2. Meditate upon the meaning of Matthew 10:29–30. Since God knows the number of hairs on your head think of what else he knows about you. What does he know about you that you do not know about yourself?
3. Review Luke 11:1–13. How does this story emphasize the knowledge and the goodness of God? How can it be an encouragement for Christians to pray "Your will be done" when they are talking with God about their needs? What would make the difference for one to pray "Your will be done" instead of verbalizing a specific request to meet a need?

Personal Investigation

1. What happens when you say "Speak, Lord, for your servant is listening?" How does he speak to you? How do you hear him? How do you respond?
2. How do you differentiate between a carefully thought out decision which seems to be right and knowing that God has spoken and given you direction?
3. Think of an unanswered prayer of your past you are now glad did not happen as you prayed. How did the fact that you did not know the future distort your ability to pray for what was best? How did the fact that God knows the future make his answer so much better than if he had answered your request as you had made it?

DOES IT MATTER IF GOD EXISTS?

4. It is easy to "let God be God" when he does what we think he should do and when he does not do what we think he should not do. Examine your relationship to him and place trust in him that will help you recognize more of his knowledge and goodness as it is focused on you.

For Further Thought

1. Think about the author's question ". . . couldn't God work things in such a way that the best would always come to everyone?" Why does he write that, if this were the way things happened, "character would be virtually impossible"? Why is there a need for **punishments** and **rewards**?

2. We may be quick to offer a prayer of thanks when we see clearly that God has protected us from some danger or disaster (note the illustrations the author uses). Think about God's care of you. Thank him for the many times he has protected you from dangers that you were not even aware of.

7

Have You Checked
Your I.D. Lately?

Cases of amnesia are not numerous, but they are genuine. Imagine awakening sometime and discovering that you did not know who you were. Whether as a result of an injury or some psychological trauma, your awareness of your identity and your place within the world had been wiped out. What would that be like?

For one thing, you would not know where to go. Somewhere, presumably, there is a place where you belong, people who love you, a set of relationships that form the framework of your life. Not knowing who you were, you would not know where you fit. Houses on a street or towns on a map would all be the same to you. You might drive your car (if you had one) aimlessly, with no sense that this is where you should turn. In a sense, you literally would not know where you were.

You would not know what you could do, either. Perhaps you are a skilled mechanic or an accountant, or something of that type. While you might stumble upon one of these abilities and notice your facility with it, you might go on for some time without any such awareness.

You would not know your value, either. This would be true in a broad and a narrow sense. Perhaps you are a surgeon with unusual ability to restore people's health and preserve their lives, but since you don't know that, they would not be able to benefit from your talent. In the narrower sense, perhaps there are people to whom you are very precious, who love you very much. Not knowing that, one might think himself quite dispensable in the world.

Suppose this happened on a larger scale. Imagine a group of tourists in an airport were suddenly struck by amnesia and simultaneously deprived of all forms of identification. A plane would be ready to depart for their home city, but not knowing who they were, they would not know that they were to get on that plane. It would depart without them while they wandered aimlessly throughout the airport, looking at one flight destination after another.

Suppose, however, that amnesia took place on a truly mass scale so that everyone in the entire human race lost their memories and their identities simultaneously. What would happen then? In the usual situation of amnesia, the victim is surrounded by persons who know who they are, and, perhaps, who know who he is. This becomes a check upon the effects of his dislocation, serving to provide some external stability and objectivity. Now, however, this would not be the case. What would that be like?

To deal with this question we need to ask a bit about what usually constitutes an identity. When a child is lost, what are the questions usually asked of him or her? What is your name? Where do you live? What is your telephone number? What are your parents' names? That last one is especially significant, for frequently we identify ourselves in terms of who our parents are. In fact, in American society, for the most part, the child simply has been given the father's last name plus one or more "given" names. This is changing somewhat, just as a woman frequently does not merely take her husband's last name, but retains her own or compounds her name with his.

This practice is found in a number of other cultures. In Sweden, where my ancestors came from, prior to the nineteenth century, the person's last name was formed by taking the father's first name and adding -son or -dotter to it. This meant that last names were rather fluid. When I went to do genealogical research in the archives in Östersund, Sweden, for example, I found that records were kept only by first name and date of birth. When that system of naming began to break down, interesting things occurred, especially when persons emigrated to the United States. My great-grandfather, named Eric Kullstrom, had four sons, one named Kullstrom, two named Erickson, and one who took a totally new name, Nordvall. Prior to that time, however, the significant thing about you in the

DOES IT MATTER IF GOD EXISTS?

little boroughs in which those rural persons lived was who your father was. Peter Johnson was literally, Peter, John's son. This phenomenon is found in biblical times as well. Simon Peter was Simon, bar-Jonah, or Simon, Jonah's son. King David was David, son of Jesse.

As our knowledge of developmental psychology grows, especially on the popular level, this interest in knowing one's parentage is also growing. This is part of why illegitimacy has such a negative effect upon the future of young persons but especially young men, for it involves a deprivation of the knowledge of who one is. Similarly, there is a growing desire on the part of adopted persons to find their biological parents, to know in that sense who they are.

When, however, we have identified ourselves with our parents and other ancestors, we have not really answered the question, "Where did I come from?" This is only a short-range answer. There are more ultimate answers. When children begin to ask, "Where did I come from?" that may be a clue that the time has come for some very basic or elementary sex education. To many people, then, the explanation that the life of a new person begins with the fertilization of an ovum by a sperm is all that is needed to understand the mystery. In a more inclusive sense the explanation of the origin of the human race in terms of evolution, or the beginning of human life in terms of basic protein molecules, is not really a sufficient explanation for it does not go back far enough.

These proximate explanations remind me of the answers to the question, "Where does milk come from?" One answer would be, "Milk comes from a bottle or a carton." A slightly more complete answer is, "Milk comes from the refrigerator." More perceptive persons may answer, "Milk comes from the grocery store or the supermarket." When asked where those places get milk, however, the answer would be, "Milk comes from the dairy." Yet, those answers really only deal with what happens to milk after becoming milk. Anyone with more acquaintance knows that milk comes from cows, assuming we are talking about cow's milk. This was a lesson learned early by the cats on our family farm. We milked by hand and the cats would gather at the barn at milking time, stationing themselves in the center of the barn, between the two rows of cows' stanchions. They received their milk by aerial delivery, and it was very fresh, the elapsed time from cow to cat being measured in tenths of a second. They understood who made milk. Actually, of course, the answer would probably be, "Milk comes from grass, hay, or silage," after processing by a cow.

So it is with human life. To answer that an individual comes into being because of sexual union of a male and a female human being is to give a rather incomplete answer, as are other "scientific" explanations of the origin of life in general. Something within us finds this unsatisfactory. There is something more to a birth than merely another biological occurrence. Each of us senses the wonder and mystery of a new person present who did not exist before. The question, "Where did this little life come from?" is an expression not so much of curiosity but of awe in the face of the unknown.

This is virtually intuition, and it has been known to contradict the more rational or scientific explanation a person may have of it. This affects even quite naturalistic and humanistic persons. So, for example, consider the scientist at the birth of his first child. Logically, he should say, "Well, another Homo sapiens has been born," with about the same degree of wonder as he displays when his poodle gives birth to a litter of puppies. But there is something more to this experience. His discovery, "This is my daughter," is more than just a scientific statement. It transcends his usual framework of understanding. There is a quality to this experience for which mere scientific explanation cannot account. This has a sort of "supernatural" quality to it.

In the first chapter of the first book of Samuel, we find the interesting story of Hannah. Even though she did not have a modern education complete with explanation of biology, biochemistry, and physics, Hannah understood about children. She knew that children were more than mere products of a sexual union between a male and a female human being. She and her husband Elkanah had been married for several years and had attempted to have a child but had experienced only futility in that regard. Something was missing, and she knew the solution. If Hannah had lived in our day, she would probably have gone to a fertility clinic, the gynecologist would have prescribed a fertility pill, and perhaps even a multiple pregnancy would have resulted. She, however, had a more profound understanding of the origin of life than that.

Hannah shared the Hebrew understanding of children in that day. Children were regarded as a gift from God, his blessing upon them. In part this may have been a practical social and economic matter. Children were a necessary part of the working crew in that agrarian society. They were also one's "social safety net," one's means of provision for widows, the disabled, and the elderly. The psalmist put it best: "Sons are a heritage from the LORD, children a reward from him. . . . Blessed is the man whose quiver is full of them" (Ps. 127:3, 5). A man and woman could not simply make children by their own efforts. The needed additional component was the Lord. Without his blessing, there would be no children. So one turned to God if one was barren. Hence we find Hannah in this passage pouring out her heart to the Lord, beseeching him to hear her prayer and give her a son. And this he did.

The value we place upon something is related to its origin. Who made it? What is the reputation of the source? When, for example, a violin is certified as a genuine Stradivarius, it is understood to be of exceptional quality, and the value is made accordingly high. This fact has led to various forms of imitation and counterfeiting. A painting that is established as being the genuine product of a famous artist is of much greater value than a forgery, even if the latter is of a very good quality. One of the major problems for legitimate importers is the fake articles, whether designer jeans or imitation Rolex watches, which are shipped into our country. Even diamonds are valued by the process of their origin. Synthetic diamonds may be chemically identical to natural diamonds and may be more perfect crystals, but they are not of similar value.

The question becomes more important when we ask about the identity of the human being. Is the human simply a highly developed animal, the highest product of the evolutionary process? If so, as strongly attached as we may be to certain persons, especially the members of our own family, that is simply something of an emotional attachment, not unlike the way we may feel about a favorite pet who has been with us for a long time. If this is simply the result of the sexual union of two human beings, then the person's value is dependent upon who those two humans are. If they are royalty, or famous people, or persons of accomplishment, then the child will immediately be someone special, sought out for the attention of the press. If the person is the child of very ordinary people, however, then in this thinking the person is of very ordinary value as well.

Suppose, however, that the human is not just an animal, not just an offspring of human parents. Suppose that there is a Supreme Being, God, who has made everything that exists and has made human beings, giving them life. Suppose beyond that, however, that when God created human beings, he made them different from all other creatures that he brought into existence. Suppose that he made each of the other creatures according to the pattern that was appropriate to them, but that when he made the first human beings, he made them like himself, in his own image, and that this image and likeness has been transmitted to every human being that has ever lived. Now we would have a very different situation. Now the human would have a much greater value than anything else.

In our society, we have seen a gradual decline in the sense of value of an individual human life. This is reflected in a number of ways. The first and most obvious is the practice of abortion. Today in the United States about one out of every three pregnancies ends with a decision by the mother to terminate it short of a regular birth, a decision that ends in the death of the fetus. The product of the abortion is discarded. A life, or at least a potential human life, has been thrown away. Babies are unwanted. This is particularly true in countries like China, where a very low value is placed upon girls, and they are aborted or given up for adoption whenever possible. If, however, they are simply additional human animals, then what real basis is there for objecting? They represent simply a surplus, and this is one way of getting rid of them.

In one of the suburbs of Minneapolis along the Minnesota River bottoms, deer periodically present a problem. Multiplying in abundance with no natural predators in the vicinity, they threaten to overrun the community. They eat people's gardens, become traffic hazards in the streets, and generally constitute hazards. At one church, an outdoor wedding reception was attended by some uninvited guests, a family of deer, which ate almost everything edible within sight. So from time to time, a "harvesting" of the excess creatures is arranged. A few hunters are granted permits to hunt these deer within the city limits, thus "thinning the herd." There are always objections, but one of the responses generally given is that this hunting is also for the benefit of the deer, thinning the herd to the size where it can survive upon the natural food resources available, thus preventing death by starvation.

Perhaps, however, we can find some guidance from this incident for a human problem which is parallel and in many ways similar. In many parts of the world, excess population is a major problem. The number of persons exceeds the available supplies of food and other necessities for sustaining life. This is also true of some families even within quite affluent cultures. Would not the solution to these problems be similar to that followed with respect to the excess deer population in that Minneapolis suburb? Why not simply allow the killing off of enough human beings to bring the population down to a manageable or sustainable number? Or could we not greatly assist society by simply taking the nonproductive members, those unable to provide for or care for themselves, lining them up, and shooting them? With only the more productive persons left, certainly everyone else would benefit, would they not?

This attitude does seem to be showing up in our society in some ways. The discussion of the cases of people who have ended their lives with the assistance of Dr. Jack Kevorkian has revealed some interesting differences. While the debate over the right of hopelessly ill persons to bring their lives to an end voluntarily has produced sharply differing perspectives, some other themes have emerged. Some persons evidently regard older persons beyond the age of economically productive activity who draw a disproportionate share of the health care resources as drags upon society. Perhaps, they argue, it is not so bad if they do leave membership in the race.

What, however, would be the next step in the thinking of such people? Will they go on to suggest that people should not be given excessive opportunities to live beyond certain points? Perhaps the provisions of Medicare for elderly persons should exclude certain extraordinary resources for life maintenance. Is there really such value in persons that they should have an unlimited right to life, as it were?

There are other indications of a loss of the sense of value of human lives. For example, the calculation that takes place regarding human lives reveals this sort of callous approach. Whenever the risk of a certain action or substance is measured by the cost in human lives, we are experiencing something of this phenomenon. Similarly, we can measure the value our society assigns to a human life in an easy economic fashion. Suppose that we could calculate the number of lives that would be saved annually by lowering the speed limit on all highways, including interstate highways, to thirty-five miles per hour. It probably would not be possible to calculate this very precisely, but at least some sort of rough estimate could be made. Then, suppose we could measure or estimate the economic cost of such a change. If we then divide the latter figure in dollars by the former figure in persons, we have the value our society has tacitly assigned to a human life. This is a not pure calculation of course, for there also presumably would be some loss of human life as a result of the lowered speed; for example, patients who would die because medications were not available in time. Yet the point is nonetheless made: we have assigned an implicit value to human life whether we can ascertain what that value is or not.

We see this in one other practice within our society. It is the practice of triage. This is a French word, meaning to divide into three. In French field hospitals during World War I, when wounded were brought into the hospital, a determination of their condition was made, and they were assigned to one of three groups. The first group was those who would live, whether treated or not. The second group was those who would die, whether treated or not. The third group consisted of those who would either live or die, depending upon whether they were treated. The medical personnel then concentrated their efforts upon this third group. Of course, these decisions were more or less relative. Some in the second group would probably live if extraordinary means were employed on their behalf, but probably at the cost of the lives of some in the third group. The underlying assumption of this scheme seems to be that all human lives are inherently equal in value. Therefore, the effort is made which will assure the maximum number of survivors. Otherwise, a judgment might be made to spare the life of an officer over an enlisted man, or perhaps even a medical doctor over a foot soldier. Such decisions are faced quite regularly in medical practice. When there are several prospective donors, all desiring and needing the one available organ, who receives that organ? Is it the person who can pay the most for the operation? The one who has the potential for making the greatest contribution to society? Or the one who has the best medical chances of surviving the surgical procedure? These are important decisions that are being made in our society. There is no question that some people are, in practice though not in theory, more equal than others. Perhaps all humans are created equal, but by the time they reach adulthood, that equality has been lost. The people who can afford the best medical care, the best legal counsel, and the best education fare better in practice than do those who cannot afford them.

This type of issue comes up in connection with certain other discussions, as well. With the observance in the 1990s of the fiftieth anniversary of numerous events of the latter part of the Second World War, there has been a reminder of many of the atrocities that were committed in that war. The popular film *Schindler's List* gave vivid reinforcement to the understanding of the six million Jews who were exterminated by Adolf Hitler's Nazi government. The murder of millions of Russians by command of Joseph Stalin was part of the reason for the renaming of Stalingrad. The "ethnic cleansing" in Bosnia has brought cries of protest. At an earlier point, in the late 1960s and early 1970s, the moral outrage over the killing in the Vietnam War was powerfully expressed, especially on college campuses. We have to ask ourselves, however, on what basis such indignation could be justified.

One of the contentions of Hitler was that the German nation was a super race. They were the superior people, and were engaged in cleansing the human race of its inferior members. He believed that the Jews were such, and that, as the superior people, the Aryans had the right to eliminate them.

Suppose, however, that Hitler had been successful in his war. Suppose that he had invaded Britain in 1940, instead of attempting to bomb the British into submission in retaliation for the bombing of Germany. Suppose that the Eastern campaign of the invasion of Russia had begun earlier, so that Moscow and other major cities had fallen before the devastating winter weather began. With simply a change in these and perhaps a few other areas, the outcome of the war might have been quite different than proved to be the case. What then?

If Hitler had become the dominant ruler of the Western world he would have been able to continue his policy of exterminating Jews, and for that matter, of any other groups he had chosen to destroy. No one could have prevented his doing that. On what basis could one have objected? It certainly would not be possible on the basis of an evolutionary view of the origin of the human. For if one holds to Charles Darwin's principle of the survival of the fittest, then victory of this type would have proved that the Germans were indeed the fittest, or the master race. As such, presumably they would have had the right to do to the lower members whatever they pleased.

In the struggle for survival in nature, the higher, that is the more powerful, shrewder, more intelligent, do to the lower whatever they please. This is not only permissible, but is practically required by the scheme of things. Without this, the process could not move on to higher levels of selection. Certainly the lower living forms, insofar as they are conscious of what is happening to them, do not like this. Everything struggles to survive, so that no cow likes being barbecued, no fish likes being broiled. But feelings have no bearing upon it. In evolution, of all places, might does make right. If Hitler had the ability to dominate other members of the human race, he also had the right to do so on purely evolutionary grounds. Most people, however, react strongly and negatively against such a suggestion. While an argument might be made on the basis of the value of the human being, if there is a super race, then all that really matters is what benefits that superhuman being.

What, however, could give a human being the value which we all seem to want to assign to it? The Bible has a very different understanding of the human than does the evolutionary scientist, for example. We noted earlier the creation account in Genesis 1, where it says that God created the human in his own image and likeness. How that relates to the value which God attaches to the human is then spelled out elsewhere in the Bible. The biblical commands about human life indicate how precious each is to God. Murder is especially vigorously condemned. The reason for this is interesting to note. In Genesis 9:6, we are told that people who take the lives of other humans are themselves to forfeit their lives, because the human is made in the image and likeness of God. Thus, in a very real sense, God values us, at least in part, because we are like him. He can love us because there is in us that which is like him and, consequently, he loves himself by loving that in us which is like him.

The value God places upon us is further seen in his concern for our eternal life as well. We are told that the reason God sent his son into the world to live and die was that "God so loved the world" (John 3:16). We also realize that this extends to everyone. Paul wrote, "who desires all men to be saved and to come to the knowledge of the truth" (1 Tim. 2:4). Peter put it this way: "The Lord is not slow about his promise as some count slowness, but is forbearing toward you, not wishing that any should perish, but that all should reach repentance" (2 Peter 3:9). The real measure of our worth is the value God places upon us, and that is because he has created us, made us like him.

DOES IT MATTER IF GOD EXISTS?

But what does all of this mean, then, in our understanding of ourselves, and our understanding and treatment of other human beings? Our friend Hannah understood that since God had given the life of that little child, he was also the one to whom that child belonged. Hannah could have thought, "I and my husband Elkanah produced this child. I am the one who bore him, who went through the pain of the childbirth process. I should have the right to keep him, to raise him, to enjoy him, to benefit from him." Yet she understood that the child had not been given to her by God. Rather, he had simply lent or leased the child to her and Elkanah for a period of time. The child did not ultimately belong to her. While she had in a sense given life to this child, it was God who was the ultimate grantor of such. Consequently, his loyalty, his service, was to be to God, not to his mother. He did not exist for her benefit, but for God's.

This understanding was revealed in the name which Hannah gave her son. In our society, names mean relatively little. They simply serve to distinguish one person from another and can easily be interchanged, much like numbers. They may have been chosen because of a family name, or perhaps taken from the lists of names distributed by greeting card companies and others. Things were different in ancient Israel, however. The names were chosen to indicate something of the parents' understanding of the identity or qualities of the person. Actually, in our society, nicknames sometimes carry this sort of significance, being chosen because of a unique aspect of the person. So Hannah named her son *Samuel,* which means, "heard by God." It was her testimony that this child existed because she had prayed for God to send such a child, and he had heard and answered her.

This means that for parents who are Christians, there is a certain understanding of their children that is different than if they were not Christians. They do not see their children as really theirs, in the fullest sense. They belong to God, who gave them life and sustains them in that life. What they become in life is not the preference of the parent, or even of the child. God had some definite plans in mind for Samuel, for he called him to become a judge. Hannah had promised the child to God, to do with as he chose. The same will be true of believing parents today.

There was a time when devout Christian parents desired nothing more strongly than for their children to enter some life of special service for God. In some popular (mis)understandings, the highest calling one could receive was to be a foreign missionary, and the second highest was to be a pastor. Overall, our understanding of these things seems to have improved so that we now see that all roles in the kingdom of God are equally important and honorable, and that the real test is simply whether one is what and where God intends him or her to be. Yet, an interesting development appears to have taken place. Unlike an earlier generation, a number of Christian parents now hope that their children will not go into what was once termed "full-time Christian service." The ministry may, overall, have risen somewhat in economic status among occupations in the United States, but it is still well below the income level of others with comparable educational preparation. Also, the prestige attached to members of the clergy has declined markedly. Thus some parents discourage their children from considering such an option for their lives. As one of them put it, "He has too much talent to throw it away on the ministry when he could be a physician or an attorney." The point is not that God prefers people to enter the ministry. It would be just as wrong to want someone to be a missionary or a minister if God wants him or her to be something else. The point is that God as the ultimate giver of life is the one whose will in the matter should be most important.

There is also the question of our own understanding of ourselves. Our identity is as God's children, and thus our final loyalty is to him as well. This should govern both how we conceive of ourselves and how we conduct ourselves. Paul reminded his readers, including us, "You are not your own; you were bought at a price. Therefore honor God with your body" (1 Cor. 6:19–20). This is also put in terms of the identity of the believer as a soldier. Paul wrote to Timothy, "No one serving as a soldier gets involved in civilian affairs—he wants to please his commanding officer" (2 Tim. 2:4). As a soldier of the living God we owe a certain loyalty and obedience to our master, and we live to please him and obey his orders, not to please ourselves.

As citizens of the kingdom of God, we have both obligations and privileges. Recently, I applied for renewal of my passport. The application form asked several very important questions: Had I ever renounced my citizenship in the United States of America? Had I ever taken an oath of allegiance to any other government? In short, was I still a citizen in good standing with the government of the United States of America?

DOES IT MATTER IF GOD EXISTS?

That citizenship involves certain duties and responsibilities. I am made aware of those every April 15, as well as at numerous other times. Accompanying such responsibilities, however, are also certain privileges. I am entitled to protection by my country. I am entitled to justice, to participate in electing officials and passing laws. If I am in another country, the embassy of the United States can be contacted for help. That help, however, is forthcoming and deserved because I have evidence of my identity as an American citizen. Were someone to present himself at the embassy without proof of his citizenship or his identity, and without ability to establish that identity, no help would be forthcoming.

In our modern world, there are many situations in which our identity is important. Take, for example, the Automatic Teller Machine. When one inserts a card and requests a withdrawal, a very important query is made by the machine. One is to enter one's Personal Identification Number. PINs are very important to ATMs. They establish that one is who one claims to be. Fraud can take place in these situations, however. Some persons unwisely leave their receipts lying at the machine. If someone obtains their PIN (as by looking over their shoulder when the number is entered), and has the account number from the receipt, a counterfeit card can be manufactured and money withdrawn. There are numerous other situations in modern life where identity is important. With the prevalence of security systems, when someone's alarm is activated, the monitoring office ordinarily calls immediately. When someone answers, they are asked to give a password, known only to the legitimate occupants of that dwelling. That is the proof that the person answering the telephone is who he or she claims to be, and has a right to be there. Similarly, with electronic mail, a password must be given to obtain one's messages.

These forms of identification leave something to be desired, however, for the password or PIN can be stolen or discovered. More foolproof forms of identification are being developed which cannot be severed from the proper owner. Fingerprints have been used for a long time. Now, however, they are being supplanted by DNA, which is a virtually infallible test of identity. Voice prints are also used, and seem to possess a degree of personal uniqueness that makes them excellent tests.

It is, however, important that the identity be in agreement with the source that properly determines identity. If one were to be given a PIN by a source falsely claiming to represent the dispensing agency, this would be of little avail, for the person or institution which ultimately controls the account or the mailbox would not recognize it. On one occasion I went to refuel an aircraft at a self-service fuel station at our local airport. I inserted my card, followed by my PIN, only to find that the machine did not recognize me. I called the attendant and found that the computer had recently been reprogrammed, with my number being incorrectly entered. I knew who I was, but the computer was in error.

This is why it is so important to know who we are. If we understand our identity in terms of mechanical or biological factors, the true and living God will not answer our prayers. We will be like an imposter, for we will not know who we really are. To see ourselves as the creatures of God, made in his own image, and then to conduct ourselves in the light of this, is to find the true way of life.

DOES IT MATTER IF GOD EXISTS?

Study Guide

Key Questions

1. What do you know about yourself? Write a short summary in answer to the questions "Who am I?" and "Where did I come from?" In the first part write about your parents and your ancestry. In the second, write your thoughts about your origin, how human life began.
2. What is the difference between explaining the birth of a child as a **biological occurrence** and as a **gift from God**? How do the two views affect one's attitude with regard to the value of the child? About the responsibility of the parent?
3. The author discusses three ways in which we in America are seeing a decline in the sense of value of human life. What are they? Do you agree?
4. Hannah looked at Samuel as a **gift from God**. She also spoke of him as being **leased** or **lent** to her. Was she confused? What is the difference between them? Does the latter indicate a sense of greater value? Does it require greater responsibility on her part?

Bible Investigation

1. In your study of chapter 6 you read 1 Samuel 1–3 focusing on the child Samuel. Now, read the same passage and focus on the mother Hannah. What was her view of the origin of life?
2. Be sure to read Genesis 9:6, John 3:16, 1 Timothy 2:4, and 2 Peter 3:9. How do these verses help you to understand the value God places on each individual human being?

Personal Application

1. **Abortion** and **euthanasia** are currently much discussed issues. Reread the section dealing with **callousness**. What is your response? Are you as quick to speak out about this as you are about the other two issues? Think about it.
2. If you are a Christian examine your attitude toward "full-time Christian service." Do you encourage young people making life-time decisions to consider areas of ministry as well as emphasizing that "all roles in the kingdom of God are equally important and honorable"? How can you better your involve-

ment to help others determine to consider God's will for their lives?
3. Memorize 1 Corinthians 6:19–20. Meditate upon its meaning to you.

For Further Thought

1. Are all children **gifts from God**? What about children of the ungodly? Illegitimate children? Think about it.
2. Think about the problem of **overpopulation**. Back away from your own views and consider the result of doing nothing. How can the Christian become involved and diminish the **calloused attitude**?
3. What obligations and privileges can you list as you think of yourself as a United States citizen? Contrast these by listing the obligations and privileges of being a citizen of the kingdom of God.

8

Is That
All There Is?

"Is that all there is? Is that all there is? If that's all there is, my friends, then let's keep dancing. Let's break out the booze and have a ball. If that's all there is." Those words of a popular song sung by Peggy Lee a decade or more ago have a haunting quality to them. Stanza by stanza she traces some of the "big" experiences of life: a circus; the burning down of her family's home; falling in love; losing the love of the one loved; and after each one asks, "Is that all there is?" Finally, she says, "When I lie dying, I'll still be singing this song, 'Is that all there is to life?'"

That question is one that we often don't ask when we're young. At that point in time we are concerned with some of the most immediate questions: having a good time, getting into the right college, whom we are going to marry and when, what occupation or profession we will pursue. But the really important question is not only: What is life itself? but: Is there anything beyond this life that we can know and experience? Many people do not face that question, often because they are too preoccupied with other matters, but also frequently because that is too unpleasant a question to ask.

Yet this is a question which must be asked. I recall Ben Haden telling a story on his radio broadcast about traveling on a plane seated next to a young man. The young man had just received a new position, and was quite excited about it. It involved a major increase in salary, and Ben Haden asked him what he planned to do now. He responded that the first thing he would do was to buy a new, larger car. "What will you do then?" asked Ben. "We'll move into a larger home in a nicer neighborhood." "And what will you do then?" came Ben's next question. The answer was, "I'll send my kids to the best college possible." "And what will you do then?" persisted Ben. "I think we'll join a good country club, and do some traveling." "And what will you do then?" came the familiar question. "Eventually I'll retire." "What will you do then?" asked Ben. "We'll probably move to a warm climate, and I'll do some fishing and golfing." "What will you do then?" asked Ben again. "I suppose I'll die," said the young man, becoming a bit impatient with this seemingly endless repetition of the same question. He need not have become impatient, however, for the question was asked just one more time, and this time without any reply from the young man: "And what will you do *then?*"

There are indications that the main problem frequently is our unwillingness to face the fact of death and its reality. During my last two years as an undergraduate student, I worked as a night attendant in a funeral home. In addition to answering the telephone, my job when there was a reviewal (formerly known as a "wake") on my night on was to stand at the door and open it for visitors, say "good evening," and be as helpful but as unobtrusive as possible. I noticed that the visitors, after first going up to the casket to "pay their respects" to the deceased, would then get as far to the back of the room as they could, and would enjoy visiting with other friends and relatives who were there. Sometimes their laughter and merriment would become quite boisterous. There were times when I was attempting to study in my second floor room and the commotion was so loud that I had difficulty concentrating. I once asked my boss, the funeral director, about this behavior. "Yes," he said, "people do everything they can to avoid the fact of the deceased's death. I think they are trying to avoid thinking about the fact that they will someday have to die themselves."

I have thought about that observation, and have noticed how we have managed in our society to avoid thinking about the fact of universal and unavoidable death. One of the symptoms is the "positive language" that we have devised to soften the harsh, stark reality of death. Have you noticed, for example, that we no longer have any old people in our society? Instead, we have "senior citizens" and "golden agers," honorific titles. Perhaps that is because old people traditionally were among the best prospects for death of anyone within our society. No one ever dies anymore, either. Instead, people "pass away" or, in more neutral and clinical fashion, "expire." In an earlier time, when dying was more fashionable, an "undertaker" handled the arrangements, and the corpse was buried in a grave in a "graveyard." The undertaker was replaced by the mortician, and then by the funeral director. And after the funeral, the undertaker took the body to what came to be known as the cemetery. Then, however, the funeral director began taking "the remains" to "memorial parks." One becomes a golden ager, passes away, and the funeral director takes the remains to a memorial park. How pleasant it sounds! Almost like going on a picnic! Surely, however, this is an effort, whether conscious or unconscious, to deny the reality of the fact that we are all going to grow old, die, and be taken to a cemetery and buried. No amount of "positive language" can extinguish that fact.

In contrast to this, existentialism has insisted upon the stark reality of death. All of this positive language is "inauthentic existence," failure to recognize and accept the realities of life. Existentialists insist that death is an inherent part of life without the recognition of which there is no genuine life. Sometimes they dwell upon death or, more correctly, the contingency of life, in ways which seem to more positive thinkers to be morbid in nature.

On existentialism's grounds, Christianity is a very realistic religion. It does not deny the fact of death, or its permanence. Indeed, it emphasizes death. Hebrews 9:27 states, "And just as it is appointed for men to die once, and after that comes judgment." Death, at least in our present state of affairs, is considered a normal or invariable accompaniment of life. Yet it is not normal in the more ultimate sense. Not only is it not desirable, but the impression is given that it is not how life originally was intended to end. It is an abnormal condition which has entered the human race because of sin. Whether humans would have died if sin had not come is a debated topic among Christians, but one thing is certain. The universal presence of sin gives death its particularly ghastly quality. It has acquired what Paul calls, "the sting of death" (1 Cor. 15:55–56).

This sting, this extraordinary unpleasantness, takes several forms, with several dimensions. One is the sheer fact of extinction. Everything that is seeks to live. To be alive is to wish to continue to live. This is instinctive in the lower forms of life below the human, and although we usually do not refer to instincts with respect to humans, there is a similar ingrained tendency or drive toward self-preservation, and it is a powerful force.

At times this statement appears untrue. What about the suicide or attempted suicide? And what about the elderly person who prays that God will "take him (or her) home?" Certainly this is evidence that life is not always desired or sought or preserved. Yet even these people witness to the inherent desire for life. For what such a person is protesting is not life but the distortion of life, the alteration of what life is intended to be. Life as these people currently experience it is not life as it is supposed to be or, perhaps, as it has been. It is grief over the loss of that life or a sense of despair over whether such a life can again be experienced, that results in this attitude and action. No, such persons are actually witnesses for, not against, the point that we are making here.

Death is, then, the threat to all of this. It ends life, the most precious commodity that the human can have or seek for. It can be deferred, but not avoided. I recently heard a discussion between doctors on the possibility of prolonging life. There is apparently hope by some doctors of determining the factors which cause aging and acting to neutralize them. Indeed, there is hope of isolating the genetic factors and using genetic engineering and treatment to negate the aging process. In some cases, the process of replacing organs might be extended and expanded to prolong life. One doctor, however, stated that there is a practical limit to all of this. Even if it were possible to prevent the aging process, he calculated that the likely upward limit of human life, under the present societal conditions, would be about six hundred years. For by that time, said the doctor, the odds are that one would die an accidental death. So inevitable is death that, one way or another, sooner or later, it claims each of us as victim.

Part of the sting of death is extinction. This is the idea that we would simply cease to be, would pass out of existence. What we have been would perish. But that in turn is related to the problem of futility. Death cuts off all our hopes and ambitions and goals and projects. Whatever is done when death comes is done; whatever is undone is forever undone. One of life's frustrations is that there is so much more living one would want to do. For some, there are goals to be achieved, inventions to be made, victories to be won, that can never be. In some ways, death is a greater frustration for the good people, the contributors, than for the takers. For they are the ones who want to do more, contribute more to this world and to the human race, and are prevented from doing so.

Beyond that, however, is the question of whether what we have done in this life, what we have contributed to the world, has any real lasting value. May it be that death not only cuts short anything further that we might do, but also negates the value of what we have done? May it be that the world will really, in the long run, be no different, and specifically, no better, for our having lived in it?

One way humans seek to perpetuate their influence in this world is through their descendants, through having offspring who will make a contribution to life. They consequently give themselves to teaching and modeling for their children in such a way as to help assure that their children will be what they would want them to be. The problem, however, is that one cannot be assured of what one's children will be and will do. Even the most moral, virtuous, and conscientious of parents may find that their children rebel and go their own way. Even the Lord himself found that his children, Israel, regularly rebelled against him and went their own way. The Old Testament as a whole is a record of this rejection and rebellion. We cannot count on our children and their children to do what we have not done. It must be our own accomplishment.

But what of this? May it be merely futile? May even our own contributions to good be wiped out by the triumph of evil some day? Would not this be the bitterest of experiences, to have labored for naught? Albert Camus has captured aptly this situation in his *Myth of Sisyphus*. Sisyphus was a character from Greek mythology who had died and gone to the nether world. The gods, however, sent him back to earth to accomplish certain tasks which they assigned him. Then they summoned him to return to the place from which they had sent him. He ignored these summons. He enjoyed the warm sunshine of this world. Repeated entreaties went unheeded. Finally, the gods had to go and fetch him from the world and bring him back. As his punishment for this disobedience, he was sentenced to push a large rock to the peak of a mountain. Straining, exerting himself, he managed to accomplish this. No sooner had he achieved this goal, however, then the rock rolled from the summit, down the other side of the mountain. He was forced to trudge down to the base of the mountain and put his shoulder again to the rock, pushing it slowly and painfully to the top. When it reached the peak, however, it again rolled down the side. He repeated this effort, again with the same results. And so he must continue, through all eternity, pushing his rock, and seeing his efforts endlessly fail.

Is this, then, what life is really like? Is this the ultimate commentary upon life? Are we condemned to doing that which has no lasting value? Will the rock that we have pushed simply roll back to where it was before us, leaving the world no different? Since death cuts off life, it may be that for all practical purposes it will not really matter to the world that we have lived at all. Or may it be that life does not make any sense, that what we do does not seize upon anything of real meaning, so that what we have done was miscalculated or even mistaken? Perhaps what we have thought to be good was not actually that. Perhaps there really is no meaning to life. Perhaps Shakespeare was right when he wrote regarding life: "It is a tale told by an idiot, full of sound and fury and signifying nothing."

This sense of meaninglessness has been held throughout all ages of the world's history, although with special force and greater adherence at some times than at others. Even some of the ancient Greeks had this philosophy of despair. Writing in the golden age of Greece, some five hundred years before Christ, Sophocles said, "Not to be born at all—that is by far the best fate. The second best is as soon as one is born with all haste to return thither whence one has come." And in a more contemporary note, Saul Bellow wrote in *Herzog*: "But what is the philosophy of this generation? Not God is dead, that period was passed long ago. This generation thinks—and this is its thought of thoughts—that nothing faithful, vulnerable, fragile, can be durable or have any true power. Death waits for all these things as a cement floor waits for a falling light bulb."

There is, moreover, a sense of incompleteness in life for many people. Even those who have had happy families and success in their work, and in some cases have distinguished themselves by attaining great accomplishments in life, often have the feeling that something is missing. There is a vague sense of an essential element being absent. One is reminded here of Augustine's life experience. He had sought for satisfaction in sexual gratification. He had sought for an explanation of his nature in Manicheism, but that had not satisfied him. Then he turned to Neoplatonism, but this philosophy did not bring termination of his restless search, either. Finally, he turned to the God of Christianity, the God of his mother who had prayed for him, and finally found the satisfaction for which he

DOES IT MATTER IF GOD EXISTS?

was looking. He later wrote, "The heart is restless, O God, and it does not find rest until it finds it in thee." This is similar to the empty spot, the "God-shaped vacuum" that Pascal claimed was within every human being. It was felt as well by C. S. Lewis, who had a vague longing for something which he called joy. It was a sort of nostalgia for something that he could not precisely identify, yet he knew there was something missing, something unsatisfied.

So it is with some persons today. There is a sense that they have missed out on the meaning of life. They cannot sing, "Ah, sweet mystery of life, at last I found you." Perhaps it is that their accomplishments do not seem really to be what they had thought they would be, or that they have not brought the anticipated satisfaction. It may be like Alexander the Great who, having conquered all of the known world, reportedly then sat down and wept because there were no more worlds to conquer. Whatever form this experience takes, death accentuates it, for death means that life's search for that meaning is over.

But what if death shows one what that object of one's search was, but also cuts off any opportunity of receiving it? What a disappointment that would be. Probably it would be better never to realize that there is something unattainable that one has been seeking for than to make such a discovery. Although the old saying states, "It's better to have loved and lost than never to have loved at all," that may not really be the case. One woman who had never found romantic love became convinced that there was no such thing, or at least that there was not such for her. Her married sister told her, "If a good man whom you can respect asks you to marry him, do it." Just such a man came along, asked her to marry, and she accepted. Several years later she met and fell in love with a married man. She said, sadly, "All my life I've been looking for something, and now that I've found it, I can't have it." Might death reveal life to be that way? The Bible contains Jesus' story of a rich man who died and found himself in torment. The poor man, Lazarus, was in Abraham's bosom. No one, however, could pass from one to the other. Their situations were fixed for all eternity. Perhaps life is that way and death seals one's fate so that it not only ends the opportunity for finding life's satisfaction but also confirms its existence, thus heightening the frustration.

There is another major sting of death. It is the pain of separation. Who of us has not felt the pain of having someone very precious taken away from us by death, and thus never to be seen again? The sorrow, the empty place in our hearts, the loss of someone who was so important to us, together with the realization that we will never see that person again, is one of the deepest forms of pain to be encountered in this life. This sorrow is proverbial. It is found in the fear of the Christians in Thessalonica that they would never again see their loved ones who had died (1 Thess. 4:13–18). It has been expressed colloquially in the song, *Clementine:* "You are dead and gone forever, dreadful sorry, Clementine." It has been expressed considerably more elegantly by Alfred, Lord Tennyson, in his poem, "Break, Break, Break", written upon the death of his friend, Arthur Henry Hallam:

> Break, break, break,
>   On thy cold gray stones, O Sea!
> And I would that my tongue could utter
>   The thoughts that arise in me.
>
> O, well for the fisherman's boy,
>   That he shouts with his sister at play!
> O, well for the sailor lad,
>   That he sings in his boat on the bay!
>
> And the stately ships go on
>   To their haven under the hill;
> But O for the touch of a vanish'd hand,
>   And the sound of a voice that is still!
>
> Break, break, break,
>   At the foot of thy crags, O Sea!
> But the tender grace of a day that is dead
>   Will never come back to me.

Is this what death does? Does it have the power to take from us that which is most precious in life, with no hope or recourse? Will we never see them again? Perhaps this is the cruelest of all of death's stings. Possibly this is why we tend to deny in practice death's reality, acting as if it does not exist. It may be that the death we really fear is not our own but the death of those whom we love most.

Death has one more sting. It is one that many people are not certain of, or in many cases, do not even think about. Whereas it is apparent that death does these other things that we have been discussing, this one may not actually be the case. But the very possibility of its truth is enough to be troubling to the serious-minded person. Suppose death is not the end of existence. Suppose it is merely the termination of life as we find it here. And suppose, further, that there is a supreme being, and that we will meet him in the existence which comes beyond death. What, then? If we find that we fall short of his expectations for us and that there is nothing we can do after this life ends to fulfill those expectations, then death is a very serious matter indeed. For then death ushers us into God's presence and brings judgment based upon our beliefs and actions in this earthly life, beliefs and actions which we cannot now negate. This is the sting of death known as judgment, and it is in many ways potentially the most serious of all these adverse effects of death.

But what of these questions and problems? Is there any answer to them in the Christian doctrine of God? For Paul, the key was found in the resurrection of Christ. For if God brought Jesus back to life from the dead, then there is basis for expecting that we also will find life beyond this life in terms of the resurrection.

Death is not merely the end of all, says Paul. There is a God, and he waits for us beyond death. There is an eternity to come, following this time, in which we will live on. And our situation in that life to come is definitely related to what we have believed and done in this life. The Bible indicates that we were made in God's image or likeness, and made to have fellowship with him. That is our end, our reason for being. That intention was not merely for each of us to have such a relationship with God for just a few short years. His desire was that the relationship should continue forever. Although this fellowship was unlike that within the Trinity since our fellowship with God has a point of beginning, it is to be like it in not having a point of ending. Thus, God made humans as immortal souls, that is, capable of living throughout all eternity. This life is not merely a cruel joke played by God which comes to an end just when we are beginning to enjoy it. It is just the prelude to something even better.

Have you ever had the experience of finding that something could be even better than you had already experienced it to be? For example, take walking through the grass versus taking off one's shoes and walking barefoot through the grass, or watching an event on television versus being there and seeing it in person. As enjoyable as the first experience might be, the second member of each pair is so much better simply because it is without the limitations involved in the first variety.

This is what the Bible teaches about the life to come. The point is not simply that we will be alive, but that we will be more alive then than we are now. We will no longer have the limitations we now experience. For one thing, we will have new bodies quite different in nature from the bodies which we now have. These bodies become ill, wear out, and die. The bodies which we will receive in the future are what Paul called "spiritual bodies." They do not wear out, break down, become old and diseased.

Much of our enjoyment of life is hindered by the imperfection of our bodies. We sustain injuries or become ill, preventing us, either temporarily or permanently, from doing things that we enjoy or, at least, doing them as vigorously or fully as we might wish. That is because these bodies we now have are what Paul calls "perishable bodies," bodies that wear out. Even as I write these pages, I am lying on my back in bed with a notebook computer propped up against my knees. In the life to come, however, there will be no influenza, no strained backs, no fractured arms.

One of the interesting things, however, about this life to come is that it involves very specialized activities. Have you gone to some place or event of which you really were not a part? Perhaps you were at a ski resort although you don't ski or have an injury and can't ski, or perhaps you were at a dog show when you really don't care that much for dogs, at least not with the intense fervor of most of the people participating. In those situations, usually we are there with someone who has that interest but we do not, possibly a friend or a spouse. It is hard to be among persons who are rabid about something, whether antique automobiles or a certain kind of cooking, when one either has not engaged in the activity enough to be very good at it or else is not very interested in that matter. Probably one would prefer to be somewhere else and doing something else, like those bumper stickers which say, "I'd rather be sailing" (or "flying" or "fishing"). Heaven and the life to come is not necessarily merely a continuation of all the activities people engage in here. The life to come is much more specialized, in many ways. The pictures that we see in the Bible of people in the future life show them all engaged in basically the same sort of activity. They are worshiping or serving the Lord. They are not engaged in bowling, shopping, or gorging themselves with rich food, nor in the first century equivalents of those activities.

Some who are familiar with the Bible might, however, object that there is a reference to the marriage supper of the Lamb (Rev. 19:9). Surely here is feasting of a type such as we find here on earth. Note, however, that there are reasons to consider that this may be a figurative or symbolic usage of the term. For it is the Lamb, certainly not a literal lamb but the Lamb of God, that is involved. And presumably this is not to be a literal wedding, either. While Paul speaks of the church as a bride and Christ as the bridegroom, that certainly is not to be a literal marriage, with a literal wedding ceremony accompanied by a wedding banquet, such as we find here on earth. In fact, Jesus said at least of humans that in the resurrection they "will neither marry nor be given in marriage, and they can no longer die; for they are like the angels" (Luke 20:35–36). Jesus also spoke of his disciples eating and drinking at his table in the judgment and sitting on thrones judging the twelve tribes of Israel (Luke 22:30). That, however, is in the context of a discussion among the disciples as to who was the greatest. Jesus responded by talking about how the Gentiles exercise authority and how his disciples should seek to serve rather than be served. Those who do so, as he has done, will then also share in his glory. The reference to sitting at his table seems to be an idiom for that special role of dignity, as does sitting on thrones, and consequently should probably be understood figuratively rather than literally.

The type of activity engaged in throughout all eternity is not, therefore, merely an extension of what people naturally most want to do here. Eternal life is on Christ's terms, not on ours. It is not an experience of endless self-indulgence or of any kind of sin. Those who experience and enjoy the life to come will be those who have been transformed here, and that transformation involves an interest in and an enjoyment of spiritual things.

This, however, may not seem like something that is all that much to be desired. To many people, worship and service of the Lord don't seem especially attractive, and may even be boring. The experience of eternity with the Lord, however, involves a higher level of satisfaction than anything ordinarily experienced. Certainly each of us can think of experiences which we found completely satisfying at the time, and could not really imagine how a given other experience could surpass it. For example, as a young person, riding a tricycle was a source of real enjoyment. Perhaps you tried prematurely to ride a bicycle, and your lack of balance meant that instead of it being a happy experience, it was a downright painful experience. When, however, you had developed the skills necessary to ride a bicycle successfully, that experience so transcended tricycle riding that there was no regret about giving it up, no desire to cling to it. And when the time came to learn to drive a car, the bicycle's pleasures were gladly foregone. So it is with the worship and service of the Lord in the life to come. Its joy, for those who have been converted, will be incomparable to those merely temporal pleasures that seem to mean so much.

We said that this involves one's higher nature or one's true being. All of us have presumably experienced the happy experience of doing the right thing. There is a satisfaction that comes out of doing what is right and what is for the benefit of the other person that exceeds the enjoyment of doing something for one's own benefit. Returning to its owner something of great value that one has found rather than keeping it for oneself is an example of this. This satisfaction is on a deeper level, a level of self-respect which cannot be compared with the pleasure one would obtain from using that for oneself. It is fulfilling the higher moral standard that even society in general recognizes. It is the joy of knowing one has character, rather than the temporary gratification these things could provide.

There is another way of looking at this. We spoke of the sense of something being absent from one's life. This is encountered in various ways. Sometimes it comes from the feeling that one has not found one's *thing*, one's niche in life. It may be the feeling of being in a vocation for which one is unsuited. One component in many midlife crises is of this nature, resulting in a change of jobs, partners, and even faiths. Or it may simply be the sense that there is something more to life than one has found. It was this which drove Augustine from one satisfaction to another until he found rest in God. And it was this which C. S. Lewis was searching for and which he had such difficulty in describing, but which he called "joy," and which he found in God through faith in Jesus Christ. As the title of his autobiographical account, *Surprised by Joy,* suggests, this came from an originally unexpected source.

DOES IT MATTER IF GOD EXISTS?

This was what Jesus was talking about in his conversation with the woman at the well in John 4. She had been married successively to five different men, and was now living with a man who was not her husband. Yet Jesus told her that if she believed in him, he would give her living water so that she would never thirst again. It is characteristic of these other supposed sources of satisfaction that they do not bring lasting satisfaction, or even complete satisfaction, and leave still that sense of something lacking. What deep down we long for, even in a vague way, we receive from the Lord, and are able to enjoy it, not for just a period of time, but for all eternity. Some of the pleasures which people pursue most aggressively can only be enjoyed for part of one's life, while physical and mental health and strength are present. A former neighbor of mine once said to me, "I want to have fun while I'm still young enough to enjoy it." Some of these pleasures lose their ability to satisfy as they once did, requiring a search for still more intensive experiences. We will never outgrow or lose the capacity to enjoy eternal fellowship with God.

But what of the futility that death seems to place upon our work? May the possibility that nothing permanent will ever come of our work render it worthless? Should we simply "eat, drink, and be merry, for tomorrow we die"? That is the philosophy of a good many people these days, and perhaps they are justified in that view.

Jesus recognized that there is validity in this view, in certain respects. Certain goals that many people pursue are bound to be frustrated because the things sought after will simply fade away. That is why Jesus emphasized the importance of choosing one's goals carefully. So he said, "Do not store up for yourselves treasures on earth, where moth and rust destroy, and where thieves break in and steal" (Matt. 6:19). Today Jesus would perhaps state it somewhat differently, perhaps like this: "Do not store up for yourselves treasures on earth, where they are subject to inflation, depreciation, devaluation, and the fluctuations of the Dow-Jones average." What Jesus said of money could just as well be applied to any of the temporal values. One might well measure his or her earthly life and the values sought by how long they will last. Some cannot be assured for even a full lifetime. What does someone have that could not disappear in a very short time, perhaps overnight or even in a moment? Fortunes can be lost very quickly. A job or position within one's profession can also disappear rather quickly. Health, even one's mind, can be lost in a split-second accident. And any of these values, even if they last throughout life, are left behind at death. As Paul put it, "For we brought nothing into the world, and we can take nothing out of it" (1 Tim. 6:7). The answer to the old question, "How much did he leave?" is still the same: "He left it all." Reputation, influence, money, and position cannot be taken with us.

Yet there is something that can be done that lasts. It is a matter of simply making one's choices wisely. Jesus said, "Store up for yourselves treasures in heaven, where moth and rust do not destroy and where thieves do not break in and steal" (Matt. 6:20). Preparation of oneself for heaven and service of the Lord are permanent. Nothing can destroy them.

Paul recognized this same concern. He said, "If only for this life we have hope in Christ, we are to be pitied more than all men" (1 Cor. 15:19). What if there is nothing beyond this life? Then we have thrown our lives away in any kind of temporal satisfaction. For then they will take us to the graveyard, or the cemetery, or the memorial park, lower us into the ground and cover us and leave us there. And that is all there is to our lives. However, in the end of that chapter he speaks of how Christ has overcome death and says, "Therefore, my dear brothers, stand firm. Let nothing move you. Always give yourselves fully to the work of the Lord, because you know that your labor in the Lord is not in vain" (v. 58). Not in vain! Not futile! Not empty! Not wasted!

Think how sad it would be to give one's self, and perhaps one's whole working life, to accomplish something which ultimately would fail and lose all its resources, or to strive for a revolution which would fail. Here, however, we are assured that we are on the side which will succeed, the side that will prevail. We are contributing to a cause which will go on through all eternity. Our lives are worthwhile when given to a work that will survive our death.

But what of the power of death to separate us from loved ones? That was the pain that Martha felt. Even though she believed that her brother Lazarus would be raised in the resurrection in the last day, that did not compensate for the sadness she was feeling; her beloved brother was not there to love, to embrace, to talk to. Even Jesus felt that sorrow. For in the verse which in our English Bibles is the shortest verse and yet one of the most powerful, John says of him, "Jesus wept!" (John 11:35). He felt that pain of sorrow and separation as genuinely as we do. Yes, that is one of life's greatest losses. A unique person is gone, and no one else can replace that person.

It is bad enough to miss someone because they are gone. We feel that whenever we must separate for a time in this life. What softens the pain in those situations, however, is the knowledge that we will again see the person, even if not for some time. But on the other hand, if that person is gone forever and we will never see him or her again, then how great is the sorrow. Then surely we must continue to grieve. This was what caused grief to the Christians in the church at Thessalonica. Some of their number had died and they faced the prospect of never seeing them again. Paul, however, reassured them by telling them that we would not precede them if we were alive when the Lord returns. Those who have died in the Lord will be resurrected. They and we will together be caught up into the air to meet the Lord. That is how it will continue throughout all eternity. And therefore Paul urged his readers not to grieve as those who have no hope, but to encourage one another, using these words (1 Thess. 4:13–18). Those who have died in the Lord are not simply gone or perished. If we also have that same love for the Lord we will see them once again. We have the hope of David. When his infant son was desperately ill, David grieved. When, however, the boy died, David gave up his grieving. He said, "I will go to him, but he will not return to me" (2 Sam. 12:23). That is true. No one has ever come back from the dead, except for Jesus and the people whom he raised. If we are to see them, we must make certain that we make the arrangements in this life which guarantee that we will also go to that presence of the Lord.

That brings us finally to the last power of sin, the power of judgment and the fear or, at least, the apprehension or anxiety that it causes. Suppose there is a God and a life hereafter, and death cuts off the last opportunity to prepare for it. Final judgment, if there is one, is, however, like a final examination in a course. In fact, one might even think of it as life's final examination. And because the time of the examination means that one has no more opportunity to prepare and the present state of one's knowledge must be revealed, its arrival often causes some anxiety. That anxiety is primarily for those who are not adequately prepared, however, who have not exercised good stewardship of time and opportunity earlier in the semester. The good student who has worked diligently and is confident of his or her knowledge actually looks forward to the examination as an opportunity to demonstrate that preparation and knowledge.

So it is with judgment for those who are ready for it, who have already met God's requirements by accepting his Son, Jesus Christ, as Savior. In Jesus' picture of the last judgment in Matthew 25, he says to the "sheep," "Come, you who are blessed by my Father; take your inheritance, the kingdom prepared for you since the creation of the world" (v. 34). They are even surprised by the favorability of his judgment, or at least by its criteria, since they had served him without actually knowing it was service of him. For them, judgment brings vindication and joy.

Is that all there is? No, that's not all there is. For the believer, death does not end it all. It is really the beginning. Death, as Paul acknowledges, is an enemy, out to bring harm to us. That enemy, however, has been conquered and now serves the Lord, carrying out his purposes—not bringing an end to all things, but bringing all believers into the blessed and everlasting presence of their Lord.

Study Guide

Key Questions

1. What is your answer to the question "What is life?" Ask yourself if "there is anything beyond this life that we know and experience." How would you have responded to **Ben Haden** had you been traveling and encountered him?
2. The author discusses four **forms** or **dimensions** of what Paul calls the **sting of death** (1 Cor. 15:55–56). Which do you or have you experienced—the fact of **extinction**, the problem of **futility**, the pain of **separation**, or the understanding of future **judgment**? Which is the most difficult for you to accept?
3. As you think of eternity and your eternal future, how are you preparing now? How will preparation now help you to anticipate more fully your entrance there and eliminate fears about it?

Bible Investigation

1. Read 1 Corinthians 15:42–58. The concentration of this study is on living so that **the sting of death** does not control us. How do these verses raise expectations of joy in eternity and how do they instruct one to prepare for it?
2. Do the same with 1 Thessalonians 4:13–18. Notice how the final verse (18) instructs you and me.
3. What was the basis of Paul's belief in life beyond this life? What was his view of resurrection? Study Romans 5:17, 2 Corinthians 4:14, 1 Thessalonians 4:13–18, and 2 Timothy 2:11.
4. Study Matthew 6:19–21. What have you stored up on earth? In heaven? Think about verse 21.

Personal Application

1. Write down questions you have about life, death, and eternity. Reread the chapter with a determination to find help in answering your questions. Pray about it.
2. If you have found answers to your questions, and are able, apply the instruction of 1 Thessalonians 4:18. Talk with someone else about knowing Christ and the life he gives, both in time and in eternity.

3. If you have further questions, don't ignore them. Go to some-one who, with their Bible, will help you find the answers you seek.
4. Learn Matthew 6:20 and 21 or 1 Corinthians 15:58. Reread the author's comments on the verse you choose. Think about its meaning for you. Act upon it.

For Further Study

1. Think about the statement "Heaven and the life to come is not necessarily merely a continuation of all the activities people engage in here." What Bible verses or passages can you find to indicate activity in heaven? What will **worship** and **serving the Lord** be like?
2. The author pointed out that the passage on the **marriage sup-per of the Lamb** (Rev. 19:9) is to be interpreted figuratively. Why is this? How do we know when to understand figurative language in the Bible? Why do we not accept it literally?

9

Strength
Out of Weakness

Things are not always as they seem, are they? Sometimes what we expect at first glance turns out to be very different when we examine it more closely. I remember sitting on a church platform one Sunday evening, waiting to speak, when the soloist came up to sing. He was a tackle on the local college football team, standing 6'5" and weighing 270 pounds. He had a chest like a barrel. I had come to associate large instruments, such as bass horns, bass drums, and cellos with low pitched sounds and I naturally expected to hear a deep bass voice. When he opened his mouth and began to sing however, out of that huge body came one of the most beautiful high tenor voices I had ever heard. There was, of course, no logical connection between the size of the body in this case and the pitch of the sound, but it did seem surprising.

There are a lot of things like that in life, aren't there? Sometimes what looks like a weak and flimsy item turns out to have unusual strength and continues in use long after we had thought we would need to discard it. At other times, seemingly well constructed objects break down, sometimes expiring shortly after the warranty expires. And that is true of life as well. Some of the most satisfying experiences actually end up being disappointments, and some of the most frustrating times prove eventually to be sources of great satisfaction.

So it was that Paul wrote this unusual statement, "When I am weak, then I am strong" (2 Cor. 12:10). This is what we call a paradox. It is a seeming contradiction. On the surface of it, the statement makes no sense. That very paradoxical character of the statement, however, forces us to stop and think. It requires that we probe more deeply into its meaning. I think that is why Paul used this particular literary device. It is impossible for us simply to read past it without giving any more thought to it. It offends reason. We can't digest it intellectually, and so we are forced to ask what this could possibly mean: How could it possibly be true that when I am weak I am strong? After all, when I am weak, I am weak; when I am strong, I am strong. But, when I am weak, then I am strong? How can such be? Yet here, hidden within this paradox, is one of the most profound truths of human experience. When we find ourselves weak, is there some way in which we can find strength within that experience?

All of us can probably identify with the list of terms Paul uses to describe these conditions, in verse 10. One of them means literally, "unable to stand." Do you ever feel that way? Perhaps it is literal physical weakness at times, when you are so fatigued and weary that you simply cannot go on. Or perhaps it is an illness which robs you of your strength. Another of these words speaks of a tight space. Do you ever feel as if you are in a small room, and the walls are closing in upon you? Paul here introduces this "psychological claustrophobia" to us as something which is a key to strength.

What Paul tells us is that there first must be discovery of weakness. We live in a day which emphasizes positive thinking, which affirms one's ability to do what needs to be done. A realistic assessment of one's own needs and shortcomings is essential to finding strength. To find out only in the situation of stress what we should have discovered earlier is a painful and possibly panicky matter. There is a place for a type of "power of negative thinking," as it were. This kind of negative thinking is not pessimism. Rather, it is realism. It is neither overvaluing nor undervaluing one's own abilities and resources.

Paul had discovered vividly what this meant. He was beset with a condition which he refers to as a "thorn in the flesh." Actually, that terminology is much too weak. The word refers to something considerably large and more prominent than just a little thorn or sliver. A more accurate translation would be, "stake," rather than "thorn." This was a virtual beam in the flesh. There have been many attempts to identify just what this was that Paul was referring to.

Some have thought it was a particular individual who opposed him and thus hindered his work. Some who hold this theory believe they can even identify this person as Alexander, the metalworker referred to by Paul in 2 Timothy 4:14. My understanding is that this was a physical condition, based upon the description of it as "in the flesh," and was a major matter. My own conjecture, and that is all that it is, is that this was a disease of the eyes. If he was referring to this thorn in the flesh in Galatians 4:13, then we may well have an intimation there as well of the nature of the ailment, namely, an eye disease. For Paul says that he first preached the gospel to them because of an illness (v. 13), and then goes on to testify of them that if they could, they would have plucked out their own eyes and given them to him (v. 15). In any event, when this came upon him, he was unable to function in his ministry.

Paul had discovered the truth of necessity of insufficiency with respect to both his spiritual life and his ministry. He had much to boast about with respect to his own spiritual qualifications. In the religion of that time, he had everything going for him. In Philippians 3, he recounts some of his virtues and qualities. He claimed to have more reasons for putting confidence in the flesh than did anyone else. He had fulfilled all the law's requirements. He had been circumcised on the eighth day, as the law stipulated. He was of the people of Israel, of the tribe of Benjamin, the one tribe that had remained true to the king of Judah. He was a Hebrew of the Hebrews. He was, with respect to the law, a Pharisee, that is, one who was meticulous in his observance of its demands. When it came to zeal, he had demonstrated this to the point of persecuting the church. With respect to legalistic righteousness, he was faultless. Certainly, if anyone could have pleased God by his own strength and accomplishments, it would have been Paul.

Despite all of this, however, Paul had found himself insufficient. And so long as he continued to rely upon his own spiritual strength, there was no hope for him. He would continue on his way displeasing God. He had to come to the point where he would consider all of these things of which he might have been so proud as being "loss." He even referred to these as "rubbish" (Phil. 3:8).

In this respect, it is helpful to note the parable Jesus told about two men, a Pharisee and a tax collector, who went up to the temple to pray. The first man, the Pharisee, was like Paul before his conversion. He took pride in the things he did by way of fulfilling the law, trying to please God and earn his favor. He thanked God that he was not like other men such as robbers, evildoers, adulterers, or even like the tax collector. He told God that he fasted twice a week and gave a tenth of all that he had (Luke 18:11–12). The other man, the tax collector, approached matters much differently. He did not have anything to offer to God, or any virtue to claim. He was so ashamed of himself that he would not even look up to heaven. He simply beat his breast and said, "God, have mercy on me, a sinner" (v. 13). Jesus' comment, however, was that the second man was the one of the two who went home justified (v. 14).

It is thus in spiritual matters. The common way of approaching this issue is the idea that those who somehow are good enough are the ones accepted by God. God is pictured almost as if he sits at a great conveyor belt like an inspector of manufactured products or of commodities of one type or another. He looks over the items that come by him and selects the best to keep. He is like an electronic appliance manufacturer which has a contract with the manufacturer of a certain variety of electronic semiconductor to receive the top five percent of its semiconductors as they are rated by an electronic testing device. What God is inspecting as they come down the assembly line are human beings, and their lives. Although there are differing opinions as to how selective God is, that is, whether he takes few or many, or perhaps all, the same basic conception is nonetheless there. The belief of most Americans seems to be something like this: If you have lived a good life, been honest and reasonably kind to people, then you will go to heaven.

Most world religions are based upon something the individual can do, some effort or ritual. The conception of what the person is to do may vary greatly, but it is still this same type of idea. Yet, the Bible tells us that no one is saved this way. Paul wrote, "No one is justified before God by the law" (Gal. 3:11). It is not just that it is difficult to please God by being good enough ourselves. It is that no one succeeds in the endeavor of pleasing God. The attempt to go that way is a fundamentally mistaken notion.

Weakness in one's own spiritual life is therefore essential. Failure has to come. Without this, there really is no hope. Without failure, one will not give up the effort, and it must be given up, because absolutely no one succeeds through that means. It is not merely that very few pass. It is that no one ever succeeds.

DOES IT MATTER IF GOD EXISTS?

In this respect, there is a parallel to Alcoholics Anonymous's efforts to help alcoholics. The alcoholic has to "hit bottom" before he or she can be helped. So it is with the Christian life. There was no hope for the Pharisee as he was. As long as he took pride in his achievements, morally and spiritually, and even thanked God for the difference between him and the tax collector, salvation was impossible. He would have to come to the point of the latter, of praying, "God be merciful to me a sinner," before there would be hope for him.

Søren Kierkegaard described the human life under the categories of "stages on life's way," or as I would prefer to label them, "orientations to life," or ways of life. The first stage, which he calls the aesthetic, is the person who seeks for life's satisfactions in the immediate pleasure and satisfaction of the moment. Sooner or later, however, that ceases to have its effect or to give satisfaction. Then the person either slumps down into the boredom of pursuing that which no longer really satisfies, or else the person leaps, choosing without intellectual basis the next stage, the ethical. In this stage, or way of life, one orders his life around strict ethical rules or demands and seeks to fulfill certain self-adopted standards. The inevitable result of this attempt, however, whether sooner or later, is frustration and despair. The person realizes his inability to live up to the very high standards he has adopted for himself.

This is what the apostle Paul also apparently felt. In Romans 7, he said, "I have the desire to do what is good, but I cannot carry it out. For what I do is not the good I want to do; no, the evil I do not want to do—this I keep on doing" (vv. 18–19). That is the experience of any truly conscientious, sensitive person who seeks to do what is right. Inability to do what we know we ought to and want to do—that is the problem.

I once heard a theology professor tell about his attempt to live a good life prior to becoming a Christian. He divided life into a set of virtues and vices and managed to reduce those to about thirty in number. Anyone who could successfully achieve those virtues and avoid those vices completely would be a perfect person. Then he assigned one of those to each day of the calendar. On the first day he concentrated on that one area of the moral life and completely achieved it. The next day he went on to the second virtue, and managed to fulfill it perfectly. So he proceeded, day by day, through each of the areas of life until on the thirtieth and last day of the month he could say that he had mastered the last of the virtues. Now, surely, he had achieved perfection. Then he looked back to see what was the virtue for the first day, and realized that while he was concentrating upon other matters, this one area had gotten completely out of control, and so had the second, and the third, and. . . . It is, to paraphrase Abraham Lincoln, as if "you can master some of the sins all of the time, and all of the sins some of the time, but you cannot master all of the sins all of the time."

It is not just with respect to moral and spiritual accomplishments that this failure is necessary, however. In terms of coping with life, we often tend to want to do things ourselves. We are like little children in this respect. Then we grow up and are taught to be self-sufficient. Many of us have jobs where no one tells us what to do, perhaps because no one could know what to do unless they had the job. We are taught to be problem-solvers, not to delegate upward. Perhaps failure to solve our own problems is thought of as a weakness. This is particularly a problem in the Western Hemisphere, and perhaps especially in the United States of America, where strong individualism is part of the culture. Unlike an earlier period when people lived in smaller communities in which everyone knew everyone else and people depended upon mutual help from one another, we are now in a situation in which each person does things for himself or herself.

There are many problems which we can solve, of course. There are do-it-yourself books and seminars on almost every conceivable subject: how to lay sod, apply vinyl siding, paint, etc. Anyone engaged in selling building materials on the retail level is also usually involved in educating people on how to do that same work or install that material. Courses on computer science, estate planning, investing, foreign languages, sewing, and dozens of other subjects fill the curricula of community education programs. Adult education is big business these days. Beyond that, many vocational courses are offered that teach people welding, accounting, auto body repair, hairdressing, and the like. All of this adds to the philosophy that one can learn how to do anything.

This carries over to the larger societal scale as well. In the United States, we have developed a sort of "can do" philosophy. Certainly we can solve any problem, if we simply put ourselves up to it. Science will find a solution to any of the difficulties which perplex us.

We don't really need to worry about any of the predicted disasters, for we will find a way out of the problems.

There are, of course, many areas which one can learn to master, some of which are not at all simple in nature. But, unfortunately, some of the biggest problems of life cannot be solved that way. If I have a sliver in my finger, it may be a challenge to me to remove it myself, and a source of satisfaction when I do. But if I am told that I have a brain tumor, I can scarcely undertake to solve that problem myself. I once knew a man who cut his own hair using a series of mirrors, but most of us would not try something like that. And many of the other problems of life go beyond the level of our capacity to cope with them. Who of us can guarantee his or her own health or success in whatever one undertakes? Who can even be certain that their children will turn out exactly as they have hoped?

But can we turn to others or to society as a whole to solve them? Here we find a mixed record. To be sure, we have solved some of the most serious problems of our society and our world. Polio and smallpox are now extinct. We have seen dramatic increases in the life expectancy of the average citizen. We have seen amazing changes in the speed of transportation and communication. It is now possible to travel to any part of the world in a few hours, and a fax transmission can place a piece of paper in the hands of another person far away in seconds. We can see live coverage of news events in other parts of the world or even on the surface of the moon at the very moment the event is occurring (or at least, very shortly after its occurrence, in view of the speed of electromagnetic waves). Yet, solutions to the most difficult problems still seem to elude us. We have not solved the really important problems of human conflict. Crime is on the rise in the most technologically developed nations. War is always with us, so much so that someone has estimated that, on average, during one year in twenty of world history, worldwide peace breaks out. And just when we conquered some of the most feared killer diseases of the past generation, AIDS threatens to reach epidemic proportions in some parts of the world with no known cure yet reached. We have made great strides in the economic development of our world, and yet large numbers of people around the world still live in poverty. And together with development have come ecological problems which still threaten our world. Waste, especially nuclear waste, is a major problem. We inevitably must come to the realization that we are not sufficient to deal with all the problems of the world, especially those we have created or aggravated. We are smart enough to solve many problems, but in the process we outsmart ourselves by creating further difficulties which we cannot solve.

For the Christian, there is yet another problem. It pertains to the necessity of realizing our weakness or insufficiency in matters of service. We are taught from many sources that we are to have self-confidence, maintain a positive attitude. This may lead to difficulty, however. For we may come to think that the things which happen in connection with the ministry which we perform in seeking to serve the Lord are our doing. This is what I call the "coincidence causation" theory. Because something happens at just the time that something is done, we may think that the former is caused by the latter. And because we were present when the former happened, or were the ones responsible for the latter, we may think that we caused the result.

The situation is something like what happened to a woodpecker. He alighted upon a telephone pole and reared back to peck. At the very instant that his beak touched the pole, lightning struck the pole, shattering it and knocking the woodpecker unconscious. After a time he regained consciousness and found himself lying in the midst of what resembled the discards of a toothpick factory. Surveying the damage, he said to himself, "I didn't think I had it in me!" That may happen to us as well. We may speak or teach a lesson, or talk one on one with someone, and something remarkable happens. There is a natural tendency in that situation to assume that we were the cause of the event which occurred.

Sooner or later, however, we will be divested of that illusion. We come up against a much more difficult problem and, like an athletic team playing a stronger team than it has ever before encountered, we find our own insufficiency. Although painful, that discovery is important.

The reason these experiences of failure or weakness are so crucial is because they bring us to the end of our strength. They force us, or at least they should force us, to turn to someone more powerful for help. Life, you see, was never intended to be lived in our own human strength alone. It was intended and designed to be lived by drawing upon the resources of a higher being who has revealed himself as the God of Abraham, Isaac, Jacob, and of the Lord Jesus Christ. His strength and grace are sufficient for us, but we are likely

DOES IT MATTER IF GOD EXISTS?

only to turn to him for that strength when the limit of our own strength has been reached.

This was what Paul had found. He found it first with respect to spiritual standing in relationship to God. When he was engaged in the pursuit of the Christians whom he was persecuting and killing, God stopped him in his tracks. A bright light came upon him, and he fell to the ground. A voice came from heaven, saying, "Saul, Saul (his name at that time), why do you persecute me?" When Saul asked who this was that was speaking to him, the voice said, "I am Jesus, whom you are persecuting." He became blind for a time and was taken to Christians who led him to faith in this Jesus. Suddenly, what he had been trying unsuccessfully to achieve by his own effort was given to him. He was given salvation. It was a gift, not an achievement; an obtainment, not an attainment.

So it must be. As long as we think we can somehow be good enough to please God, we will never succeed. When we see the standard of what God really expects, we then become like the tax collector rather than the Pharisee. We cast ourselves upon God, saying, "Lord, be merciful to me, a sinner." That is a prayer that God always answers in the affirmative when it is prayed sincerely. It is, however, a prayer that often is not answered simply because it is not prayed. Failure, morally and spiritually, has to precede this kind of success and will lead to such success.

A story is told of Mr. Religious, who appeared at the admissions desk of heaven and was told by St. Peter that to enter he must have 1000 points. That did not seem excessive to a person of his moral and spiritual achievements, so he immediately told of what a community leader he had been for thirty years, and how he had worked for better government and general societal improvement. Peter's response was to tell him that such an excellent record qualified him for one point. Taken aback, the man added that he had been a good family man, had always been faithful to his wife of forty years, and had raised three children whom he had sent to the best of schools. Peter commended him, indicating that this record was worth another point. Perspiring profusely by this time, the man pleaded the fact that he had been a scout leader, attended church every Sunday, served as a member of the church board, and taught Sunday school. Peter's response was that this was worth another two points. In virtual panic, the man blurted out, "Good Lord! But for the grace of God, no one would get in this place!" whereupon Peter answered,

"You have just been awarded 1000 points." Although the details of the story are not to be taken literally, the point is sound. Until people come to the discovery of their own spiritual and moral inadequacy and cast themselves upon the mercy of God, there is no hope for them. But when they do, God's grace is more than sufficient.

It is hard to come to that point, isn't it? Do you know what are the most difficult words in the English language to pronounce? Not "supercallifragalisticexpialidosious." That word, Mary Poppins notwithstanding, is relatively easy to say, compared to really difficult ones like "I was wrong." And the next most difficult ones are almost as hard: "I am sorry." Now there certainly is nothing inherently difficult about those syllables. In different combinations, they are quite easy to say: "You were wrong. I was right." But "I was wrong"? That costs something. That is psychologically difficult. It is costly to our egos. That is essentially what is involved in coming to God for salvation by grace. It is admitting our own wrongness, our sin. It is admitting our failure to live up to God's expectations and requirements for us. That is confession. It is also telling God we are sorry for this failure—sorry not only because it may have resulted in unfortunate consequences for us, but because it is fundamentally an offense against him. That is what God calls repentance. Without this, there really is no hope of pleasing God. John the Baptist preached this to those who came to him, some of whom were quite proud of their own spiritual attainments. Jesus preached this as the necessary condition for acceptance by God. He preached it to common ordinary sinners as well as to highly revered spiritual leaders. It was to Nicodemus, a Pharisee, that Jesus said, "You must be born again" (John 3:3). And the statement was made in the plural: "You (all) must be born again" (v. 7).

It was not merely with respect to salvation that Paul made this discovery, however. The affliction which is referred to here as a "thorn (or stake) in the flesh" evidently prevented him from ministering effectively. Consequently, he prayed three times for God to remove it (2 Cor. 12:8). He was sufficiently concerned about this that he repeated the prayer twice after the initial prayer. One who is familiar with Jesus' threefold prayer in the Garden of Gethsemane, that the "cup" (the crucifixion) should be taken away from him, cannot help but be impressed with the similarity of this prayer to that. The answer came, but it was not the answer Paul expected or wanted to hear. It was not that the thorn would be removed, but that the grace of the Lord would be sufficient for him. The force of this response is apparent in Paul's writing, for the word "sufficient" is put in the first position in the sentence, the place of greatest emphasis in Greek word order. He was saying, "*Sufficient* is my grace for you." Further, the personal pronoun in verse 9 is of the emphatic variety, rather than the more common ordinary form. He is saying, "that the grace of Christ may rest upon *me*." This was not just a general promise that Paul understood, in the way in which we sometimes think of God as blessing everyone, but not us. This was Paul recognizing that the promise was to him.

The point was this. It seemed that the problem was too great for Paul to bear and, in his own strength, this was true. When, however, he turned to God in prayer, then the grace of God, the strength to live with and in the midst of the affliction, was given. Now it was not merely his strength, but that of Paul and Christ together. It was as if he were saying, "When I am weak, then **WE** are strong." For now he was not alone. Note, however, that the strength to bear the trouble was only given because he prayed, and he might not have prayed had there not been this problem. Hence the weakness was the means to his being strong. In a sense, it was only because he was weak that he was strong.

This is why Paul could then write what he did. He said, "Therefore I will boast all the more gladly about my weaknesses, so that Christ's power may rest on me. That is why, for Christ's sake, I delight in weaknesses, in insults, in hardships, in persecutions, in difficulties. For when I am weak, then I am strong" (vv. 9–10). Elsewhere, writing from a prison cell, he wrote, "I have learned to be content whatever the circumstances" (Phil. 4:11). This, however, was stronger. He was talking not merely about being content in these circumstances, but actually delighting in them. He did not write this because he was a masochist. Paul did not necessarily enjoy suffering. His preference, humanly speaking, undoubtedly would have been for the "thorn" to be taken away. He saw the value of this, however, because it had driven him to the kind of dependence upon God that had resulted in his strength being more than merely his own.

Throughout the Bible there are both instances and promises of men and women of God serving him with great power. None of those is a case, however, of the person simply being an example or model of great personal strength. Rather, in each case it was a matter of the power of God being expressed through the person. When David fought Goliath, the odds were greatly against him, humanly speaking. Goliath was larger, stronger, more heavily armed and armored, and much more experienced. Yet David is never credited with having won that battle by his sheer skill with the slingshot. In fact, he is quick not only to credit God for past victories over a lion and a bear but to predict that the Lord will give him victory over this Philistine (1 Sam. 17:37). He makes clear to Goliath himself that it is the Lord who will give the victory (vv. 45–47). Jesus' promise to his disciples that they would do great works even greater than the ones he had performed was tied directly to the coming of the Holy Spirit (John 14:12; cf. 16:7) whom Jesus said would give them power (Acts 1:8).

I don't know about you, but I must confess that the amount of praying I do tends to be in direct proportion to the amount of trouble I have. I suppose on a subconscious level I tend not to want to bother God when I have no major needs, since he has so many other people to look after. This altruism, of course, is misplaced on two grounds. First, it rather anthropomorphically seems to assume that God cannot really attend to more than a few concerns at one time, whereas he is actually omnipresent and omniscient as well as being omnipotent. It also, however, tends to restrict the point of prayer simply to praying for the granting of our requests or meeting of our needs. Prayer includes that, but is much more besides as well. It includes praise, adoration, confession, and much more.

Perhaps this is why God does not always grant us everything we need far in advance. Jesus had to remind his disciples of this, when they were anxious about what they would eat and drink and with what they would be clothed (Matt. 6:25–30). He told them not to worry about tomorrow, but to trust God for it. Sometimes God does not give us what we need for tomorrow until tomorrow, perhaps to keep us dependent upon him. The people of Israel, for example, had their need for food provided for in the wilderness by God sending a little white wafer-like substance which they called "manna" (actually two Hebrew words meaning, "what is it?"). They were told that each day they were only to gather enough food for that day. They were not to try to keep any over for a second day. The next day they were again to rise early and there would be another day's supply of manna. Some, thinking they could improve upon the system, tried to save enough for the second day and found it rotten and inedible.

On the day before the Sabbath, however, they were to gather twice as much as usual, so that they would have enough to eat on the Sabbath. Again there were those who did not obey, and when they went out on the Sabbath to gather manna, found that there was none. Those who had obeyed the instructions, however, discovered that their manna was as fresh and delicious and nutritious on the Sabbath as it had been on the previous day. Certainly God, who is a miracle-working God, could have made that two-day manna any day of the week, but he did not. For he knew that the Israelites' need for food was as great as their need for faith and trust in him, and each time they picked the manna, that faith was strengthened by the reiterated and underscored affirmation, "It is by the hand of Jehovah that we are fed."

So it is for us. We may feel quite self-sufficient and may be going along quite well, even serving the Lord, taking relatively little thought about our need for total dependence upon him. Then, however, he allows some problem, some failure, some special difficulty to come along which forces upon us an awareness of our own short-comings, needs, and dependence. We may find a rather painful, even bitter experience, and our natural reaction will tend to be that which Paul expressed here. We may cry out, "Lord, take it away!" Logically, that may make great sense. Paul might have said, "Look, Lord, I know that you want me to serve you, preaching and evangelizing, and we both know I could do that more effectively if I did not have this thorn. It just makes sense to remove it." It may be as logically compelling in our case, even apart from our own concern for our welfare and comfort. Yet God in his wisdom is far wiser. He knows that as long as this matter is present in our lives it will compel us to rely upon him and thus to draw upon his strength.

Early in my second pastorate, I made a discovery. It was one of those things which the pastoral search committee had not told me, perhaps because they thought if I knew it I would not accept the call, and perhaps because they did not actually realize it was present. It was, however, very evident to me. It was of rather long standing duration in the church, and it definitely hindered the ministry of the church in general and my ministry in particular. I used to go to the church on Saturday evening and practice my Sunday morning sermon in the empty sanctuary, and sometimes I preached a better sermon to those empty pews than I preached at either of the two morning services on Sunday. Then, after I preached, I would pray, kneeling at "my pew," the first pew, just to the right of the center aisle. One of those nights I felt especially burdened to pray about that problem situation in the church, and I pled with the Lord to remove it, or at least to neutralize it. I have never been much of a mystic who hears audible voices from God or has angelic visitors, but that evening, although I heard no audible words, it was as if God had said to me in unmistakable fashion: "As long as you are the pastor here, that problem will be here. I won't remove it, but I will give you the grace and the strength to be able to minister, even with it present." I knew then that I would have to kneel and pray for strength not only every Saturday evening, but many other times as well. Because of that, I believe, my ministry was stronger than it would have been otherwise.

When I am weak, I am strong! How strange! We can simply puzzle over that paradox, or we may allow it to teach us the need for reaching outside ourselves and our feeble strength to trust in God, and then we too will be able to say with Paul, "When I am weak, then I am strong."

Study Guide

Key Questions

1. The apostle Paul wrote "When I am weak, then I am strong." How can one say that? What does it mean? What is weakness? What is strength? Can anyone become strong?
2. When is the **power of negative thinking** not **pessimism**? When does weakness become strength?
3. The author discussed attempts of individuals and of society to overcome failures and weaknesses. He included, for example, emphasis on education, scientific discoveries, and economic development. Then he explains why experiences of failure or weakness are important. Why are they? What do they (or should they) do for us?

Bible Investigation

1. Study John 3:1–21. What were Nicodemus's inadequacies? What does it mean to be **born again**? John 3:16, Titus 3:4–7, and 1 Peter 1:3 will help you with this.
2. In 2 Corinthians 12:7–10, what does Paul say his weakness would prevent him from becoming? Why did he welcome his weakness? How does Philippians 4:11 help us understand Paul's attitude?
3. Read 1 Samuel 17:34–54 and focus on David's **weaknesses** and how he was confident in a **strength** to overcome them. Give special attention to verses 37 and 45–47.

Personal Application

1. List areas of weakness and failure in your life. Think about where you have gone for help in the past. When you have had strength, where has it come from?
2. Ask yourself: Do I find it easy to identify and admit failure and weakness? Is it hard or easy to say "I was wrong" or "I need help"?
3. Read Philippians 3:7–11. Think about why Paul looked to his human achievements as "rubbish" and counted them as "loss." Examine your desire to have the strength of Christ.
4. Identify an experience you've had where God definitely gave you strength to endure and to cope in that situation, rather

than removing the weakness. Thank him for what he has taught (or is teaching) you! Memorize 2 Corinthians 12:9. Repeat it often.

For Further Thought

1. Study the parable of the Pharisee and the tax collector (Luke 18:9–14). How does this illustrate "When I am weak, then I am strong"?
2. Read about Paul's (Saul's) conversion experience (Acts 9:1–19). Note the weaknesses of Paul and the work of God that produced strength.
3. Using a Bible concordance and the study text, discover ways the Holy Spirit helps us in our weaknesses. Start with John 6:63; 14:16, 26; 16:13; Acts 1:8; Romans 8:26–27; 1 Corinthians 12:4–11; and Titus 3:5.

10

Will Evil
Finally Win?

Prime time scheduling came to an abrupt halt. Even the telecast of what might have been the final game of the National Basketball Association championship series was brought to a standstill as nearly one hundred million Americans watched on their television the drama of the accused being pursued across Los Angeles freeways by the police. This, however, was no ordinary accused, and this was no ordinary crime. A professional football Hall of Fame player, sportscaster, and movie actor was charged with the brutal killing of his former wife and her friend. Finally, the car driven by his friend made its way back to O. J. Simpson's home and pulled into the driveway. Following a long period of waiting and negotiations, the accused surrendered to police.

The drama, however, was only beginning. With the arrest, the media continued their intensive coverage of the case. The arraignment, the preliminary hearing, the addition of defense attorneys, and the trial all came in for detailed exposure to the public. Story after story was written analyzing the case. Some told the story of the fallen public hero; others delved into supposed racist dimensions in the story. A full length book appeared on bookstore counters within ten days of the chase and apprehension. It seemed as if the public had an insatiable hunger to know more about this story. So great was the public attention riveted upon these events and persons that the opposing attorneys virtually despaired of being able to find twelve people who would be impartial enough to serve as a jury.

Why, may we ask, should there be such fascination with a tragic story of this type? Why is the public so strongly drawn to this type of story? Many suggestions have been offered, but I propose that this interest was not unique to this case. The interest was maximized because the alleged murderer was a celebrity, but the real interest can be seen in any one of a number of slayings that have mesmerized the public. There seems to be a fascination with evil on the part of the general population.

To test this hypothesis, watch the evening news for several successive nights with a pencil and pad in hand. Keep a rough count of the number of stories dealing with basically positive matters and those which emphasize negative matters, a sort of good news/bad news ratio, as it were. It appears that the emphasis upon the bad news items is out of proportion to the actual occurrences of such matters. For example, when crime statistics are reported, the number of husbands who did not murder their wives last night is not mentioned, nor are the number of teenagers who are not pregnant or on drugs. Why should this be? It seems that bad news makes better news than does good news.

Television gives us other clues to the human interests, beliefs, and tendencies. Many of the popular programs involve violence in one form or another. Even the so-called family comedy programs frequently depict conflict of some type among family members. Movies seem to reflect even more strongly this interest in violence.

Yet, when the question of evil and even of sin is raised, a rather different reaction takes place. Many persons deny or at least ignore the idea of evil, as if it did not exist. If they do believe in it in theory, it nonetheless makes no real practical difference in their lives or in the way they view reality.

In our society we are willing to go to great lengths to avoid admitting the reality of evil, of the harshness or ugliness of life, of even the very unpleasant. Our language reflects this. Elsewhere in this volume, I have focused our attention upon this tendency of our society with respect to death and the increased age which frequently precedes it. Any sort of lack or problem which could suggest a value judgment is treated in different language. For example, we used to have disabled persons in our society, people who because of some physical problem were unable to do certain things which other persons, "normal" persons, could do. Disability, however, has tended to disappear from our language, except in the vocabulary of insurance companies. "Handicapped" is still a word used, although largely in connection with specially reserved parking spaces. This softens the concept. Persons are not really disabled, or unable to perform the actions that others can. They simply have to do them under certain disadvantages, which makes doing them somewhat more difficult. This speaks of a functional difference, not a real difference of condition.

The change in ways of thinking and speaking in this regard came home to me rather vividly a few years ago when we were considering purchasing a new automobile. We visited a new car dealer's showroom, where, before we left, the salesperson (probably now a "new car counselor") gave us a brochure about the particular model we had looked at. On the inside back cover was a reference to a program the manufacturer had for a certain class of customers—the physically challenged—to supply automobiles with special equipment. Similarly, there are no disabled persons, for this might suggest an advantage for those who are not disabled. The former are now more correctly referred to as the "differently abled."

This whole concept of challenge or disadvantage has come into strong play as a factor in our society of late. There was a time when people were distinguished from one another on the basis of their height. Greater height was usually considered positive, so that lesser height (or shortness) was negative. This, however, is not the current way of thinking in these matters. Persons who are below average in height are "vertically challenged," while those above average are thought of as "vertically gifted." Similarly, there was a time when some people were thought of as "fat," a very negative concept in our society. Then came the concept of "overweight," or in extreme cases, "obesity." Now, however, such persons can be referred to as "horizontally gifted," or, if attention is focused upon a perceived cause, as "dietarily enhanced." I was pleasantly surprised to learn recently that I am not getting older; I am joining the ranks of the "chronologically gifted." The connotations of words shift with our orientation to them. There is, for example, an invisible line in our life charts. I do not know just when it comes, and that point probably varies with different people. I do know how to detect its passage, however. Before that point, "youthful" is a negative concept, and "mature" is a positive idea. After passing that point, "youthful" becomes positive, and "mature" becomes negative. I learned this the hard way when a director of personnel informed me that she had appointed a "more mature" woman as my secretary. I found that in this case, "more mature" meant fifty-nine years of age, which to me, thirty-five years of age at the time, seemed aged. The official publication of the American Association of Retired Persons, whose minimum membership age is fifty, is "Modern Maturity," suggesting that at least in our time, one is not mature until fifty.

This tendency is carried over to references to inanimate objects as well. I can remember when it was possible to purchase a "used car" or a "second-hand tire." Now, however, one shops for a "previously owned" automobile, as if the person had possession of the vehicle but was simply engaged in safekeeping for us rather than submitting it to any use which might result in wear and which would in turn reduce its usefulness to us. Alternatively, one will find advertisements for "pre-driven" automobiles. The imagery conveyed is that of a parking attendant who brings the car, perhaps warmed by the heater or cooled by the air conditioner, to the driver so that it is comfortable and ready to drive without further waiting. One of the most extreme versions I have ever seen of this type of advertising, however, was a banner across a service station which proclaimed: "Tire sale—new and experienced." Who would want to entrust his life and that of his passengers to a green, inexperienced, novice tire when a seasoned veteran tire which had been around the block a few times, so to speak, was available?

Evil, no matter how strongly believed in, does not seem to get translated into the idea of real human perverseness or defectiveness. Belief in radical evil in the world seems to coexist with belief in the inherent goodness of individual human beings.

Here is one of the great wonders of our time: belief in the inherent goodness of human beings. At one time when orthodox Christian theology was widely held, the belief was rather in the sinfulness of human beings. This was sometimes referred to as depravity, or the idea of the defectiveness of humans. Sometimes it even had the adjective "total," suggesting that the infection which beset the human was thorough, extended into every part of the person, and left no facet of human behavior untainted. It even was conceived of as a condition with which every human being began life, termed "original sin," and traced its origins to the sin of the first human

DOES IT MATTER IF GOD EXISTS?

beings in the Garden of Eden long ago. That is an unpopular belief today, however, despite the fact that empirical phenomena have certainly not done anything to disprove it. Indeed, it could more accurately be suggested that an observation of human behavior down through the centuries and surely at the present time, would rather serve to confirm this idea. G. K. Chesterton said once that he could not understand why Christianity has given up the idea of original sin since it was the one doctrine that can be empirically proved.

This positive belief goes back a long way. Even among those who saw imperfection within humans, there was a sense that this was incidental or easily disposed of. The end of the nineteenth century and the early twentieth century was a time of great positive thinking. Numerous self-improvement schemes were developed. One of these was expressed by the Frenchman Coué, who taught his followers to recite, "Every day, in every way, I'm getting better and better." There was a strong confidence, even in Christian and other religious circles, that things were moving in the right direction. Thus, one religious periodical renamed itself *The Christian Century*, which was what its publishers believed the twentieth century would be.

It is difficult to believe, at this point in human history, in the innate goodness of human beings. The twentieth century soon proved that it was not to be the idyllic time that many had hoped for. The World War, a war of such magnitude as had not previously been experienced, broke out. Rather than simply involving European nations, it also drew in North American countries, most notably the United States of America. Those who fought in this war and those who experienced it resolved that the lesson learned therein would not be forgotten. A League of Nations was established to preserve peace and justice globally. The World War was to be the war to end all wars.

This effort to bring war to an end soon proved fruitless, however. Within fifteen years a powerful war machine was again growing in Germany, and war began again, first on a rather limited scale and then in a truly global fashion which eclipsed the preceding war. Nomenclature had to be revised. What was simply, "the World War" now came to be called "World War I," as "World War II" supplanted it in terms of destruction and loss of human life. Estimates of the number of casualties vary greatly, but even a conservative figure includes 26 million persons killed.

It was not merely the number and variety of persons whose lives were lost that was most disturbing, however. It was the way in which some of these deaths took place. In particular, the genocide of at least six million Jews because of a concerted effort by Adolf Hitler to do away with them horrified the world. In many concentration camps Jews were gassed to death and incinerated. Some simply died of starvation. Seldom had such unnecessary cruelty on a large scale been witnessed.

V-E day and V-J day in 1945 brought a great sense of relief and rejoicing to a world wearied of warfare, destruction, and killing. Even in the defeated nations there was a profound sense of gratitude that the conflict was at last concluded. This time, surely, the world had learned its lesson and would put war in the past. What the League of Nations had been unable to do, largely because its major advocate, Woodrow Wilson, had been unable to convince his own country to join, the United Nations surely would accomplish.

It became apparent almost immediately, however, that conflict was not obsolete. It had merely taken a new form. Instead of a hot war, with military fighting, the world was gripped in a "cold war." Europe was divided between the communist Soviet Union and the nations which it controlled as satellites, and the democratic nations of western Europe and the Americas. Winston Churchill spoke of an "iron curtain" having descended upon Europe, an image which soon took visible and concrete form in terms of the Berlin Wall and other literal boundaries sealing off East from West. Although the communist leaders claimed that these barriers had been erected to keep out the persons from the West, it was apparent to all that the desired movement was Easterners trying to escape to freedom. Ingenious ways were found by East Berliners to make their way out, as documented by the Museum of the Wall, still to be found near where Checkpoint Charlie, the entrance to the American zone, stood. It was illegal to purchase or sell diving equipment in East Berlin. On the other side of the world, mainland China was a huge communist nation, with its own brand of Marxism. These two large blocs of power, the communist and the democratic, struggled to draw unaligned nations into their sphere of influence. At times the ideological battles broke out into actual fighting in Korea, Vietnam, and other places.

DOES IT MATTER IF GOD EXISTS?

Nor was the conflict restricted to the struggle between communism and its opposite (capitalistic and socialistic democracies). It took other forms: sometimes religious, sometimes ethnic or racial. In Northern Ireland, conflict between Protestant and Catholic forces became severe. Actually, the conflict was more in terms of this area's continued loyalty to Great Britain versus its possible union with Ireland. In the Middle East, a group of Arab countries surrounding Israel engaged in continual warfare and raids against that nation, some of them publicly vowing to exterminate it. Israel itself, successful most notably in the Six Day War of 1967, treated some of the Arab people in occupied territories with less than humane concern.

Civil wars, inexplicable in many cases to those outside the countries involved, raged recently in several nations. In what was known as Yugoslavia, war broke out as Serbs sought to exterminate Bosnians through "ethnic cleansing." Similar civil conflicts brought great suffering and hardship to countries such as Ethiopia and Rwanda.

On more domestic scenes, it also should be apparent that not all is well. Even with all of the supposed progress in education, welfare, and technology, some areas of difficulty remain resistant to change. Areas especially affected by scientific research have responded well. For example, some diseases have been wiped out, most notably smallpox and polio. The only smallpox viruses still in existence are in storage in laboratory vaults, with the great debate among scientists being whether to exterminate them or keep them alive. Great progress has been made in infant mortality, in treating heart disease and certain types of cancer, as well as in organ transplants.

Some other human problems are not so easily solved, however. Crime continues to increase at a frightening rate so that many Americans now consider it the major problem of our society. Crowded prisons and court backlogs result in early discharge, plea bargains and convictions without significant sentences. In some sections of some major cities, police are not in control. Out-gunned and outnumbered by gangs, they do not even enter some areas under certain conditions. Use and abuse of habituating drugs is growing at a rapid rate, and because of the need to finance drug habits, this leads to other crimes such as robbery.

Even disease is not fully subject to our human control. AIDS is a rapidly growing disease for which no cure has yet been found, although more money is being spent in the United States on research into the treatment and cure of this disease than on research on all forms of cancer. Yet we know the causes of the overwhelming majority of AIDS cases in this country: use of unsterilized intravenous needles and unprotected sex with someone infected with the HIV virus. Both of these are avoidable with change of behavior. AIDS, in other words, is an eminently preventable disease. Yet activistic homosexual groups such as ACT-UP continue to demand that the government invest more money in AIDS research rather than altering the behavior that is resulting in the infection. In other words, they wish to continue the behavior but not experience the consequences of it, and have someone else pay for it. It begins to appear increasingly that the problem may be a human problem rather than a health problem: a problem with human behavior, rather than viruses.

Some have concluded, in light of the foregoing types of considerations, that something is indeed wrong with the human but that it is curable circumstantially. That is to say, given a different set of circumstances, the person's behavior would be different. The person is not somehow evil or sinful or broken; rather, it is only a matter of the setting of the person. The behavior is what is wrong, not the person, and the source of the difficulty is external to the person, not internal. Thus, the changes desired in the person are to be effected by external factors as well.

One frequent candidate for this role has been education. If only the person can be properly educated, then he or she will see what is the right thing to do and will do it. Part of this results from seeing that the action that one is engaged in contributes to evil of the whole and thus is ultimately self-destructive as well. It is a matter then of enlightened self-interest to live differently.

In some cases, the difficulty is believed to be partially in the type and nature of the education that was being practiced. So-called progressive education, developed especially by John Dewey, felt that education had been too concerned with facts, with rote memorization, with "academic skills." It proposed instead to help students learn to live in an adaptive and useful way. Some theorists of higher education felt that the individualistic type of education being practiced was inducing the very opposite attitudes from what were desired and needed. This encouraged students to achieve at the expense of the performance of others, a tendency which they then

DOES IT MATTER IF GOD EXISTS?

carried over into their everyday practices in life. More was being learned, in terms of actual life changes and attitudes by how students learned, rather than by what they learned. Instead of this individualistic approach, what was needed was a cooperative learning experience in which students worked as a team and the success of each contributed to the success of others. This, it was argued, was far better preparation for the life which lay ahead.

This approach appears not to have achieved its professed goals, however. Rather than decreasing crime and conflict, these seem to be increasing in American society. And, unfortunately, preparation for further education and for the basic skills of earning a livelihood is being revealed as inadequate. So, for example, in terms of ability to use their native language, to say nothing of knowing another language, and in knowledge and skill with respect to science and mathematics, American students do pitifully poorly. To be sure, there is in some cases a considerable good feeling on the part of many of these persons regarding their competency. So, for example, public school students (high school level) from ten different countries were tested in terms of mathematics skills. They were also asked to assess how well they felt they did in mathematics. The United States students ranked themselves the highest of the ten groups, while the Koreans ranked themselves lowest. When the actual performance on the tests was assessed, however, the Koreans ranked first and the Americans last! When our youngest daughter lived in Germany, her best German friend (who spoke excellent English) said to her, "The thing that bothers me about many Americans is that they cannot even speak their *own* language correctly!" To be sure, her experience of Americans was largely with G.I.s, who may not be the best products of American education, but the remark is nonetheless disturbing. In an increasingly globalized economy, American students who are partially illiterate and largely innumerate stand little chance of competing effectively. Thus, the problems that do result from economic needs are not solved, but rather compounded, by the educational system which was supposed to remove problems.

One other major difficulty looms for the thesis that education is the solution to societal problems. If this thesis is correct, then we would expect to find a direct positive correlation between education and ethics. Such, however, has not proved to be the case. To be sure, more educated persons generally do not perpetrate the more violent or gross types of crimes, the "blue collar" crimes. There is, however, a whole culture of "white collar" crime. Aided by knowledge of law, economics, and computer science, highly sophisticated forms of theft, fraud, and embezzlement are performed. It appears that education does not eliminate crime; it merely enables the person to practice it with greater skill and sophistication.

The same is true of science and war. Science is capable of producing amazing technology. This technology, however, is morally neutral. It can be used either for good or for evil. The difference lies in the moral character of those putting it into use. The growth in knowledge in our day has not eliminated war. On the contrary, it has only enabled war to be waged more efficiently, to kill larger numbers of persons, and destroy more property in a single blow than was previously the case. An atomic reaction is based upon an extremely sophisticated understanding of the laws of physics which govern our universe. It can be used to generate electricity, doing great good (although it may have some unfortunate by-products). On the other hand, it can be used to manufacture an atomic bomb with immense destructiveness. Power multiplies the force of ethical decisions, but it does not make them.

Another candidate, self-appointed, for the role of solver of the problems of human evil, has been communism, the popular application of the philosophy known as dialectical materialism. As its name indicates, this view considers matter to be the most fundamental component of reality. Thus, matter and the laws which bear upon it or govern it explain what occurs within the universe. The whole movement of history is a working out of these tendencies of matter. This is true of human behavior, as well.

When applied to the understanding of human beings, this means that all human activity is motivated by material factors, whether direct or indirect, conscious or unconscious. Human beings are to be understood as primarily economic beings. The story of history is the story of changes of the means of economic production. This could be seen as a tension or struggle between forces until they are reconciled. So, for example, in the feudal period, the lords owned the means of production (primarily the farms and lands), which were only lent to the vassals and must revert at death to the feudal lord. This was followed by the age of capitalism, in which the property owners also owned the factories, but in which there were also free farmers who owned their own lands and were able to earn their own income. Here, however, the employees had to work for whatever the employers would pay and to work under whatever conditions the employers stipulated. Then came the age of liberal capitalism. Here, government intervenes in the relationship between employer and employee, stipulating conditions under which such relationships are to take place. Employees are given the right to organize, or form unions, in which they bargain as a group with the employer. The employer either pays what the employees ask, or is unable to find anyone to employ. Still, there are classes, the owners and the employees. If the owner or employer is able to make a larger profit, he alone benefits from it. Finally comes the classless society, in which there is no private ownership of the means of production. At this point, since the state owns the factories and other means of production, there is mutual benefit from any economic advantage achieved.

In this whole process, there is conflict or struggle between the two groups involved, or what is called the dialectic (or interaction between the two). At each stage, the result of the struggle is a synthesis between the two parties, which is not simply the elimination of one and the preservation of the other factor, but a new entity which arises from the interaction. It is this struggle which moves the processes of history, and the conflict is the source of evil in the world.

When the final stage, the classless society, is reached, this struggle will cease. With the distribution of means of production among all the members of society, there will no longer be any need for such competition and struggle. The slogan of communism is, "From each according to his ability; to each according to his need." With this distribution, no one would lack for the necessities of life. Thus, there would be no need for theft, for example, in order to feed one's family. Further, there would be no struggle out of envy or jealousy. If one's neighbor had nothing that one did not also have, there would be no need to engage in theft or embezzlement. The major causes of hatred and violence would be removed if there were equality and justice. The state would see to it that injustices were redressed. So evil would simply wither away. The real reason for this is that the fuel of evil, economic inequality and strife, would be gone, and so would have nothing to sustain it. It would, as it were, die of starvation.

It was usually acknowledged that there would be some limitations upon the realization of this ideal. For one thing, it would have to become universal, or at least, worldwide. As long as pockets of society were still organized on the basis of competitive capitalism, there would be difficulty, and the process of eliminating this corruption of human society would inevitably be conflictual and even at times violent. It would have to occur, however, so that the universal conditions of the classless society could be realized. The architects of communism also conceded that there were people alive who were so hopelessly warped by the old ways of thinking that they could not be changed. The hope for the future lay in the education of a whole new generation of communist believers. The older generation, hopelessly and incurably infected with the disease of private property, must die off. It was also recognized that from the beginning of the revolution until the classless society was fully realized, it might be necessary to have a sort of transitional phase. During this time, some of the older characteristics of domination might be necessary, in a reversed relationship. Then, however, following this "dictatorship of the proletariat," the new age could dawn.

These hopes, however, were destined to be disappointed. Although the worldwide rule of communism was never realized, it did become sufficiently complete in some large societies (notably, the Soviet Union and the Peoples' Republic of China) so that it could function much as its creators had intended. Yet here there was great disappointment. Evil did not fade away. It simply was repressed on the part of the ordinary citizen. The state became so powerful that it was able to curtail its members' freedom. In so doing, it engaged in activity that surely, on the old standards, would have been judged evil. For example, the revelation of the atrocities committed at the command of Josef Stalin made clear that in many ways these were the equal of what transpired under Adolf Hitler. Further, the obvious judgment of many within these societies was that this regime was oppressive. The extreme lengths to which people went to escape were the most impressive evidence of this sentiment, as were the lengths to which these societies went to keep persons from leaving. The Berlin Wall was not built to keep Westerners out, but to keep East Germans in. Dissent was not allowed and was severely repressed whenever attempted. The uprisings in Poland, Czechoslovakia, Hungary, and the Peoples' Republic of China were quickly suppressed, in rather forceful and even cruel fashion.

Beyond that, however, it appeared that the classless society had not really arrived. Those who were in privileged positions of leadership within the communist societies engaged in lifestyles more

DOES IT MATTER IF GOD EXISTS?

like those of the capitalistic upper class than like the ordinary persons in their own societies. It appeared that the greed which supposedly results from capitalism was still present, and rather conspicuously so. Thus, what occurred was more an inversion of the older exploitative society rather than its abolition.

Also, communism seemed to be an economic failure pragmatically. Instead of raising the level of all its citizens, the communist society appeared rather inefficient. The overall standard of living was impeded by this new approach. This was most apparent in those places where communist and capitalist societies of the same people ethnically existed side by side. One dramatic case was found in Germany, where the German Federal Republic and the German Democratic Republic adjoined, and in particular, where West Berlin existed as a free island surrounded by communism. The contrast in the two standards of productivity and of living was astounding. This could also be seen in such places as North and South Korea and Taiwan and Hong Kong, adjacent to communist China. In the final analysis, it was not so much the theoretical conception of communism that failed as it was the practical outworking in the economy.

Today, communism is largely a thing of the past. The entire series of Eastern bloc countries shed the domination of the Soviet Union; the Baltic countries of Latvia, Lithuania, and Estonia secured their independence; and even the Soviet Union broke apart into its member republics, with free elections and new constitutions arising even in Russia. China, although still officially communist, is rapidly transforming its society into capitalism. Only in a few places, such as North Korea, Cuba, and some university faculties in the United States, does anything of old line communism live on. The grand experiment, if not disproved, has at least been abandoned as a solution to the world's ills.

Within the United States, social action and legislation has been another means by which our society has sought to rid itself of its ills. The theory behind this effort was that persons are not bad but are the products of a bad or unfavorable social environment. If their circumstances could be altered, so would the people and their behavior. If unemployment, poverty, illiteracy, and lack of job skills are the problem, government can solve it. From the New Deal to the Great Society to the latest reform of welfare, much legislation has been passed seeking to set right what is wrong with our society including new programs of education, public housing, job training, headstart, child care, and on and on. Yet not too much can be seen by way of improvement. School scores continue to drop, gang activity and other forms of crime increase, and welfare rolls swell. It appears that the evils that were to disappear with modification of the social environment are much more resistant than some had thought.

A very different philosophy, expressed both on the philosophical and the very mundane level, related human problems to repressed sexuality. Stemming from Sigmund Freud, this view, in its intellectual version, saw the human as primarily a sexual being. The libido, the powerful sexual energy, seeks expression in many ways. Our society, however, places taboos and other restraints upon human behavior of this type. Consequently, persons are forced to repress these drives. They are told that such energy is only to be expressed and satisfied in the most complete sense within marriage. People are to wait until marriage and then restrict those practices to their own mate. Further, sex is only to be practiced with persons of the opposite sex. This repression, however, leads to all sorts of difficulties. Anxiety and guilt are induced by such dictums, leading to other problems, neuroses, and even psychoses.

On the popular level, many young people and even some older people have reacted in what is sometimes called the "sexual revolution." Premarital, extramarital, homosexual, and other sexual practices have been engaged in, often without any real limitations. The percentage of young people engaging in unmarried sex during their teens has increased greatly. Sexual freedom is a very real matter in our society. One may see the change by watching an assortment of current network television programs, and then comparing them with the standards of a generation ago, perhaps by watching Nickelodeon. In the latter case, sex was something practiced within marriage, and persons in love married. Now, at least to judge by the popular television programs, people simply move in together and live together, without marriage.

What has been the result of all this? One result is a sharp increase in the number of unmarried teenage pregnancies. Further, there has been a significant increase in venereal disease. And, because many of these people practice unprotected sex, there has been an increase in the incidence of AIDS, and we can anticipate a continued growth of this problem. All of this is happening despite the fact that sex

DOES IT MATTER IF GOD EXISTS?

education programs in the public schools are more widespread and explicit than ever before. Has this solved the problems that were supposed to result from repression of the sexual drive? Teen suicides continue to increase, with suicide now the second leading cause of death among teenagers. Nor does the overall mental health of young people seem to have improved. Indeed, many are now finding a sense of emptiness and meaninglessness, having experienced virtually everything that adults do by the age of sixteen. The future does not hold much for such people.

Are things really getting better? Can we expect that our world will get better and better? This hope seems to be ill-placed. About twenty-five years ago, I participated in a series of ecumenical dialogues on a television station in Chicago. On one of the programs, one of the other participants, now the editor of a leading liberal periodical, kept talking about "celebrating the bright moments in the history of mankind." I finally asked him if he would specify a few of these from the twentieth century. He fell strangely silent. I think he would have an even more difficult time listing such today. Oh, to be sure, there have been notable accomplishments: the discovery of penicillin and of polio vaccines, space travel, the computer, and satellite television, just to name a few. When it comes to the really important matters of personal and social human behavior, however, the situation is quite different. It is questionable what, if any, progress we have made in these areas within this century.

This, however, brings us to a very sobering thought. What if, rather than disappearing, evil continues to increase in power and ultimately is victorious over good? What then will become of our world? Is that a world that one would wish to live in? Suppose that the conditions that prevail within the worst sections of the inner cities, or within nations torn by civil war, were to become universal? What then?

May it be that this is what is actually happening? Some persons are predicting a time of economic chaos, in part because we have not had a really severe economic downturn for more than sixty years, in the face of the historical record of some type of crisis every sixty years, approximately, since 1540. Think, for example, of the financial panic of 1873 and the stock market crash of 1929 and the ensuing Great Depression. To be sure, mechanisms which were not present at earlier times are now in place to ameliorate the effects of such developments. Yet, one can well see a restlessness and discontent already in place within our society which might well be pushed to an explosion by serious economic developments. Under such conditions of widespread lawlessness, the looting and killing that some envision may not be out of the question.

Consider the news one sees on television, hears on radio, and reads about in newspapers and newsmagazines. Are we to conclude that good is prevailing, or is evil gaining the upper hand? It is difficult to decide. What is clear, however, is that we have tried a wide variety of human efforts to stem the growth of evil and to encourage the growth of good, but with little real positive consequence. If we are to be assured of any real hope, it will have to be based upon something other than merely human ability. And that is where God fits in.

The announcement and promise of Scripture is that God is able to transform human hearts, which it clearly declares to be in need of radical change. Paul put it well when he wrote, "If anyone is in Christ, he is a new creation; the old has gone, the new has come" (2 Cor. 5:17). This had been the experience of the author of those words. From being a headstrong, self-righteous person who opposed the things of Christ, hunting down and even murdering Christians, he had become a loving follower of Christ. Even his name was changed, from Saul to Paul, to indicate the change which had taken place in him.

This same transforming grace of God is available and effective today, as well. Consider the testimony of Charles Colson. One of the Nixon officials convicted in the Watergate scandal and sent to prison, he became a born-again Christian. In his position as head of Prison Fellowship, a ministry program among prisoners, and as an author, he speaks out sharply against sin, whether outside or within the church. He is as active in promoting the cause of Christ as he once was devious in attempting to cover up the crimes within the administration. Humans may only be changeable when changed by God, but he is continuing to do that very thing, for those who allow it.

God will deal with evil on a much larger scale, however. The Bible tells us that a time is coming when God will bring history to a close. There will be a time of judgment in which wrongs are righted. God will triumph over all the evil in the world. The leaders and sources of evil, the devil and his cohorts, will be forever vanquished. There will be an eternity of love, joy, and righteousness. For God, who created everything that is, has the power to bring it all to his conclusion.

DOES IT MATTER IF GOD EXISTS?

Study Guide

Key Questions

1. When you first read the title of this study, "Will Evil Finally Win?" what was your answer? Why? What beliefs and what external observations helped you in answering? Was the question easy to answer?
2. The author says that our society seems willing to go to great lengths to avoid admitting the reality of sin. Why is this? What is the basis for belief in "the inherent goodness of human beings"? How do people who believe this explain evil?
3. What is the doctrine of "total depravity"? Of original sin? What is the basis for these beliefs? How do adherents of these doctrines explain evil?
4. Think about society's attempts to overcome evils in the world. Our study discusses wars (both hot and cold), education, welfare programs, the development of technology, and scientific research. What is the success rate? How is **moral character** or **ethics** a key to success?

Bible Investigation

1. What does the Bible teach about **sin** and **sinfulness**? Study the following: original sin (Rom. 5:12–19), the effect of sin (Rom. 1:21; Gal. 6:7–8), the consequences of sin (Gen. 2:17; Rom. 6:23), the forgiveness of sin (Pss. 32:1; 103:8–12; 2 Cor. 5:19; Eph. 1:3, 7; Col. 2:13).
2. Read Psalm 51. Think with David as he responds to the discovery of his sin of adultery when the prophet Nathan confronts him. Notice his plea for forgiveness, his acknowledgment that he was a sinner, his sense that God could make him a new person, and his insight into the kind of life God desires.
3. How does God change our lives? Look up Jeremiah 24:7; Ezekiel 11:19–20; and 1 Peter 1:3. Use a concordance or a subject encyclopedia to find additional help.

Personal Application

1. The author emphasizes the interest and fascination of people today with tragedy and violence. The media most often

emphasizes the bad news over the good news. Examine your own use of time. Do you spend too much time on the bad? Think of ways you can encourage good things to happen.

2. Think about your own attitude toward evil. Are there good ways society is combating evil? What is your church doing? How are you involved? What more can you do?

3. Meditate upon Psalm 105:1–5. Write down the steps it gives in order to be an ambassador of hope in a world of evil.

For Further Thought

1. Do the exercise suggested in the text. Listen to the evening news for three or four nights in succession. Think about your response. How do you feel about the world and the future? Then, reread Psalm 105:1–5, 2 Corinthians 5:10, and the concluding three paragraphs of the study text. Look around you and think about what you see God doing for good in the lives of people. Contrast your feelings now with the feelings you had after doing the newscasting exercise.

2. Reread the study of communism included in this chapter. Learn how to explain how communism tries to solve problems. In what ways does it sound good?. Think about the Marxist slogan—"From each according to his (her) ability; to each according to his (her) need." Why does it not work?

11

Give Me Liberty or Give Me Death!

You can see the indications of it on every hand: signs, voices, and actions, all expressing the desire to be free. It comes in many forms. Some of these are simply a reaction against anyone telling anybody what to do. Young people go through a period of rebellion during adolescence, when they seek to shake off the shackles of parental domination. A two-year-old's first word learned is "no!" which she then uses to express her intention to do her own desires, rather than those of her parents. The protests of taxpayers are objections to the way the government is spending their money. A driver flagrantly violates a law of the state governing how one shall drive or where one shall park. A student complains, "why do I have to do this assignment, which I don't want to, and which I don't think will do me any good?" These and countless indications point to the desire of humans to be in control of their own lives, to be independent of external restrictions upon them.

This may take a much larger scale and more elegant expression than the rather mundane examples we have given. William Ernest Henley captured the idea in his poem, "Invictus," written in 1875:

Out of the night that covers me,
Black as the Pit from pole to pole,
I thank whatever gods may be
For my unconquerable soul.

In the fell clutch of circumstance
I have not winced nor cried aloud.
Under the bludgeonings of chance
My head is bloody, but unbowed.

Beyond this place of wrath and tears
Looms but the horror of the shade,
And yet the menace of the years
Finds and shall find me unafraid.

It matters not how strait the gate,
How charged with punishments the scroll,
I am the master of my fate:
I am the captain of my soul.

Some have even elevated freedom to a sort of worldview. The French existentialist Jean-Paul Sartre, for example, built his whole philosophy upon belief in his own freedom. That was the one indubitable point of his understanding in light of which everything else must be understood and evaluated. If there were a God, Sartre reasoned, he would surely be a limitation upon my freedom. Consequently, God must not exist, for I know that I am free. So this freedom led Sartre to atheism.

Great wars have been fought over this principle of freedom, as one nation or group of people struggled to become free of the domination by another. Patrick Henry may have put it very dramatically, but he spoke the concerns of oppressed people everywhere when he said, "Give me liberty, or give me death!" Theological debates have taken place over whether a particular type of divine action would deprive humans of free choice. Political struggles occur over whether government is encroaching upon the free lives of its citizens, or whether regulations are unduly restricting the ability of business to accomplish its goals. Whether we as humans are really free is one issue that is difficult to resolve, but that we desire to be free seems quite clear.

What are most people referring to when they speak of their personal freedom? The concept is an illusive one, and may mean different things to different people, but certainly it at least involves the idea of absence from external constraint, or the idea that nothing or no one can compel my action, or my thought.

People go to great lengths to achieve freedom. They will risk their lives attempting to escape what they perceive as an oppressive government. During the days of the Berlin Wall, for example, persons made attempted dashes across no man's land to flee. In many cases, they failed and paid with their lives. At least one young man was shot down and then left to bleed to death while those on the free side of the wall looked on helplessly. The Latvians, Lithuanians, and Estonians sought a separate existence for their republics, freed from the dominance of the central government in Moscow. Large numbers of Haitians have attempted to flee their native country in boats, risking their lives at sea for a chance at freedom. Others have gone to war in civil conflicts, seeking to free themselves from the government of the country. These were people who reckoned that their lives were possibly not worth saving and living if they could not be lived in freedom.

There are certain realities of life which seem to place limitations upon our freedom, however. One of these is the sheer physical limitation which makes it impossible to do some of the things that we might choose to do. For example, I may, in one sense of the word, be free to leap thirty feet in the air. There are no federal, state, or local laws prohibiting such an action. I will not be fined or imprisoned if I am apprehended doing such a thing. Yet there is a law that I can choose to violate but cannot succeed in violating, namely, the law of gravity. There are other very real limitations, as well. For example, I may aspire to be the world's greatest pianist. There is nothing barring me from this externally. No law prohibits me from this, the way the constitution of the United States of America prohibits a foreign-born person from becoming president. There is no one who stands in my way, using force to keep me from ever playing publicly. Yet, the reality is that while some persons can become accomplished musicians, I cannot. I learned that early in my boyhood piano lessons, and I learned through a musical aptitude test in laboratory psychology class in college why I cannot. This is one of the limitations which I must accept.

There are other limitations which are very real parts of life. The ambition of some people is to live much longer than the normal life expectancy, and the fulfillment of some of the other goals many people have requires living longer than we usually have. What may I do to achieve either of these? Suppose that my goal is to live to the age of 120. I sometimes say that I will live to an advanced age simply because I want to get my money's worth out of social security, and having paid as a self-employed person most of my life, and having been at the maximum covered earnings most of those years, and knowing how the computation of benefits is made, I will have to live a long time. The desire to live that long, however, does not make it possible. The odds are that I will die long before that time. There are, of course, various sources of help that claim to make possible such a long life. One of these is a form of dieting. If one eats seafood, especially fatty fish such as mackerel, salmon, tuna, and herring; if one eats considerable amounts of fruits and vegetables, including half a raw onion a day and the equivalent of three cloves of garlic; if one avoids saturated fats, and follows certain other stipulations, then the odds of one's life being increased beyond normal are considerable. Note, however, that we are only speaking of improving the odds. Suppose that instead of the age of 120, I set my sights on 150. What would happen then? In all likelihood, the proposed solution would fail. The same could be concluded for any of the other goals people set for themselves in life, whether the ability to win friends, to be successful at sales, to negotiate well, to speak a foreign language, or whatever. The ability to be truly free to do these things, not simply to be free from external restraints, requires the help of a force far greater than is usually available to us.

Yet all around us we see people endeavoring to overcome the limitations that prevent them from being or doing what they really aspire to. For example, many people dread aging or, at least, the revelation of the fact that they have aged. So we see numerous advertisements on television for hair replacement in one form or another, or for hair coloration. Surgical procedures such as face lifts and tummy tucks can mask the reality of aging. In the final analysis, however, these only delay, rather than eliminate, the inevitable.

We spoke a moment ago of the attempt to postpone death. Modern medicine has found some interesting ways of doing this. One of these is the organ transplant operation. When one has lived long enough to have outworn the usability of his or her heart or kidneys, if it is possible to find a suitable replacement, that organ can be transplanted into the person and give a second chance to live, by means of a replacement part. It is almost as if the person were a machine, where new parts can be substituted for worn or broken ones by the mechanic, known in this case as a surgeon.

Attempts are made to alter the effects of what ordinarily would be termed inevitable conditions of life. To many, the genetic equipment which they received at conception has gone far to circumscribe the conditions of later life. Yet, through genetic engineering, gene splicing, and other techniques, even these conditions can be modified to some extent. Those who are not as physically attractive as they might wish can have plastic surgery and become more nearly their ideal selves, but this has limitations as well. One of the most interesting developments are those of transsexuals. Ordinarily, the sex with which one was born is considered one of the boundaries of life, sometimes (especially in earlier periods of history) imposing rather severe limitations upon what one can be and do. Yet recent medical history has seen the development of the sex-change operation so that, with varying degrees of success, a person who has male physical equipment but feels female psychologically can be transformed into a completely female person, physically as well as psychologically, and vice versa.

What must be borne in mind, however, is that there are limitations upon the effectiveness of all these attempted modifications of life's circumstances. If one is free to the extent that the limitations are transcendable, then human or natural efforts can only succeed to a certain degree, and one cannot be truly or fully free.

One of the paradoxical and even tragic aspects of the desire for freedom is the way in which it often does not lead to freedom but to enslavement, or at least to restriction of freedom. Some of the major restrictions young people react against are the standards, practices, and expectations of society as embodied in the older generation. So dissent is registered in some interesting ways, often visible, such as grooming and dress. Yet the interesting thing about this is that one can often tell the nonconformists by their similarity to one another. They all nonconform in the same fashion. Their new dress or hair style becomes almost a uniform, in some cases. While known as countercultural, it is definitely a culture. It is not simply that this is contrary to the prevailing culture, but that it is a counterculture, an alternative. It is well known that peer group pressure to conform is most powerful among young people, who in the process have simply exchanged their conformity to one group or standard for conformity to another rather than for freedom. This is what Martin Heidegger referred to as "the everydayness of the they," the virtually automatic acceptance of what everyone else is doing and thinking. This becomes, in Heidegger's opinion, a substitution for genuine or authentic existence, in which one sovereignly chooses one's own values and actions.

It is particularly instructive to see the power which gangs have over their members. Strict codes of conduct are developed and rigidly enforced, with serious consequences to those who deviate from them. The conflict of gang against gang is an indication not only of the cohesive force of the group toward those within, but also the exclusionary power of the group toward those thought to be their rivals.

One form that rebellion against authority or against the prevailing culture or ethics often takes is in the use of forbidden substances. This is one way of showing parents and other adults that they, the younger people, need not conform themselves to the desires of the older persons. They are free from the shackles of domination, as it is conceived of. Yet, sadly, the expression of freedom too frequently becomes the means of a new enslavement. It was expressed in the words of a woman ahead of me in the checkout line at a supermarket. She was buying a carton of cigarettes, and asked the young checkout girl if she smoked. When the latter replied that she did not, the older woman said, "Good! Don't ever start!" With the restriction and prohibition of smoking in many buildings, one can see these smokers standing outdoors smoking their cigarettes. They are victims of a habit most wish they could now break. Alcohol dependency programs are growing in number because of the large numbers of persons who need help in controlling a habit they easily acquired, perhaps as a means of displaying their independence. More than one outstanding entertainer or athlete has come to a tragic end of life because of an overdose of a substance that was first sought for its enjoyable qualities.

For some people, the restriction upon their ability to be what they want to be and do what they want to do is found not outside, but within. Powerful forces within one's own personality seem to dictate one's actions. The attempt to choose and then to do what one chooses founders upon the shoals of one's own nature. Habits, drives, and cravings may prove irresistible. When the goal of the person is not just for accomplishment in career or society, but in moral character, then the frustration becomes all the more apparent.

This phenomenon has been described by Søren Kierkegaard, in the second of his "stages on life's way." This stage is called the ethical stage. It is the approach to life to which one moves after trying the self-satisfying hedonism of pleasure in the esthetic stage. Abandoning this emphasis upon stimulating and satisfying experiences, he resolves to become an ethical person, to govern his life by certain rules or principles that exist independently of him. The ethical person, however, who is sensitive and conscientious, soon finds the frustration of falling short of the standards which he sets for himself. Whether internal, as in this case, or external, as in some of the other areas described, freedom is subject to the realities of existing unalterable factors.

It appears that freedom is more elusive than was at first thought. It may be used to choose something which it cannot then be used to unchoose. The choice is an irreversible choice. Certain actions are permanent in nature. A person who freely chooses to murder a member of his family cannot subsequently choose to have that person back alive again.

There are, of course, some people who reject freedom. They realize that freedom comes with a certain type and amount of responsibility and, being unwilling to accept that responsibility, these people settle for something less. They may do this by denying that they are able to change the state of affairs, or in particular, to change their own behavior. Various excuses or explanations of their behavior are offered. The genetic excuse assumes that our behavior has been predetermined by our genetic makeup. As one young woman told her father, "I'm that way because you're that way; and you're that way because Grandma is that way." If the truth were known, maybe Great-grandma or Great-grandpa was that way as well. Environmental conditioning is another explanation. "Growing up in this society, and in this part of it, I really didn't stand a chance to be any other way" is one explanation given. Or perhaps luck is offered as explanation. "I just didn't get the breaks" is a frequently recited litany. Social contacts are another explanation. If I had known important people, like so-and-so did, I would have succeeded as he did.

This type of person denies his or her freedom by failing to attempt the thing at all. This is really a sort of forfeit. The person slumps down into the ordinary routine, or the complacency or even despair that may come, and never even tries. In a sense, the self-assessment becomes self-fulfilling. Being sure one is unable to do something virtually guarantees that they will be unable to do so. Perhaps we need to look more closely at the concept of freedom. We have tended to think of it as absolute absence of any external constraint. Yet, as we have seen, such freedom is an elusive idea, at least in terms of what we can do ourselves. Perhaps it would be better to think of freedom as the ability to become, or to achieve, our highest potential. In real estate, there is the concept of highest and best use of a piece of property. While one may choose to use the property for a lesser purpose, such as by building a windowless warehouse on a potentially beautiful residential site with a breathtaking view, that is less than the best or most valuable use of the location. While one may choose to build a home on what would be an ideal commercial location, that is not its most valuable utilization. These are, in a sense, wasteful ways to employ the land, bypassing uses which are unique to it and using it for purposes which could themselves be better pursued in another place.

The same idea needs to be applied to human beings. Aristotle once expounded the concept that something is not really that thing unless it is fulfilling the end for which it is destined. While it may serve well in another purpose, that source is less than its reality. So one may use books for paperweights on one's desk rather than for sources of information, or one may use one's head simply as a rack on which to hang objects. So it is with humans. Humans may simply function as animals, perhaps work animals. Some humans are used to draw farm equipment. Others are used to serve as fences, to restrain groups of people. These, however, are not unique to them as human beings, and are therefore not their best and highest use.

The achievement of one's greatest potential is not easily accomplished, however. Indeed, it generally requires considerable restriction of some aspects of one's life. A professional musician, for example, must spend many hours of practice and forego other activities. The same is true for athletes. One young woman who had been a star of her high school swimming team chose not to compete in swimming in college. It would have required six hours of practice a day, which would have squeezed out too much of the rest of the college experience. All of these, however, are freely chosen limitations of one's activities for the purpose of maximizing one area of life, one set of aptitudes. While some would see this as enslaving, it is a voluntary choice of limitation for the sake of becoming able to be something more.

DOES IT MATTER IF GOD EXISTS?

This may well involve surrendering some of one's own free choice to another for the sake of gaining what that other can give. An outstanding example can be found in the realm of international Olympic athletics. One that particularly comes to mind is Mary Lou Retton, who won the gold medal in the women's all-around event in the 1984 summer Olympics. Her coach was Bela Karolyi, who had also coached Nadia Comaneci. For a full year before the Olympics, Retton lived away from her family at a secluded gym, where she had two long workouts under Karolyi's direction every day. He had control over virtually every aspect of her life: what she ate, when she slept, when she worked out, what she did in those practices, and particularly, how she did it. Some might see this as a terrible slavery, a major curtailment upon her freedom. It was, however, a step that she had taken with full knowledge of what was involved and for the sake of what she could become. Her discipline and the restriction of her life enabled her to become truly free to do that which she had not before.

These types of stories abound in the Olympic village. The figure skaters, the pole vaulters, the distance runners, and many more have submitted themselves to the control of another, and in the process have become free to become what they potentially could be. Indeed, this is the case with anyone who attempts to improve his or her athletic performance. Years ago I took a class in elementary golf. We were taught such basic matters as how to stand and how to grip a club. We were instructed to follow certain procedures to try to attain a repeating golf stroke: keep your head down; don't bend your left elbow; don't sway; swing inside-out; follow through. All of this seemed terribly restrictive, but we were assured it was necessary. It seemed that we had all we could do to keep all these matters in mind, let alone hit the ball. There were times when I wanted to scream, "I want to be free. I want to sway if I feel like it, bend my elbow when I swing, hit the ball anyway I want to." Under such conditions I would, in one sense, have been free. That would have been freedom, however, to hit the ball in the rough, in the water trap, or in the sand trap. By accepting the restrictions which the instructor placed upon my swing, I was beginning to receive the freedom to hit the ball far and accurately down the center of the fairway. Real freedom is the freedom to become, to realize one's best possibilities. It liberates one to achieve by enabling one to overcome some of those seemingly inevitable limitations that otherwise loomed before. Similarly, with respect to health, I may want to be free to live a sedentary life, to eat a heavy fat diet, to neglect having regularly scheduled physical checkups. Under such conditions, however, I am not free to overcome or to escape the natural forces that bring on death, and perhaps at an early age. Accepting limitations in my lifestyle is rather a way of becoming relatively more free to live in ways that are more satisfying in the long run.

Even with inanimate objects, restriction is a necessity to best performance. A railroad locomotive, for example, functions best when it moves upon its tracks. This may seem a very restrictive type of motion: always in the same plane, and moving over the same path. It is, however, motion that can be continued. Should the locomotive be freed from the restriction of its tracks and lurch off on its own, it would soon come to a halt and would in all likelihood be severely damaged in the process. In other words, it might not only lose the ability to travel, but even to exist as a locomotive at all. A mechanical device like an engine must have movement, but there is a practical limit upon the amount of free play that is consistent with efficient operation of the device. Careful tightening and adjustment are necessary for it to fully function as an engine.

This is a kind of discipline of movement, as it were, channeling it so that it is useful. Disorganized energy is of little use and may actually be destructive. For example, when a flame or a spark of electricity is introduced into the presence of gasoline fumes, the result is an explosion. This can have terribly destructive effects, both of property and human life. That is why one sees signs at gasoline stations that say, "Shut off your engine while refueling." That is why it is not wise to light a match to look down the fuel filler tube of the gas tank of one's car to see how full it is. When, however, this energy is harnessed, wonderfully useful results can occur. If the spark of electricity is introduced into the combustion chamber of a cylinder of the engine, into which a vaporized mixture of gasoline and air has just been sprayed, the resulting explosion has just one major effect: to drive the piston back down in its cylinder so that it then turns the crankshaft, and together with three or five or seven other such pistons provides torque to the transmission, which in turn transmits it to the wheels, then we have locomotion.

Other analogies come to mind. A river may flow freely and swiftly. When rains increase its flow, it may overflow its banks, bringing great destruction. In the summer of 1993, for example, a heavy and prolonged rainfall struck the midwestern part of the United States, producing severe flooding of the Mississippi River and its tributaries. Homes were destroyed, farms were inundated, in some cases the flood swept away valuable topsoil or covered the land with thick deposits of sand. The following year, the same destruction occurred in the southeastern United States. This was a major and uncontrollable example of what happens frequently on a smaller scale in many places. The excess water is of no value to anyone and, on the contrary, is exceedingly harmful to the earth and to many of its different inhabitants. When, however, dams are built, very positive use can be put to a river. Although many people do not realize it, the major benefit of dams is flood control. Beyond that, however, irrigation can be managed from the reservoirs, as well as drinking water for large populations in many cases. The lakes resulting from the damming of rivers provide recreational property for many. Moreover, hydroelectric generators can be constructed, thus producing electricity. All of these benefits, as well as the prevention of destructive floods, result from the simple containment and channeling of a wild, uncontrolled river.

In many ways, this is a sort of parable of the lives of some people. Their energies, whether physical, emotional, or intellectual, may be randomly disbursed and so are accomplishing nothing useful. This is what some people think to be freedom, the absence of restraint or discipline. In reality this is dissipation, or wastefulness, like pouring out precious water upon the sand. At worst, this can be very harmful, to themselves and others.

Thus far, we have argued that freedom is the ability to become what one can be and to become the best of what one can be, or to realize one's highest and best potential. We have further argued that this realization of potential is accomplished not simply by a random or unfettered expression of energy, but that it involves the disciplined harnessing of that energy into useful channels. That in turn involves the voluntary submission of oneself to something external, whether that be a conception, a cause, an organization, or another person. Indeed, we have hinted that there really is no such thing as completely untrammeled energy. One is directed or driven by something, whether internal or external, constructive or destructive, intelligently chosen or blindly accepted. But where does God fit in all of this? It is our contention that, rather than being a limitation or restriction of freedom, God is the true source of freedom, in the sense of being the one capable of enabling the human person to realize his or her own highest potential.

We note first that God is the one who is capable of doing anything which is the positive expression of power and goodness. By that we exclude the ability to be untrue, cruel, etc. This includes the ability to change human hearts, minds, and personalities. It was with respect to changing persons, not manufacturing or lifting rocks, that Jesus said, "With man this is impossible, but with God all things are possible" (Matt. 19:26). He used radical language to describe what God could and would do on behalf of those who became believers in Christ. He told Nicodemus, "you must be born again" (John 3:7). Paul used similarly strong language: "Therefore, if anyone is in Christ, he is a new creation; the old has gone, the new has come" (2 Cor. 5:17). These statements suggest a degree of transformation exceeding anything of which the person would be capable himself or herself.

But what is this potential, this capability that God enables? It is not a finite goal but an infinite goal. Suppose that one's objective in life is the attainment of some particular ability or skill. In this case, one would desire to become like some outstanding person in that field, some outstanding representative of that ability. It is not uncommon for persons, especially young people but also persons of all ages, to have "idols" or heroes whom they seek to emulate. To be able to be called another Michael Jordan or another Michael Jackson is the desire of many. In the world of politics, some desire to be another John F. Kennedy, or in business, another John D. Rockefeller. Usually, the higher the status of the person, the greater the honor to be like that person.

In the present case, what we are talking about are moral and spiritual qualities, qualities of the very character of the person. Here, there are also great heroes of many, such as Albert Schweitzer, Martin Luther King, Mohandas Gandhi, Mother Teresa, or Billy Graham. These are persons widely admired for the quality of their lives, or of their very persons. But for all of their good qualities, each of these persons also has some significant flaws which generally are not mentioned by their biographers. While there is much in the life of each of these paragons to emulate, there also are some aspects which one would not want to take as a model. Suppose, however, that one had as one's model, not merely an imperfect human being but the highest of all beings, the perfect and complete one, God himself! Certainly to aim to be like the one who is higher and greater than any human being would be the loftiest of hopes.

The Bible tells us that God created us with the intention that we would be like him. Indeed, the creation account says that God made the human, both male and female, in his own image and likeness. Think of that! Whereas he made all of the other creatures "after their kind" (or type), when he came to give life to the human, God used himself as the pattern or model. Humans, in other words, were to be as holy and righteous, as loving and kind, as merciful, fair, compassionate, and forgiving, as God himself. This plan and intention rather quickly went awry for God. The first human beings chose to use their freedom to rebel against their God, to go their own way. They thought that in so doing, they would become something more than they already were. The tempter suggested that they would become like gods, knowing good from evil, and that this was why God had forbidden them to eat of the one tree in the Garden of Eden that was off limits. Yet, when they took his advice and sought to break through the limitations upon their freedom, they found that rather than becoming more than they had been and becoming like God, they became less than they had been and partially lost the likeness to God that they already possessed. Through all of this, however, the image was never completely lost as a human possession, for in Genesis 9:6, God prohibits murder on the grounds that the human is the image of God. So, an attack upon a man is in effect an attack upon God himself, albeit indirectly.

It is apparent that God's image and likeness that the humans had at the very beginning was not the final completed version of what they were to be. It was merely the beginning. It was the promise of what was to be rather than its possession. The salvation that Jesus Christ came to accomplish and to confer was the restoration of what had been present originally in Adam and Eve from the creation, and the fulfillment of the likeness to Christ, who was himself described as the "radiance of God's glory, and the exact representation of his being" (Heb. 1:3). Paul makes it clear in Romans 8:29 that God has planned and destined humans "to be conformed to the image of his Son, that he might be the firstborn among many brothers." In 2 Corinthians 3:18, he speaks of the glory of the Lord, and says we "are being transformed into his likeness with ever-increasing glory, which comes from the Lord, who is the Spirit." To bear the likeness of God is an incredible privilege and possibility.

This is not something we accomplish by our own decision, determination, and effort, however. It is a transformation God produces in us. It then leads on to a growth process, and in this growth we are active participants. Paul expressed something of a paradox when, with respect to this growth in likeness to God, he wrote, "work out your own salvation with fear and trembling, for it is God who works in you to will and to act according to his good purpose" (Phil. 2:12–13). The mystery is that as we will and as we work, God is at work even in and through these actions on our part.

Two questions then must be asked of ourselves regarding this freedom and our desire for it. The first is: What do you wish to be or to become? Are you like the singer who wishes simply to be able to sing in the shower without the limitations which a professional voice coach would impose and the restrictions brought on by long hours of practice, or to be an accomplished and expert singer? Are you like the golfer who is satisfied with bogeys and double bogeys so long as he can swing in any fashion he wishes, or like the one who will follow specific directions from a golf pro in order to be able to play par golf, or at least close to it? What do you wish to be, an undisciplined, self-indulgent person, or a highly principled and highly admired person of integrity and moral character, of the very holiness of God himself? The choice is one's own, but the latter alternative in each case is an increased freedom to become something greater in one's life.

A second question is: Will you insist upon being able to do everything yourself, or are you willing to allow someone else to bring out and to amplify the best in you? Does freedom mean that one must painstakingly dig by hand a piece of land, or does it mean that one is also accomplishing the same result oneself when one uses a piece of power equipment such as a Rototiller by operating, directing, and handling it oneself? Is one only truly speaking when one speaks with her unaided human voice, or is she also speaking when using an electronic amplification system which reproduces that voice with greater volume and with only the slightest modification of its quality? The analogy is this: When God supplies the power for us to be and to become what he has intended for us as his pattern and goal, it is not a loss of what we really are, but the fullest sense of its attainment.

DOES IT MATTER IF GOD EXISTS?

All of us want to be free. Some are seeking that by a reaction against God, a desire to be completely independent of him. That freedom, however, may not be a freedom to achieve, to arrive, to be, but rather a freedom to become controlled by lesser forces, and to be something less than the best one could be. On the other hand, the choice of God as one's sovereign is the choice of what one really can best be and the choice which most fully enables that. It was Jesus who said, "and you will know the truth, and the truth will set you free . . . So if the Son sets you free, you will be free indeed" (John 8:32, 36). True freedom, in the fullest sense of the word, is not the avoidance and rejection of God, but the seeking and acceptance of him.

Study Guide

Key Questions

1. What do most people mean when they speak of freedom? How does the author define **freedom**? Why are the two definitions so different? What is, or has been, your definition and why?
2. How might persons, void of responsibility and goals for achieving their potential explain their behavior? The study text lists five.
3. Does being **free** demand the acceptance of responsibility? Does **responsibility** put **limits on freedom**? What are some things that limit freedom?
4. The author believes that true freedom that results in developing our full potential involves the ". . . disciplined channeling of our energy into useful channels" and that doing this involves ". . . a voluntary submission of ourself (ourselves) to something external." Do you agree? What is meant by **something external**?
5. What is it like to "realize one's highest and best potential"? What does God do for the person who asks his help in reaching that goal? What are the responsibilities and limits the person will place upon himself or herself in order to reach that goal?

Bible Investigation

1. Reread the section of the text explaining how "God is the one who is capable of doing anything which is the positive expression of power and goodness." Study Matthew 19:26 (a good verse to memorize), John 3:7, 2 Corinthians 5:17, Galatians 5:1 and 1 Peter 1:3. How do these references suggest a **transformation** that is greater than anything a person can do for himself or herself?
2. Study 2 Corinthians 3:18; 5:15, 17; Galatians 5:1; Ephesians 2:10; Philippians 4:7, 13; Colossians 3:9; and Hebrews 7:25. Focus your thoughts on being free to achieve your highest potential. What is your responsibility? What is God's?
3. What does it mean that we are made in the image of God? Gain a deeper understanding by studying the following Scriptures: Genesis 1:26; 5:1; Romans 8:29; 2 Corinthians 3:18;

Ephesians 2:10; 4:21–24; 5:1; and Colossians 3:8–10. Since God made us to be like him, how does this influence our view of freedom?

Personal Application

1. Think of demands for freedom that you have made in the past. Did they really make you free? Were there responsibilities and limitations that were placed upon you because you chose that "freedom"?
2. In the next few days, look for freedoms that have restrictions and limitations for which you are thankful. Express your thanks.
3. Pray for a clear understanding of what "achieving your highest potential" would be like and ask God for help in finding it.

Further Thought

1. In the quest for freedom, what really happens when a person escapes the restrictions of one culture and becomes engrossed in the rules and expectations of a counterculture? List some examples.
2. Think through the meaning of "**automatic acceptance**." Why is this not freedom? What is it?
3. How might you choose to surrender to another person some of your own free choice in order to gain what that person can give?

12

Getting Out
the Spot

The most painful experiences of life are not necessarily all physical in nature. It is quite possible to experience intense pain in psychological and emotional realms. One of the most severe of these is the experience of guilt. We all know what it feels like: an awareness of having done wrong together with a sense of remorse for what we have done. Frequently, there also is a consciousness of someone being disappointed in us or angry with us for that. There may also be a sense of having been caught doing something and being liable for punishment which one does not want to experience. It may be cosmic in its import: there may be a sense of having disrupted the very order of things in the universe. It is one of those experiences of tension of which we wish to rid ourselves.

I recall a painful and frustrating experience of guilt in my childhood. My sister, who is five years older than me, had done something which irritated me. I felt wronged and sought some way to get even with her. Then I saw my opportunity. There sat her bicycle, with two large balloon tires, fully inflated. I found a sharp nail and a brick and when no one was watching, I pounded the nail into her front tire, then watched triumphantly as the aired leaked from that tire. My revenge was achieved. She would be unable to ride her bicycle.

Soon, however, that feeling of satisfaction was replaced by a different emotion. I felt regret for what I had done and a painful sense of responsibility as well. I wanted relief from that emotion, and that required forgiveness. I went to my sister and my parents and confessed what I had done, asking for forgiveness. To my surprise and disappointment, they did not grant it. They did not believe I had done what I confessed, being convinced instead that Eileen had simply run over a nail. I am not sure whether they thought me incapable of committing such an act, or were simply unconvinced that I would confess it. In any event, my plea for forgiveness went unheeded. I was unforgiven, and it was a painful experience. To be unable to obtain forgiveness for one's misdeeds is indeed a painful experience. Lady Macbeth, obsessed with the fact of her guilt, is a picture of more than one person today. All of us at times feel like her, trying unsuccessfully to remove the spot of guilt.

If guilt is a painful experience, then forgiveness must be equally pleasant, enjoyable, and rewarding. For the strength of the emotion relieved is the measure of the joy experienced when that relief comes. What a wonderful relief to know that an offended person no longer holds any resentment or sense of being wronged. Beyond that, however, there is often also an awareness of renewal of positive fellowship, friendship, and love. A relationship healed is often stronger than before the break took place. One's own sense of self-respect is often restored as well, since the awareness of guilt frequently reflects unfavorably upon the estimation of what type of person one is.

What of that type of experience that I had, of needing and wanting forgiveness and not being able to obtain it? Is this really a problem for others and for all of us on a larger scale? Are there situations in which we desire forgiveness but are unable to obtain it? And if so, what does one do in such a situation? It would appear that there may be potential for such a treatment. For large numbers of people feel a sense of guilt which continues with them throughout many experiences of life. This may not be on a conscious level, but rather simply in a rather self-effacing or apologetic approach to others.

This type of feeling has been widely dismissed as merely "guilt feelings," irrational emotions to which no objective condition corresponds. Counselors treat this as simply a sign of poor self-esteem to be gotten rid of as quickly and surely as possible. The problem does not lie with any actual condition of guiltiness, so no forgiveness is necessary.

Is this really the case, however? To be sure, there are people who feel guilt for virtually everything in life. There are also Christians who have accepted the gift of salvation from God and who have asked for forgiveness, yet still have this sense of guilt. Perhaps this answer has been too easily given on a universal basis. If one is working within a framework in which there are only other human persons to whom one has any responsibility, and hence with respect to which one could have any guilt, then if no concrete wrong against another human being can be identified, there can really be no guilt, or at least there should be no guilt. This would be the case with a naturalistic set of presuppositions, for there are no superhuman persons against whom people could do wrong, and with respect to which therefore there could be guilt. But suppose a different picture of reality, in which there is at least one superhuman person, a supreme person against whom one might do wrong and to whom one's obligation is infinite. In such a situation, feelings of guilt may be a symptom, an indication of the presence of objective guilt with respect to this person.

We might well ask ourselves about the possibility of situations of guilt in which forgiveness cannot easily be granted within a human framework. Several types of such experience readily come to mind.

1. There are cases in which the person wronged is simply not available to grant forgiveness. One of these would be where the person involved may have died and consequently is not accessible for our confession of remorse and request for forgiveness. This would be particularly the case for a murderer. No matter how great may be the sense of contrition for that wrong, there is no way to express it to that person or to make restitution or amends. More than one murderer has undoubtedly felt such a desire, but has also experienced helplessness. Even where an interval may intervene between the act and the subsequent death, remorse cannot do anything to cancel the effects of the deed. There may also be cases where a person does not realize that he has wronged someone until after that person has died, so that again there is no chance for forgiveness.

2. More common, perhaps, is the situation where one who has wronged another feels responsibility, remorse, and guilt, and expresses that repentance to another, asking for forgiveness, but that person is unwilling to grant such forgiveness. What is to be done, then? While one may and should feel a sense of relief from the guilt, having done all he can to set things right, there is still a consciousness of disequilibrium. The desire to prolong the sense of

guilt on the part of the offender is often the reason why the offended in such a situation refuses to grant forgiveness, and that technique is sometimes successful. One can only hope that with the passage of time the person's heart will be softened, but such a hope is sometimes left unfulfilled.

3. A third situation is where the person wronged does not take seriously the need for forgiveness, apparently not believing this is a matter requiring forgiveness, or not believing that the person doing the confessing is really responsible for the wrong which has occurred. In the former case, the obvious earnestness of the confessor may convince the person wronged that he should forgive, even though he does not think it necessary, but in the latter case, little can be done.

4. There also is the case where the one offended does not take seriously the expression of repentance on the part of the offender. Here it is the desire, rather than the need, of forgiveness that is taken less than seriously. The offended may feel that the offender is simply doing this for the sake of public appearances, or for some other reason of expediency, rather than out of a desire to set things right with him. This may persist even with demonstrations of sincerity which may actually result in a sense of earning the other's favor, rather than being granted genuine forgiveness.

5. There may be lack of forgiveness because the wrong is of so broad an application that forgiveness by the wronged may be impractical. It may be that the wrong is against a whole group or even against society itself. This corporate body may not have the procedures for such forgiveness. The closest thing that can be cited is when a pardon is granted by some official capable of doing so. Unless, however, this comes as the result of a widespread public outcry insisting upon such a pardon, it is merely the work of one official rather than society as a whole. What happens in those situations in which there seems to be such is either an exoneration, as when a subsequent investigation or trial reveals that the person was not really guilty, or a cancellation of the debt on the basis of the person having paid his penalty, served his time, etc. Neither of these, however, is really the equivalent of forgiveness by the corporate group, something which cannot really be done. In fact, even when a person has paid his penalty, the society against which the offense was committed often still harbors resentment against him.

6. There may be cases where the wrong has been done against something incapable of granting forgiveness. This may occur, for example, where the person has sinned against nature. The animals who have been harmed by the action are not capable of forgiving, nor are the inanimate members of the creation. This is the problem with ecological misdeeds. How do those responsible for the ecological disaster of the Exxon Valdez, for example, ever receive forgiveness from some of the victims of the spill such as the fish and birds?

7. This, in turn, may lead to feeling that one has wronged the whole of reality, or something of the sort. This may be a sense of having violated one of the most basic of rules of the universe, of having changed the whole of reality, the balance within it, or something of the type. We might term this "cosmic guilt." There is no way, seemingly, for reality as a whole to hear, understand, or accept the confession and plea for forgiveness of reality in general.

What does one do with these types of experiences, where guilt and the consequent need for forgiveness are felt, but where it is not possible to obtain that needed forgiveness? What is one to do in such a situation? A number of possibilities come to mind.

1. A first is simply to try to forget the whole matter. One could ignore the feelings or tell oneself that it is irrational to have such feelings. One could proceed on the assumption that if ignored, these feelings will simply go away. They draw their strength from our preoccupation with them. It is questionable, however, how effective such attempted disposition of the guilt would be. The very presence of the feelings usually indicates that such efforts to ignore them have already proven unsuccessful. If there is any real basis for such feelings, then ignoring them is avoidance of the problem and is like ignoring the symptoms of physical pain which are warnings of an objective condition in need of treatment.

2. A more radical solution is to concentrate upon the positive side of oneself. Guilt feelings would be considered a result of negative self-thoughts, and as such the solution is to note the positive things about oneself, emphasizing them so that the others are diminished by comparison. This may work for some people. The difficulty here, however, is that this approach seems to be most successful for those who are already basically positive thinkers or, to put it another way, for those who are not quite as sensitive to the nuances of ethical responsibility as some others. Raising con-

sciousness in moral matters may actually have the effect of making one aware of the vast possibilities that actually exist, and thus of the shortcomings one has.

3. A still stronger version of this same approach is not simply to think positively about oneself, but rather to engage in a program of moral self-improvement, stressing the completion of more and more of what would be called good and admirable deeds. If the sense of guilt is because one has not done enough good, then this would be a definite program of self-improvement. Again, however, this approach tends to be self-defeating for the purposes we are considering. When one reads the biographies of great saints, of men and women whose lives were exemplary in terms of their treatment of themselves, others, the world and the creation, one is struck by the absence of any sense of self-satisfaction or light-heartedness in them. The more they grew in their holiness, the more conscious they became of their shortcomings. It was as if they now were sensitive to matters that they were not even aware of before. The more evils in the world they labored to combat, the more evils they became aware of, and the greater was their sense of responsibility for having contributed to those ills. Consequently, their perception of their need of forgiveness was much more penetrating than those of other humans. While perhaps becoming convinced of how far they had already come, they also were increasingly aware of how far there was still to go. One may notice Paul's self-assessment, certainly one of the greatest of the New Testament Christians. Whereas he had once considered himself a righteous and exceedingly self-righteous person (Phil. 3:4–6), he now considered himself the "worst of sinners" (1 Tim. 1:16). His increasing sanctification made him conscious of the magnitude of his sin.

4. The fourth approach is in many ways more like the first approach than it is like the second and third ways. This consists of getting professional help in attempting to get rid of the irrational guilt feelings. This may have some success in that it disposes of some apparently unnecessary concerns and anxieties, giving a sense of relief in the process. Unfortunately, it may accomplish more than is intended, resulting in a sort of insensitivity to larger issues as well. Thus, there may be feeling on the part of others that this person is now a less concerned person than formerly, and that may even come home to the person himself or herself with the feeling

DOES IT MATTER IF GOD EXISTS?

that something has been lost, that one is not as altruistic as was formerly the case.

Now let us return to our earlier suggestion. That was the idea that there may be something approximating "cosmic guilt." By that we meant that if there really is a supreme being, we have great responsibilities to him, responsibilities which exceed anything we would otherwise have contemplated. Suppose, for example, that society is not merely a social contract between two people (repeated numerous times, of course). Instead, those two people may both have been given life by God. He also has established the collective grouping known as society and has designed it and its members to function on the basis of certain rules or guidelines which he has established and promulgated. If this is the case, then my social relationships are not merely dyadic, but triadic. For failure to treat the other person properly involves wronging that other person, as is generally understood. It also, however, involves wronging God, who is the one who has established the basis on which the relationship is to take place, and on the basis of which that action is wrong.

This would mean that our actions have both a horizontal and a vertical dimension. When we do wrong to other persons, they can forgive us of that horizontal dimension. They have no power over the restoration of the vertical dimension, however, and that must still be set right. That is what only God, if there is one, can do.

As an analogy to help us understand this issue, we might think about the difference between civil and criminal offenses. Suppose that one person has done a wrong, a severe wrong, to another. Perhaps it is as serious as murder. The victim does not die for several days, however, during a part of which he is conscious and his murderer comes to him, confesses his wrong, and begs for forgiveness. This is granted and there is no personal guilt in this relationship. The victim's family also share in the forgiveness, agreeing not to sue for damages for the injury to their loved one, in keeping with his fervent request to them. Thus, there will be no civil suit.

But, criminal charges will still be brought against the perpetrator of this crime. The willingness of the victim to forgive and thus not to press charges does not affect the accused's criminal condition, for prosecution will proceed regardless of the feelings of the murdered person. For the law has a status of its own, deriving from society. The law has been violated, and society insists that it consequently has been wronged. It will therefore press its case. Perhaps the victim is willing for punishment not to be meted out, but that cannot affect the district attorney's decision. He does not represent the victim as his attorney. He represents the people, as their attorney. That is why cases of this type are stated as "the people vs. X." The wronged individual does not have the power to effect pardon on behalf of the state, only on his own behalf. That must be a question of the state's evaluation and action.

Many people do not think about this dimension of their actions. They may ask what is wrong with a particular action if two parties were involved, both of whom consented to the action, and neither of whom was apparently harmed by it. They do not think, however, about the effect this action may have upon other persons, upon what may happen to some persons if others act upon the example given. They may fail to realize that actions take place within a social context, and that context must be respected and protected.

This analogy may now be carried over into the consideration of the person's relationship to God. The way in which we treat others also involves God. If he has willed that others be treated in a certain way, then we are offending not only them but him as well. Offended humans can forgive the horizontal relationship, or the violation of the responsibility to them. They have neither the right nor the ability to forgive the vertical relationship, or the violation of the responsibility to God.

This conception emerges in the biblical discussion of social wrongs, as well. A foremost case of a person who wronged another was David. He sinned against another man, Uriah, by taking Uriah's wife, Bathsheba, and committing adultery with her. In order to cover that sin, he then arranged to have Uriah, a soldier, die in battle, thus actually committing murder against him indirectly. When David prayed his great penitential prayer, in Psalm 51, however, he expressed consciousness of the wrong he had done against God. He prayed, "Against you, you only, have I sinned, and done what is evil in your sight, so that you are proved right when you speak and justified when you judge" (v. 4). He had coveted another man's wife, committed adultery with her, and murdered the man. Beyond the wrong done against Uriah, however, of which Uriah was now incapable of granting him forgiveness, he had violated God's law by breaking the sixth, seventh, and tenth commandments (Exod. 20:13–14, 17). Thus, he had to ask God for forgiveness. The same was true of Saul of Tarsus, later known as the apostle Paul. He had

DOES IT MATTER IF GOD EXISTS?

done terrible wrongs to some of the Christians whom he persecuted, had imprisoned, and even executed. Yet when the Lord appeared to him on the road to Damascus, he was on his way to find believers in Jesus to bring back bound to Jerusalem. He heard a voice saying to him, "Saul, Saul, why do you persecute me?" (Acts 9:4) and when he asked, "Who are you, Lord?" the reply that came back was, "I am Jesus, whom you are persecuting" (v. 5). Saul's persecution of Jesus' followers was also a persecution of Jesus himself.

Suppose, then, that we have done everything possible to obtain forgiveness from everyone whom we believe we have wronged, but that we still have a sense of guilt. While this might be an irrational feeling, perhaps derived from a conditioned response, it might also be an intuitive awareness of a sense placed deep within us of responsibility to someone beyond the creation, namely the creator himself, and an awareness that there is still wrong for which we are responsible.

We should observe that part of what we are after is a complete, thorough forgiveness. Some human forgiveness is not complete and final. This is found in the statement, "I forgive, but I can't forget." What this sometimes means is, "I don't quite forgive." Perhaps it means, I forgive, but I am going to be watching you, just in case you do that again. That is not forgiveness. It is cancellation of any immediate consequences of the wrong, but the roots of the resentment remain. It is like a weed that is cut off, but not uprooted, so that it grows back again. This type of forgiveness leaves the offender uneasy, on edge lest he slip and commit the wrong once again. It does not consequently lead to a sense of relief.

With God, however, forgiveness is complete. One of the most forceful statements Jesus ever made on this subject is found in Matthew 18. There he told of the shepherd who had one hundred sheep, ninety-nine of which were safely in the fold. Yet he left those ninety-nine to go in search of the one, and brought him back to the fold safely. Jesus indicated that the shepherd rejoices more over the one who was found than over the ninety-nine already within the fold. He made clear that this was a picture of the Father's attitude toward the lost.

Jesus then went on to give an interesting follow-up to the parable, however. He explained to the disciples the procedure for relating to someone who has sinned against them. They were to go to the brother, then if unsuccessful, take a witness or two along, and finally, if necessary, bring it before the entire church. In response to this, Peter asked, "Lord, how often shall my brother sin against me, and I forgive him? As many as seven times?" (v. 21). He probably thought this was an incredible number of times to forgive someone who continued to sin. Most persons would have written off the offender long before that. Yet Jesus responded, "I do not say to you seven times, but seventy times seven" (v. 22). Whether this is 490, as this translation suggests, or 77 (seven times and seven), as many commentators have thought, the point is that it is a large number of times. Jesus used the figure seven, the symbol of completeness or entirety. I do not think Jesus was saying we are to keep count: "seventy-five; seventy-six; seventy-seven. That's it! I will not forgive you any further!" He was simply proposing that we forgive and forgive, and forgive, and not keep track.

Jesus subsequently made clear the motivation for this human forgiveness. He went on to tell about a servant who owed his master a large sum which he was unable to pay, and of which the master then forgave him. The servant then went out, found one of his fellow servants who owed him a small amount, and demanded that he pay him. When the master, however, heard of this, he brought the unforgiving servant in and told him that because of his lack of forgiveness of his fellow servant, he would now be put in jail until he paid the original amount that he had been forgiven. The application of the parable is clear: "So also my heavenly Father will do to every one of you, if you do not forgive your brother from your heart" (v. 35). The point of the appeal to forgiveness is that we are to forgive because God has forgiven us. The repeated forgiveness is because that is how God treats us. And lest we think that the parable indicates that God "forgives, but does not forget," it should be observed that sincerity of repentance, something not shown by the servant here, is an essential to receiving forgiveness. Jesus did not say that the unrepentant sinner in verses 15 to 17 is to be forgiven, regardless of the attitude. Rather, that person is to be treated "as a pagan and a tax collector" (v. 17).

Peter was to find in his personal relationship with Jesus just what this forgiving spirit meant. At the Last Supper Jesus said that all of his disciples would fall away from him (Mark 14:27). Peter, however, declared that this would never be the case. Even if all the others were to fall away, he would not (v. 29). Jesus then warned him that before the cock crowed twice, Peter would deny him three

DOES IT MATTER IF GOD EXISTS?

times, but still Peter protested (vv. 30–31). After Jesus was captured, this very thing occurred, exactly as Jesus had predicted (vv. 66–72). This left Peter weeping bitterly (v. 72). When, however, the three women came to Jesus' tomb on the morning of the first day of the week, the young man there dressed in white told them, "But go, tell his disciples and Peter, 'he is going ahead of you into Galilee. There you will see him, just as he told you'" (Mark 16:7). Jesus made sure that Peter was specifically told, thus making clear that Peter was still included among his followers. The sin of denial, made all the more emphatic by Peter's forceful protest, would not be held against him. He was still one of Christ's trusted followers. Although he tested Peter's continued commitment, he reaffirmed his commission to him to do his work (John 21:15–18). Peter had discovered in his personal experience what Jesus was talking about when he gave the instruction of forgiveness.

Peter had another opportunity, earlier in his contact with Jesus, to experience this immediate forgiveness. During a night in which they were crossing the Sea of Galilee, Jesus came walking to them on the water. Seeing Jesus and wanting to be with him, Peter said, "Lord, if it is you, tell me to come to you on the water" (Matt. 14:28). After walking to Jesus on the water, Peter noticed the wind, became afraid, and began to sink. He cried out, "Lord, save me" (v. 30). Jesus' reaction is beautiful, as Matthew reports it: "Immediately Jesus reached out his hand and caught him. 'O you of little faith,' he said, 'why did you doubt?'" (v. 31). Jesus might have lectured him on his failures while suspending him with the water just below his nostrils, but he did not. The rhetorical question, "why did you doubt?" was not so much a rebuke as an indication that he would not have had to experience this danger. Jesus did not hold Peter's failure of faith against him. As quickly as Peter asked for help and deliverance, it was granted.

This same pattern of persistent and complete divine forgiveness is found throughout the Scriptures. Think of God's love for his chosen people, Israel. Again and again they strayed from him or even rebelled against him. They were so quick to forget what God had done for them, in delivering them from Egypt. They repeatedly wished that they could be back in Egypt, where they had things so good. They made idols, which they worshiped as gods. They adopted the gods of other nations about them. They disobeyed his commands. There must have been times when, anthropomorphically speaking, God was tempted to cast out his chosen people. Perhaps there would have been more hope for the Hittites or the Amalekites if he had revealed himself to them the way he had to Israel. Yet through all this, God remained faithful. Although he allowed them to be carried off into captivity as part of his chastening activity, he restored them. He gave them victories over the nations that would destroy them, and he preserved them, even under conquerors. When the Savior came, he was born from the nation of Israel and presented his message first to them. When they rejected him, he turned to the Gentiles, but this was not the end of his dealing with them. In Romans 11, Paul considers the idea that God has cast off his people Israel, and firmly rejects it (v. 2). The promises and covenant of God remain firm, even though they have temporarily hardened their hearts. This hardening, however, is only until the full number of the Gentiles come in. He states, "and so all Israel will be saved" (v. 26). This is faithful forgiveness.

This faithful forgiveness is seen as well in the Old Testament story of Hosea. God used the prophet's marital situation to reveal something of himself and his relationship to Israel. Hosea's wife, Gomer, had proven unfaithful to him, and the names he gave to his children indicate the pain through which he went as a result of this infidelity. Yet through it all, he remained faithful and even took her back to himself as his wife rather than divorcing her, as he had a perfect right to do under the law. This was a picture of God in relationship to Israel. Instead of putting their trust in Jehovah, the Israelites had sought for the favor first of Assyria and then of Egypt. Passages which express great tenderness are intermingled with those which convey the idea of harsh judgment. God would certainly have been justified in casting off his people for their faithlessness, but he stood ready to forgive them.

Another individual who found God's forgiveness to be complete was Paul. As severe as had been his opposition to the cause of God in Jesus Christ, God not only forgave him but enabled him to become the outstanding missionary and Scripture author of the early church. He expressed his amazement and sense of unworthiness of being privileged to have Christ appear to him, since he considered himself "the least of the apostles and do not deserve to be called an apostle, because I persecuted the church of God" (1 Cor. 15:9). God's forgiveness also canceled any supposed disqualification from the Lord's service.

The Bible is replete with references to the totality and finality of God's forgiveness. The writer of the letter to the Hebrews writes of the new covenant which God will make with the house of Israel and the house of Judah (8:8–13). He says, "For I will forgive their wickedness, and I will remember their sins no more" (v. 12). The same idea is repeated in Hebrews 10:17–18. The promise is the more impressive when we realize that it is a quotation from Jeremiah 31:34, where God speaks of the new covenant which he is to make (vv. 31–34). It was written more than six centuries earlier by a prophet who lived in a Judah which was so unfaithful to God that he found it necessary to allow the judgment of defeat and captivity to bring chastening upon the nation. Yet even then he was speaking of the faithfulness he would exercise on behalf of his people and the forgiveness he would grant.

The thoroughness of this forgiveness is stressed in the idea of remembering their sins no longer. God is not one who "forgives but does not forget." The opening chapter of Isaiah's prophecy makes clear that these people were sinful and faithless. Yet God's promise was of forgiveness and cleansing that would leave no traces of this sinfulness. It is put in vivid terms: "Come now, let us reason together, says the LORD. 'Though your sins are like scarlet, they shall be as white as snow; though they are red as crimson, they shall be like wool'" (Isa. 1:18). Psalm 103 is a powerful expression of the experience of God's persistent, forgiving love. It was written by David, who of course had sinned greatly against God. The central part of the psalm contains these moving words: "The LORD is compassionate and gracious, slow to anger, abounding in love. He will not always accuse, nor will he harbor his anger forever; he does not treat us as our sins deserve, nor pay us according to our iniquities. For as high as the heavens are above the earth, so great is his love for those who fear him; as far as the east is from the west, so far has he removed our transgressions from us" (vv. 8–12). One Christian told of confessing a certain sin to God and being forgiven. Some time later, he came back to God in prayer and said, "God, about that sin of mine," and it was as if God said, "What sin?" God does not keep account of sins confessed and forgiven. If they are forgiven, they are really forgiven.

The force of divine forgiveness is especially great because of the nature of the one doing the forgiving. For some people, forgiveness is relatively easy, for they do not take things like this seriously either from the offender or the offended. Forgiveness is not a difficult matter because it is almost more a question of dismissing the offense rather than actually forgiving it. In God's case, however, we are dealing with the highest, most ethically sensitive, and most serious being in the entire universe. He has no choice but to take sin seriously. He feels even the slightest sin, for he himself is perfectly holy. For such a being to forgive requires unusual powers of forgiveness. Further, with some humans forgiveness may not be quite so difficult since they themselves are also frequently sinners, and so right is not completely on one side and wrong on the other. In other words, because they contribute to the wrong, they are not so completely wronged as they would be if they never did any wrong themselves.

This fact of divine forgiveness has some powerful effects upon us as the forgiven, as well. The result of realizing the extent of God's forgiveness should be, and is, love for God on our part. This was made clear by Jesus in connection with an incident during his ministry. While Jesus was eating in the home of a Pharisee, a sinful woman came in and, weeping, began to wash his feet with her tears and wipe them with her hair. She anointed him with ointment. Jesus' comment to the Pharisee was, "her many sins have been forgiven—for she loved much; but he who has been forgiven little, loves little" (Luke 7:47). There is apparently a direct relationship between the amount of forgiveness one realizes he or she has received and the amount of love felt toward the Lord. If we find it difficult to love the Lord as we should, one answer is to reflect upon the nature and extent of his forgiveness of us.

Finally, we should also understand that the forgiven spirit is a forgiving spirit. We referred earlier to Jesus' parable of the unforgiving servant. It is apparent what the Lord expects: If we have experienced forgiveness, we will similarly show that forgiveness to others. This is the way we demonstrate that we have understood that we are forgiven and that we appreciate it. So, for example, in the Lord's Prayer, we are told to pray: "And forgive us our debts, as we also have forgiven our debtors" (Matt. 6:12). We can pray confidently for God's forgiveness when our behavior reveals that we have truly understood it and the motivation Jesus gave his disciples when he sent them forth to preach the good news, to heal and to perform miracles, telling them, "Freely you have received, freely give" (Matt. 10:8).

Robert C. Newell tells of driving late one night along an isolated road when the motor of his car stopped. A friendly traveler came

DOES IT MATTER IF GOD EXISTS?

along, took a rope from the trunk of his car, and towed his stalled car nearly thirty miles to a garage. When Newell insisted that he accept pay, he refused and also rejected his offer to fill his tank with gas. "Well," said Newell, "I must in some way return your kindness." The stranger replied, "If you really want to show your gratitude, buy a rope and always carry it in your car."

Study Guide

Key Questions

1. Is guilt something that everyone experiences in different degrees and all the time? Is it "natural" to feel guilt? Can a person ever be entirely guilt-free? How? Certainly, to have guilt feelings is unpleasant, and to have them removed is pleasant, but is having a feeling of guilt bad?
2. From the study text, list seven types of experiences in which one might seek forgiveness and yet be unable to obtain it. Though each situation is different, what is the one thing needed in order to find resolve and have the guilt removed?
3. How do people try to gain forgiveness in these various experiences (#2 above)? How is each of the four possibilities different from the others? Is one better than the others? Why don't they work?
4. Why is "cosmic guilt" different from the other six situations discussed? What does **"then my social relationships are not merely dyadic, but triadic"** mean?
5. What is the significance of the amount of love one has for God and the extent of one's pleasure in enjoying the feeling of forgiveness?

Bible Investigation

1. Reread the section of the study text that deals with triadic relationships and the explanation of the horizontal and vertical dimensions. Study the story of David, Bathsheba, Uriah, and God (Exod. 20:13–14; 17; 2 Sam. 11–12:14; Ps. 51). What were the situations David found himself in, how did he deal with them, and how did he find forgiveness?
2. Study Matthew 18:10–14 and think about the completeness of God's forgiveness. Think about Jesus' answer to Peter's question about how often one should forgive another (Matt. 18:21–22). Take time to learn more about forgiving and the removal of guilt feelings (Matt. 14:25–33; Mark 14:27–72; John 21:15–18).

Personal Application

1. Examine your attitude toward guilt and guilt feelings. How do you get rid of guilt? Seek the help of God who forgives com-

pletely. Apply the Scripture teaching we've discussed in this study.
2. How do you help others see guilt removed? Are you forgiving? Is there someone you need to forgive? Go to them today.
3. Meditate on Luke 7:47. What is your response? Determine to grow in your love for God.

For Further Thought

1. Read the book of Hosea. Focus on this subject of guilt and forgiveness. As you are thinking of Hosea, Gomer, and their situation, try to relate to God and his willingness to forgive all who will come to him for it—including you.
2. When guilt has been removed and your relationship with another person and with God has been completely restored, are you then thankful for the experience of guilt?

13

So What?

Back in the seventeenth century, the mathematician and physicist Blaise Pascal reflected on the France of his day. Pascal saw that the problem was not so much that these Frenchmen rejected God, but that they ignored the question entirely. It was this indifference, rather than hostility, that must be dealt with if they were to come to faith. He posed a challenge to his contemporaries which has become known as "Pascal's wager."

Each of us, says Pascal, is betting or wagering either that there is a God or that there is not a God. Think however, said Pascal, of the magnitude of the issues involved. Suppose that you wager that God is, and he is. If so, you have gained everything. If you wager that he is and he is not, you have really lost nothing. By implication, we may deduce the results of wagering that God is not. If you wager that God is not and he is not, you have gained only temporally, but if he is, you have lost infinitely. For what you have wagered and lost is your eternal soul.

Jesus posed a similar question in Matthew 16:26: "What good will it be for a man if he gains the whole world, yet forfeits his soul? Or what can a man give in exchange for his soul?" He was challenging his hearers to follow him wholeheartedly. This involved cross-bearing, self-denial. Those who were unwilling to follow him were apparently unwilling to give up the things which were most precious to them, namely material possessions and other earthly attainments. Jesus' concern was that they realize what was really at stake. They were either betting that he was who and what he claimed to be, namely the Messiah, the Son of God, or that he was not. He wanted them to realize that what they were betting was not simply some part of themselves or some possession. They were actually betting their lives, their souls, their very selves. In view of this, he said, is it worth betting against him? For even if they were right, all they gained were temporary material rewards. If, however, they were wrong, what they stood to lose were their eternal souls, of infinite and irreplaceable value. No matter how much they might gain, even the whole world, there was nothing that could buy back one's life or soul once it was forfeited. Jesus was virtually saying, "You bet your life," for that is what they were betting, for or against his claims. He did not ask his hearers simply to follow him blindly. He never called for such a "leap in the dark." Rather, what he was challenging them to do was consider carefully the choice they were making. They owed it to themselves not to make such an important decision by default.

Each of us is making this sort of choice regarding the claims of Jesus Christ. We are either betting that what he claimed for himself is true and he is the Son of God, the Savior and Lord of the entire human race, the head of the church, or that he is not what he claimed, and therefore must be either an impostor and fraud or a megalomaniac. But upon the outcome of this wager hangs our entire future, which is eternal if he is right. Even if the odds were very low that he is what he claims, the stakes are so very high that we dare not make this decision by default. And make no mistake about it, we are betting one way or the other. If we are not betting for him, we are automatically betting against him. Our money is placed upon the "not the Son of God" space unless we have done something to place it elsewhere.

How high a risk are you willing to take? In investing, we are often told that risk and potential gain are roughly directly proportional, ordinarily. If the possibility of loss too far exceeds the possibility of return, then that is not a prudent investment whether one is a speculator or a conservative investor. A very volatile stock which nonetheless does not carry high returns is a poor investment. That is why many investments are now rated for their "risk-adjusted return." This should be borne in mind when reflecting on the fact that what is at stake in our faith and action is our very selves, all that we are and will be.

While Russian roulette is talked about more than played, there have been instances of this sport. It was practiced by some American military personnel in high stress situations during World War II, on at least one occasion in the South Pacific. Occasionally one hears of some teenage young person being killed while playing this sport, which is something like the game of "chicken." The rules are very simple, and the equipment is relatively minimal. All that is needed is a revolver and one live bullet. The player takes the gun in hand, spins the cylinder, places the barrel of the gun to his temple and pulls the trigger. The chances are five out of six that the hammer of the gun will descend upon an empty chamber, the player will hear a click, and he wins. The chances are one out of six that the hammer will descend upon the chamber containing the bullet, the other players will hear a roar, and the player will lose—infinitely.

Would you play that game? The odds are not bad: one to five that you will win. Yet the stakes are high, and the results are so unequal. If one wins, the gain is slight: merely a bit of diversion. If one loses, however, the loss is great and even infinite: one loses all he is and has. Suppose we increase the odds. Instead of one gun with one shell, we would give you a box containing one hundred revolvers, only one of which contains one shell, the others being completely empty. Now would you play? Here the odds are 599 to 1, but the stakes are still very high. Probably most of us would still refuse, for the potential gain does not equal the potential loss or the risk.

One October Monday morning I boarded a plane for my weekly fall commute from Minneapolis-St. Paul to Dallas-Fort Worth. I settled into my usual seat, 6D, and took out my prebreakfast work. As we taxied out for takeoff, the lead flight attendant was giving the usual announcements. She told us where the emergency exits were in this aircraft. She indicated that in the unlikely event of a loss of cabin pressure, panels above our heads would open and oxygen masks would descend. One should place the mask over one's nose and mouth and breathe naturally. Then, however, she made an announcement that I had never heard before in all my years of air travel. She said, "Our maintenance department has informed us that we will lose one seat somewhere between Minneapolis and Dallas. The seat will simply drop through the floor. We do not know which seat it will be, but we have been assured that only one seat will be thus involved. Have a pleasant trip."

She did not say that, of course. I can assure you, however, that if she had, I would have headed for the nearest exit and asked to be let out. It is 852 air miles from the Minneapolis-St. Paul airport to the Dallas-Fort Worth airport, but I would walk it rather than risk the chance of losing my life. The odds would be 131 to 1 against 6D being the seat that was to be lost, but I would not want to take that chance.

This is the risk we are taking, the bet we are making. What if you gamble that there is no God, or that Jesus is not the Son of God, and you are wrong? What do you do then? As Jesus said, "What will a man give in exchange for his soul?" The literature of several countries contains the Faust theme: the story of a man who trades his soul to the devil, then is unable to regain it. What price do you place upon a human life? During the attempted invasion of Cuba by some Cuban expatriates in 1963, many of them were captured and held prisoner by Fidel Castro. Negotiations went on for their release. The question was what would be traded for the prisoners, and what the price would be. It was finally agreed that since Cuba needed tractors, they would be traded for the prisoners, but how many tractors equal one human being? This was an attempt to place a price tag upon a human life. The same is done when ransom is demanded for the release of a kidnap victim. What price would you place upon your most precious, most beloved person? What would you give to spare the life of that one? Or what would you pay for your own life? The point is that even if one kept everything one had in terms of material possessions but lost his life, he would have nothing, for the "I" which is the subject of the sentence, "I own everything," would cease to be, leaving only, ". . . own everything." For as the Bible says, "We brought nothing into the world, and we can take nothing out of it" (1 Tim. 6:7).

We consider foolish the people who do not know the value of what they have. Recently, a person purchased for five dollars at a garage sale an original Andrew Wyeth drawing, worth many thousands of dollars. The seller had no idea what it was worth, probably considering it merely "some old drawing." Probably there pass through our hands coins worth considerably more than their face value, but we do not know their value. We marvel at the American Indians who reportedly sold what is today Manhattan Island to Peter Minuet for about twenty-four dollars worth of trinkets, not knowing what that real estate would someday be worth. We shake our heads in wonder at Esau, who traded away his birthright for a bowl of vegetable stew. Yet it is just as sad when someone, not realizing the value of their life and soul, trades it away for some secondary good in this world.

What about you, reader? Have you really considered seriously the possibility that there truly is an infinite God? Or, if you believe this, are you living on the basis of the implications of such a view? It has been our aim to show in this book that God does really matter, that there is a significant difference between living in a world in which there is a God and believing in him, and in living in a world without a God. In light of the seriousness of the issue and the magnitude of the stakes, I strongly urge you to consider carefully the answer to this question.

How does one believe? I am not urging a blind leap in the dark, a hoping that it is so, or as Mark Twain defined faith, "believing what you know ain't so," in this case more correctly paraphrased as, "believing what you don't know ain't so." Rather, I urge you to inquire carefully and wisely regarding the possibility of these matters. In Luke 7, we read the story of John the Baptist, who had been imprisoned for faithfully declaring the message which included repentance. Now, however, from his prison cell he sent two of his disciples to Jesus to inquire of him, "Are you the one who was to come, or should we expect someone else?" (v. 19). Somehow the faith of John, who had so emphatically announced, "Look, the Lamb of God, who takes away the sin of the world!" (John 1:29) had changed to doubt. The apostrophe of faith had become twisted into the question mark of doubt in that situation in which John probably realized that his very life was soon to be forfeited upon the question of Jesus' identity. Jesus responded to his question in an interesting way. He did not say, in authoritarian fashion: "I am he!" leaving John to take it or leave it. He did not respond in manipulative fashion, "John, you had better stop asking these questions, or you will lose your soul." Nor did he use a nondirective response, "John, I hear you saying that you are uncertain about who I am, that you have feelings of insecurity about the future." No, Jesus responded by pointing out the evidences of what he was doing, "Go back and report to John what you have seen and heard: the blind receive sight, the lame walk, those who have leprosy are cured, the deaf hear, the dead are raised, and the good news is preached to the poor" (Luke 7:22). He did not offer overwhelming evidence, but sufficient evidence for one who was willing to believe and wanted to believe. He allowed John to make up his own mind. Christ will always respond to the person who honestly wants to know and believe the truth.

This may mean that it is sometimes necessary for us to do something similar to what John did in coming to Christ: to pray, in effect, "Lord Jesus, if you really exist, and the Bible is your message, please enable me to believe. Show me the evidences that will make it possible for me to believe." This should be accompanied by looking in the right place, being selective about that to which we attend. John could have chosen to focus upon the realities of his immediate physical situation: the prison cell, bars, chains, guards, etc. If he had done that, doubt would have become unbelief. He chose instead to focus upon Jesus' actions, and these brought about faith, as indicated by Jesus' words of commendation (vv. 23, 28). We will want to examine the evidences, historical, philosophical, and experiential, for the truth of the Christian faith. We will want to discuss our questions with a trained person, such as a pastor or a scholar whom our pastor might recommend who can help us with these matters. Part of their help will be in referring us to some of the many excellent books and other materials which present the positive evidence for the truth of Christianity.

Faith is, in this life, a path traveled rather than a destination attained. This means that we must often ask Christ for assistance in the building of our faith, even in the process of our using what faith we currently have. In Mark 9, a man came to Jesus with his demon-possessed son, who was deaf and dumb. When the man asked if Jesus could do anything for his son, Jesus answered, "Everything is possible for him who believes" (v. 23). The man's response was immediate, "I do believe; help me overcome my unbelief" (v. 24), and Jesus went on to heal his son by casting out the demon. That man may be an example for us and thus the hero of our story as well.

Study Guide

Key Questions

1. Review. Think through the answers to these questions:
   (1) Is God's Word, the Bible, your basis for **confidence** and **security**? Do you find comfort and peace in the study of the Bible?
   (2) Has fear of the unknown been replaced in your life with the **assurance** that God is the God of the future and that he is waiting for you to join him in that future?
   (3) Have you placed your **trust** in the Creator God who knows all about you? Does he call you by your name? Do you recognize his voice?
   (4) Do you feel his **love** and know his **strength** when you are going through difficult experiences? Do you remain **confident** that he is still in control?
   (5) Have you learned to "let go" and "let God be God"? Are you experiencing a life of **usefulness, honor**, and **satisfaction**?
   (6) Do you know yourself as being made in the image of God? Does it affect how you look at life?
   (7) Have you accepted Christ as your **personal Savior** from sin? Has the sting of death lost its power over you?
   (8) Does your strength come from God so that you are able to say as the apostle Paul declared, "**When I am weak, then I am strong**"?
   (9) Are you confident that evil is not going to win? Do you know that **God will triumph** in the end?
   (10) To you, is **freedom** the ability to realize your **highest** and **best** potential?
   (11) Have you learned how to have your guilt removed? Are you able to **forgive** as you have been forgiven?
2. Does it matter to you that there really is a God? As you study the study text's conclusion, go back to chapter one and rethink its content.

Bible Investigation

1. Study Matthew 16:26. What is your answer?
2. Read Mark 9:14–26. Think of your personal relationship to God as you read. Do you need to pray the same prayer as the father did?

Personal Application

1. Write questions you still have concerning the existence of God and the difference it makes to you and your life. Read John 3:31; Philippians 2:5–6; Colossians 2:9; Titus 2:13; and 1 John 5:20. What help do these verses give in answer to your questions? Determine that you will continue to study until you are confident that your questions are answered.
2. Pray a prayer of thanksgiving for the understanding you have gained from this study.

For Further Thought

1. Review the suggested **Personal Application** section of each chapter. Measure your action in response to the suggestions given. What additional steps should you take?
2. How will your life be different because of your study of *Does It Matter if God Exists?*

Teaching Suggestions

Chapter 1. A Question Worth Asking

1. Acquaint the class with the book and the author's invitation to **explore** the meaning, or lack of meaning, of God in experience, and to answer the question: "Does it matter if God exists?"
2. Make a newspaper headline titled "**God Is Dead**" and solicit comments on how **alive** class members think God is today.
3. Work with the class on exercise #2 in Key Questions. Help them understand that **death of God** adherents hold to one or more of the following four beliefs: (1) Death of the "experience" of God; (2) Empirical science "undercuts" the idea of God as inconceivable; (3) The sense of the reality of God has been lost, rendering God obsolete; and, (4) God as a separate being, outside the world, has ceased to be and is rather a part of the being of every person (as in **process theology**).
4. Ask the class to share the "tough" questions about life and existence that they struggle with. List these on a chalkboard or dri-erase whiteboard. Take a little time to discuss them.
5. Have the class find in their Bibles and read silently John 18:38–39. Then ask for responses to the following questions: (1) What evidence is there that Pilate had intellectual struggles? (2) What claims does Jesus make about himself? (3) What is taught about the eternity of Christ? (4) According to Jesus, to whom does the discovery of truth lead? Also, if time permits, do the same thing with Acts 17:16–34 and ask for responses to these questions: (1) What did the objects of worship reveal to Paul? (2) What answer did Paul have for what the "very religious" thought to be "unknown"? (3) What does the passage teach about the extremely "religious" and the "truth seekers"?
6. **SPECULATE:** Ask for a response to these questions: If you are or were convinced that there is no Christian God, by what standards would you live? What prevents chaos in society? What makes society a place you still want to be a part of? Is

the proper norm ". . . do whatever you wish as long as you do not hurt anyone"?

7. Some nonbelievers may advocate that society still use a code of ethics that contains part of the Ten Commandments or the basic teachings of Jesus. Ask: Why? Who decides? By whose set of standards are you willing to live . . . and why?

8. **ASK:** "If you believe the Christian God exists . . . how does that affect your lifestyle?" Lead the discussion from the broader "I put Christ first" . . . to specifics such as: (1) the election booth; (2) my sick neighbor; (3) treatment of spouse in a way that is an example to my children that God is love.

9. **Supplementary Scriptures**: John 1:1–3; 10:37–38; 1 Corinthians 1:24; Colossians 1:15–17, 19; 2:2–3, 9–10; 1 John 5:20. These texts will suggest questions and discussion ideas you can implement if you have time. Stress that the question of whether or not God exists is important only if the answer makes a difference.

Chapter 2. Here Comes the Future

1. Illustrate how "change and development are characteristic of all reality . . ." "No man can step into the same stream twice . . ." Get agreement by a class discussion that change is challenging but that it is also fearful, especially because the future is unknown.

2. Ask what preparation each is making to minimize future instability (a college education, life insurance, savings account, investments). List the suggestions on the chalkboard or on a dri-erase whiteboard. Ask which one on the list they would omit if they had to drop one. Now add to the list the words *God will be in the future.* **ASK:** Does this addition make any difference to how you plan for or feel about the future?

3. Ask how the church (in general or their specific church) has changed in recent years (traditional vs. contemporary). List the ways. Then ask how the problems facing the church have changed. List them (drugs, abortion, marital break-ups, alienation between parent and child). Make a third list of what the class feels the church must do to minister in a changing world.

4. Illustrate from the call of Moses in Exodus 3 and 4 that which demonstrates God's encouragement in a changing world. The

author interprets the Hebrew name for God "I **AM**" in 3:14 to mean "**I will be**," implying "**I will be there**." Ask the class: How does this interpretation give hope and encouragement for moving into the future?

5. At the last session you assigned the reading of Exodus 3 and 4. Plan a quick study on how God led Moses into the future (from the book of Exodus). Distribute pencils. Leaving space for answers, make enough copies listing these questions: (1) Whose idea is the future and what is the plan (3:10)? (2) Surely God made a mistake . . . right (3:11)? What feelings does this reflect? (3) What can I expect (3:12)? (4) How do I convince anyone (3:14–15)? and, (5) Do I get any help (3:16, 18)?

6. The author notes that in the call of Moses God makes three things clear why "change" need not overwhelm us: (1) **God understands the change that is taking place**, ". . . not only does God know and understand . . . change, but he is the very cause of it"; (2) **When it comes to moving into the future, God understands our inadequacies;** and (3) **God will be in our future** (Exod. 3:12). Again . . . emphasize that the name "I AM" means "I will be." "I will be in your future" from "generation to generation" (Exod. 3:15b).

7. Using your Bible study helps, find and use references that show that God promises to be in our futures: Psalms 91:11; 121:3; 138:7–8; Philippians 1:6; 2 Thessalonians 3:3; Hebrews 13:6.

8. Encourage that #3 in Personal Application be done individually or have someone read the hymn "Oh God, our help in ages past, our hope for years to come . . ."

9. Challenge class members to embrace the Christian God who encourages us in a fast-paced changing world. It does matter that the Christian God exists.

Chapter 3. Somebody Knows Your Name

1. Cut 3 x 5 cards in half. Print different five-digit numbers (such as 16390) on enough cards for everyone in the class. Make a master list. Give each class member one card with a number on it. From the master list call the role using the numbers. Ask that they reply "here" when their number is called. After "roll-call" ask a few to take their neighbor's card, stand, and introduce themselves and their neighbor saying, "I am 16390

(whatever) and am happy to be here. I'd like you to meet my neighbor 43972." Discuss reactions class members may have.

2. Choose from the chapter or from your own experience an example which illustrates why this question dominates current thinking: "Does anybody out there care about me?" (e.g., A social security number is more important than a name; the **baggage** approach to personhood). Stress the **depersonalization** so prevalent today.

3. Ask that each have Matthew 10:29–31 before them. From the passage indicate a dimension of God that shows he cares and that the existence of such a God is a satisfying answer to the question of the chapter (see #2 above). Through the story of the sparrows, and other Scriptures, Jesus and others speak of the Father's **KNOWLEDGE** and **CARE**. In rhetorical fashion ask the question: "When was the last time you had the hairs on your head counted?"

4. With Matthew 10:29–31 still in focus, make and illustrate the emphasis that persons have value to God because the events of a life: (1) are not unknown to God; (2) do not occur contrary to God's will or decision (**direct** will, or **permissive** will); and (3) are not something God cannot control once they happen.

5. In literature you have received from some sweepstakes offer you have read how rosy life is going to be for you when the right entry numbers are selected: a new large home, travel, automobiles, and financial independence. Read this to the class. The odds of winning are in the "fine print." In the context of a person's quest to provide for his (her) every need, stress that God is aware of our FUTURE needs. Ask the class where the most assurance comes from—in the sweepstakes letter, or, in the story of the sparrows?

6. Continuing with what Matthew 10:29–31 teaches make these two main points: (1) It is not that we avoid trial or trouble, but, "nothing ultimately bad can happen to those who are God's children"; and (2) Every individual human being is valuable to God, is more than a statistic or number, and is an object of God's **LOVE** and **CARE**.

7. Refer to the following Scriptures noting what the author says about them: (1) Luke 15:3–6, Parable of the Lost Sheep; and (2) John 10:11–18, The Good Shepherd.

8. Ask class members to focus on doing #1 in the Personal Application section. Ask that at the next session they be prepared to share any special progress they made in deepening a personal relationship.
9. Conclude with the challenge: We can TRUST the ONE who knows our name. It matters that the Christian God exists.

Chapter 4. Is Anyone in Charge?

1. Head in a direction that shows that God gives meaning to life's often unpleasant and "seemingly undesirable" events. Study the life of Joseph from Genesis 37–50, using the passage as a major source of your presentation.
2. Display newspaper clippings that headline tragedy. Then ask if class members would share personal experiences that have led to these questions: Can good things come out of hard situations?; Is there any ". . . meaningful way to think of God as being at work in the unpleasant and seemingly undesirable events of life"?
3. In the Joseph narration, pick up on these negative experiences of Joseph (how did he act, or react?): bitterness (or lack of); jealous brothers; ridicule; ill-treatment by his brothers; sold into slavery; falsely accused of adultery; imprisonment; being forgotten. Emphasize that Joseph's responses make the point that God works ". . . to accomplish his purposes in and through all of the events of life. . . ." He is in charge.
4. Ask the class to picture themselves in Joseph's shoes as you read to them Genesis 37:23–24. Then, reading from Genesis 45:4–5, and 15, ask if they would have reacted as Joseph did when he saw his brothers again years later. Ask: How would today's world act? Put arms around them and kiss them? (See Gen. 45:15; 1 Peter 2:15, 20–24.)
5. Use the following lessons the author draws from the Joseph narration: (1) Being constantly and everywhere active, "God is at work in . . . both the pleasant . . . and the unpleasant"; (2) God has an ultimate goal for us toward which he is working (see Gen. 45:5–8); (3) God is able to use evil for good (Gen. 50:20). Also see Acts 2:36 where an evil act made Jesus Lord and Christ the Savior; (4) We see the difference between the short-range and the long-range results of certain events (see

Teaching Suggestions   227

Gen. 50:20). In the long-range there was "... the saving of many lives. ..."; and (5) Avoid becoming bitter. Ask if the class agrees with the author: "It is in our own interest to forget the wrongs."

6. Stress practical lessons the author draws: (1) Be alert for opportunities for service; (2) Broaden our outlook as to what God can do; (3) Exploit the difficult and watch God work; (4) In "chance experiences" unexpected opportunities come our way without planning.

7. Expand upon the author's thoughts about **blessing through adversity**. Note his personal experiences. Again Joseph is the example here ... point out how.

8. Point out that trusting God is not a natural response. Man's view is that God must always bring good and prevent the bad.

9. For the next session ask the class to study 1 Samuel 1 and 3.

10. The lesson is: **God is at work in everything**. God is **in charge**. It matters that God exists.

Chapter 5. Something Does Not Move

1. On the chalkboard or dri-erase whiteboard draw a line freehand that you think is about twelve inches long and also level. Ask the class what is needed to test your line. Using a twelve-inch ruler and a carpenter's level check your work for accuracy and make corrections if needed. Refer to the ruler and carpenter's level as absolute **standards** necessary to determine the "truth" about the line. So, the pursuit of truth requires **standards**.

2. Finding **TRUTH** may well involve this question that you should also ask the class: Does the discovery of truth have anything to do with whether or not the Christian God exists? Take a poll to see how the class stands on this. Also, call attention to exercise #3 in Key Questions. Point out the revealing statistics of the Barna report. Ask that the class complete exercise #3 and share their answers to the question posed there. Do the class results indicate that **relativism** is alive and well?

3. Point out that relative to the pursuit of moral truth, unless it is tied to a standard by which it can be measured, an answer to what truth is can only at best be: (1) "It all depends"; (2) "One view is as good as another"; (3) "Nothing is absolutely right or wrong"; or, (4) "What is right for one person or time

may be wrong for another person or time." Ask the class: Is there ever a time when these responses are acceptable?

4. Go over the main points of **situation ethics** and then ask the class how they react: (1) There are no absolute rules; (2) There is nothing absolutely good at all times; (3) **One exception**: The only thing that is always good is LOVE; "Always do the most loving thing." (4) Our limited knowledge of all the considerations and circumstances in making specific decisions is a roadblock to belief in absolutes.

5. Ask: "Is truth something 'discovered' or is it 'created'?" Use the illustration of the three baseball umpires. Focus on the umpire who said: "They ain't neither balls nor strikes until I call them." Truth is "relative" to "how I call them." Apply.

6. Create discussion around the question ". . . is there a '**divine perspective**' upon the whole of reality?" Also ask: In a world of many viewpoints coming from limited perspectives, is there something outside of human understanding that can be appealed to as a valid measurement of truth? Ask the class: Is that "something" (someone) the Christian God?

7. Make a "plumb line" by tying a weight to a string at least six feet long. Affix the string above the floor and let the weight hang freely. When the movement stops the string is perfectly perpendicular and one can determine that a wall is straight up. Read the book of Amos. Share the "plumb line" passage (7:7–9) that implies that God's Word renders certain what the truth is.

8. Ask the class: What (Who) is the ONE measuring standard that DOES NOT MOVE? Is it (he) the Christian God? If not, who is it?

9. Ask the class to read Exodus 3 and 4 in preparation for the next session.

10. **Supplementary Scriptures**: Exodus 15:18; Deuteronomy 4:39; Psalms 31:5; 83:18; 105:7; 119:160; Proverbs 8:14; John 1:14, 17; 6:44–51; 17:17; Romans 11:36; 1 Thessalonians 1:9; 1 Timothy 6:15.

Chapter 6. The Universe Right Side Up

1. The issue here is: Are we going to let God be God, or is our belief **conditional** on whether or not God does what we want him to do? **Inverted Theology** puts man "on top" filling the

role of "god." Ask: How do men and women play the role of God? Ask: What does the author mean by, "We believe in God, but conditionally"?

2. Study 1 Samuel 1–3. Point out that Samuel and his mother Hannah had the **right side up**, and let God be God (1 Sam. 1:27–28; 3:10).

3. Break into small groups asking that someone in each group record and later report conclusions to the following: (1) From 1 Samuel 3:10b write the converse response you think might come from today's average churchgoer; (2) list pressures that rest upon anyone who presumes to tell God what he must do for them; (3) From Matthew 16:24–26 create a paraphrase of Jesus' definition of "right side up" theology; and (4) Create a definition of "self-denial" as it relates to "right side up theology."

4. Be sure it is brought out that the converse to Samuel's response in 1 Samuel 3:10b includes: "Listen to ME, Lord, for your servant is speaking to you." Also share the author's definition of "self-denial": ". . . becoming sufficiently self-detached so that one does not feel powerfully one's own needs and desires." "Pressure" in #3 (2) above includes knowledge of self and the future.

5. Point out that a man or woman needs help from outside himself or herself to understand all that is needed to meet life's challenges. Such help is found in such a source as suggested by Matthew 10:29–30.

6. Show that the main principle of "right side up" living is Samuel's principle of prayer and response to God: "Speak, for your servant is listening. . . ." (1 Sam. 3:10b). Jesus seeks the same response but says it a bit differently as seen already in Matthew 16:24.

7. Build a challenge around the author's question: "At what point do we expect God to be God?" Will the answer be: "When he does what we think he should do . . . and does not do what we think he should not do"?

8. Point out that living a "right side up" existence in the universe is, like Samuel, to do the following: (1) Giving God an opportunity to speak to us; (2) Not making God validate our self-chosen directions, but choosing God's directions; and (3) Letting God be God.

9. Develop what the author feels is the "essential issue" here: ". . . that God is really God and we are his servants. We exist to love and serve and glorify him, not vice-versa. And if that is how we were fashioned and created, then that is how we will find our greatest fulfillment and satisfaction in life."
10. **Supplementary Scriptures**: Matthew 6:19–21; 16:25.

Chapter 7. Have You Checked Your I.D. Lately?

1. Ask the class: What would it be like to suffer amnesia? You face the questions: Who am I? Of what value am I?
2. Discuss with the class: **What constitutes identity?** A name? Family relationships? Parents? An address? Include: Am I only the result of a sexual union? Can I only be explained as a "biological occurrence . . ."? Where did I come from?
3. Note that relationships seem to upgrade "birth" and "life" beyond just being "scientific statements." It means something that "this is my daughter . . . my son," and almost a supernatural quality comes into play.
4. Break into small groups asking that someone in each group record and later report conclusions to the following (If time is a factor, assign each group certain ones. You may wish to print them out.): (1) Name several situations in our modern world where one's identity is important; (2) What is necessary for someone to feel he or she is a person and has value? (3) Name some things that are valuable mostly because of their origin; (4) What practices are permitted in society that diminish the value of human life? (5) What do you have to believe about humans in order to believe they have a much greater value than anything else? (6) What would you add to this scientific explanation of what the birth of a human is— ". . . an individual comes into being because of sexual union of a male and a female"? (7) What do these scriptures tell us about why individuals have value (Gen. 9:6; John 3:16; 1 Tim. 2:4; and 2 Peter 3:9); and (8) Does the idea of God as Creator enhance the meaning of "identity"?
5. Read the account of Samuel's mother Hannah in 1 Samuel 1–2 and note her profound understanding of life (1:27–28): "I prayed for this child, and the LORD has granted me what I asked of him . . . now I give him to the LORD . . . For his whole

life he will be given over to the LORD." Samuel did not exist for Hannah's benefit. Relate Christian "identity" with "belonging to God."

6. Show the class some object that has value to you because of who made it. Make a major point out of this statement from the author: "The value we place upon something is related to its origin. Who made it? What is the reputation of the source?" Use the illustration of the Stradivarius violin. Is God the creator of life? (We say he is.)

7. Using a chalkboard or dri-erase whiteboard, write out and discuss the following syllogism: "Everything God does has value; God made me. Therefore, I have value." Included in one's "I.D." is quality and value. It does matter that God exists.

8. Ask the class: How do you see yourselves? (1) Biologically only? Then we are impostors to God; (2) Creatures of God? Made in his image? ". . . to conduct ourselves in the light of this (his image within us) is to find the way of life." It matters that God exists.

9. **Supplementary Scriptures**: 1 Corinthians 6:19–20; 2 Timothy 2:4.

Chapter 8. Is That All There Is?

1. This lesson is about the questions and despair the reality of death brings, and addresses the question: "Is there anything beyond this life that we know and experience?" Ask the class what their questions about death are. Point out that one has not sufficiently assessed life unless he or she has also assessed death. Use 1 Corinthians 15:55–56.

2. Discuss death as a "sting" in the following ways: (1) As **extinction**, bringing into question value and meaning; (2) As **futility**—life ". . . is a tale told by an idiot . . . signifying nothing" (Shakespeare); (3) As **separation**. Will we never again see our loved ones? (4) As **lack of any assurance**. "Suppose there is a supreme being . . . we will meet (and) that if we fall short of his expectations . . . there is nothing we can do after this life ends to fulfill those expectations. . . ."; and (5) As **bringing judgment** for which death cuts off the last opportunity to prepare. (See Eccles. 12:14; Matt. 25:31–46; John 5:22, 27; Acts 17:31; and Rom. 14:11–12.)

3. Plan a TRANSITION that searches out what lies beyond death: (1) The resurrection of Christ creates a basis for expecting that we will find life beyond this life (see 1 Cor. 15:22–23); (2) The apostle Paul taught that death is not the end (see Rom. 8:11; 1 Cor. 6:14; 1 Thess. 4:17); (3) Being made in his image, we are designed to have fellowship with God forever; (4) Eternity will be better . . . we'll have imperishable bodies (see 1 Cor. 15:42–54); (5) Eternity holds for the believer "specialized activities" such as worship, service to the Lord, and a high level of JOY as God is praised, self-respect is restored, and fulfillment is attained; (6) Having found what was "missing," the "living water" is experienced forever (see John 4:13–14); (7) There is something that has supreme value and is forever (see Matt. 6:20; 1 Cor. 15:19, 58); and (8) Grief when losing loved ones is tempered (see 1 Thess. 4:13–18; and David's hope seen in 2 Sam. 12:23).

4. Break into small groups asking that someone in each group record and later report conclusions to the following: (1) Can **real life** be lived apart from full consideration and implications of the **reality of death**? (2) In question #2 above, which "sting of death" do people experience the most? (3) From your personal observation, list three things society teaches or implies that will give meaning to life. Do they work? (4) Believing that death ends any search for meaning, what changes, improvements, or additions would you make for yourself starting today? (5) What Christian doctrine and truths moderate or eliminate the "'sting(s)' of death"? and (6) What is the meaning of being "surprised by joy"?

5. Point out that in God's love, fear of death is diminished. We can be prepared (see Matt. 25:34; John 3:16).

6. **CONCLUSION**: Ask again in rhetorical fashion the question in #1 above. The answer is YES. Point out a paradox: The **ENEMY** (death) is conquered by death (the death of Christ) and what has always brought an "end" now brings us a new beginning into the Lord's eternal presence by the death, burial, and resurrection of Christ.

Chapter 9. Strength Out of Weakness

1. Make a point of "paradox" (Webster): "a statement that is seemingly contradictory . . . and yet is perhaps true." **Illus-**

trate it. Ask class members for illustrations. Then refer to the paradox of this lesson from 2 Corinthians 12:10b: ". . . when I am weak, then I am strong."

2. Emphasize these key questions prompted by the paradox in #1 above: (1) "When we find ourselves weak, is there some way we can find strength within that experience?" (2) What is the first problem the Christian must solve? ". . . first must be discovery of weakness."

3. Illustrate the **self-sufficient** posture of modern society: (1) technological advancement; (2) medical strides; (3) miracles in communications; (4) transportation; and (5) social reform. Ask: "Is there any relationship between a man's weaknesses and his achievements?" Discuss #3 under Key Questions in the study guide.

4. Use David's stand against Goliath as a prominent example of strength out of weakness (see 1 Sam. 17:34–54; esp. vv. 37, 45–47). Find points on David's insufficiencies and God's sufficiencies, and ask how these are implied as you read from the following passages: 2 Samuel 22:1–4, 7, 17–19, 29, 31, 40, 44, 47, 51.

5. Make a point of how inadequacies bring us to the end of our strength. Stress how the Christian God's help comes as "free" and as "sufficient." (Share from Scriptures such as: Pss. 33:18; 46:1; 54:4; Prov. 3:5; Matt. 6:13; John 10:3; Rom. 8:28; 2 Cor. 3:5; 9:8; Eph. 1:3–8; Phil. 4:19; 1 Peter 5:7.)

6. Break up into small groups and appoint a leader for each. Have each group discuss David's circumstances of weakness and need in each of the following passages: (1) 1 Samuel 23:1–5; (2) 2 Samuel 5:19–25; (3) 2 Samuel 11:4–5, 26–27; 12:7–10, 13–14; (4) 2 Samuel 17:22, 28–29; (5) 2 Samuel 8:6b, 14b–15; and (6) implied need in 2 Samuel 22:17–20. If you wish, you can ask for responses.

7. Identify the biggest "insufficiency" man has: "The ability to earn what would bring him assurance of eternal life with God." In other words, "salvation" (see Job 14:14; Ps. 51:5; Prov. 20:9; Isa. 1:4; Rom. 3:23–24; 6:23). Note that God in Christ is the solution (see Rom. 5:1–2, 8–10, 12, 18–19; Gal. 2:16; 4:8; Eph. 3:20).

8. Have one-half the group study Nicodemus's encounter with Jesus (John 3:1–21) and the other half study Paul's conversion

experience (Acts 9:1–19), looking for their **needs** and **insufficiencies** and noting God's provision (see John 3:16; 1 Peter 3:18). Encourage that class members "reach out" beyond themselves to accept Christ as Savior and Lord (see 1 Cor. 15:22; John 1:4).

9. Get back to the questions of #2 (above). Conclude that the Christian God makes sense out of the paradox, "When I am weak, then I am strong." IT DOES MATTER THAT GOD EXISTS.

Chapter 10. Will Evil Finally Win?

1. **ASK: Does America reject EVIL as a reality?** Can we make "value judgments" anymore? Share the author's conclusion about the inherent goodness of humans. Ask what the class believes.

2. What follows is from *Christian Theology*, by Millard J. Erickson, Baker Book House, 1986, pp. 256, 628–30. Use it to assist the class with #3 in the Key Questions section. **Depravity:** ". . . human nature, including reason, has been adversely affected by the fall . . . failure to love, honor, and serve God . . . good and lawful actions cannot be maintained consistently . . . the sinner is . . . unable to extricate himself from his sinful condition. . . ."; (1) **the body:** Romans 6:6, 12; 7:24; 8:10, 13; (2) **the mind and reason:** Romans 1:21; 2 Corinthians 3:14–15; 4:4; and (3) the **emotions:** Romans 1:26–27; Galatians 5:24; 2 Timothy 3:2–4. Explore why **original sin** is an unpopular belief. Point out that in spite of objections to it, "depravity" is easily confirmed in our world today.

3. **TRACE the history that disputes inherent goodness:** The League of Nations following World War I failed; the Holocaust, six million Jews were exterminated; World War II, nearly fifteen million battle deaths; United Nations, quite ineffective; "cold war"; Iron Curtain; Berlin Wall; Communism-Marxism; Korean War; Vietnam; Bosnian Serbs' "ethnic cleansing"; the domestic scene with crime, AIDS, abortion, and homosexuality; and the attempt to solve everything through **education**.

4. Discuss: How has society "attacked" evil by altering the unfavorable environment? Refer the class to exercise #4 in the Key Questions section and ask: "To what extent has human

achievement and the problem-solving approaches of society worked?" Include: welfare reform; public housing; rehabilitation programs; job training; Headstart; sex education; crisis counseling; and affirmative action.

5. Make reference to the modern phenomenon of **SEXUAL FREEDOM**. Study the author's discussion. Stress the ills that result from this "freedom" such as: unmarried (unwanted) teenage pregnancies; sexually transmitted diseases; failed marriages; disillusioned youth; sex "education"; condom distribution in schools; and AIDS.

6. Break into small groups, appointing leaders you will later ask to report conclusions. Study 2 Corinthians 5:16–21 to find (1) an answer to the lesson's title; (2) a mandate for the church to evangelize; (3) hope for and challenge to the sinful; and (4) Christ's role in forgiveness and the demise of evil.

7. **TRANSITION:** God fits in because hope for change lies in something (someone) whose abilities are far beyond human ability. Keep the small groups and have them simultaneously study and discuss these Scriptures to show that: (1) Man is in need (see Job 15:14–16; Pss. 51:5; 94:11; Jer. 17:9; Rom. 5:6, 8; Eph. 2:1; Col. 1:21); (2) Change is possible (see Rom. 8:2; 2 Cor. 5:17; Gal. 1:3; Col. 1:3; 1 John 3:9); and (3) Wrongs will be righted (see Ps. 37:10; Acts 17:31; 2 Cor. 5:17); and (4) God will be triumphant over evil (see Matt. 25:31ff; 1 Cor. 4:8).

Chapter 11. Give Me Liberty or Give Me Death!

1. **ASK THESE LEAD-IN QUESTIONS TO STIMULATE DISCUSSION:** (1) Do humans desire to be in control? Use the quote from Patrick Henry and the last verse of the poem "Invictus." (2) How do most people define "freedom"? Seek class response to #1 in Key Questions section. (3) Can "true freedom" be attained apart from some ". . . voluntary submission . . . to something external (or 'someone')?" Can it be experienced solely by personal skills and energy? If not, what is needed?

2. **ASK: WOULD YOU AGREE WITH THE AUTHOR?** That "free to do" requires a force far greater than is usually available to us. A cause? A concept? An organization? How about a person?

3. Note how "freedom" is limited by certain realities or choices: (1) physical, law of gravity; (2) life expectancy, certain eventual death; (3) good and bad habits, we flourish accordingly; (4) aging, illness; (5) "conformity exchange," e.g., youth "escape" the current "rigid" culture, only to be "enslaved" by the "counter-culture" (dress, hair-style, substance abuse, "gang membership"); (6) choices with irreversible consequences such as: murder and other crimes, abusive behavior, deceitfulness; and (7) surrendering free choice in one area in order to achieve excellence in another (e.g., to qualify for the Olympics).

4. **DISCUSS** the author's view that: Freedom is the ability ". . . to become what (you) potentially could be." This involves: (1) ". . . channeling . . . energy" down useful pathways; and (2) "voluntary submission" to ". . . something external," which brings the Christian God into the picture as the only one capable of enabling a person to realize potential (see Matt. 19:26; John 3:7; 8:32–36; 2 Cor. 3:5b; 5:17; 9:8); and (3) Answering the questions: "What do I wish to become? (undisciplined or God's image?)"; and "Will I insist upon being able to do everything myself, or am I willing to allow someone else to bring out the best in me?"

5. Using a chalkboard or dri-erase whiteboard, demonstrate the path to freedom by printing out this syllogism:
Freedom is reaching my fullest potential;
Only God can make this to come about;
I acknowledge and obey God's will;
THEREFORE: I reach my fullest potential in HIM;
THEREFORE: I AM FREE!

6. **BE SURE TO STRESS**: God used himself as a **MODEL** when he created mankind. "Let us make man in our image . . . in our likeness . . ." (Gen. 1:26). We have the potential to be and act in godly ways. By so doing we are "free" (see Rom. 8:29; 2 Cor. 3:18; Eph. 2:10; 4:21–24; 5:1; Col. 3:8–10).

7. **CONCLUSION**: Does it matter if there is a God? Yes, without him I would not reach my potential no matter how hard I tried. QUOTE THE AUTHOR: "True freedom, in the fullest sense of the word, is not the avoidance and rejection of God, but the seeking of him and acceptance of him." Leave the class with John 8:31–32 stressing that Christ is the Christian God, "God with us" (see Matt. 1:23). Thus, in Christ I am free.

Chapter 12. Getting Out the Spot

1. **POSE THE QUESTION:** How do we handle GUILT? In one of two ways. (1) **The naturalistic approach**: no supreme being who can be wronged; think positively about yourself; only society's standards rule. (2) **The Christian approach**: there is a supreme God who sets the rules; I can "wrong" both him and his creation.
2. **DISCUSS THIS QUESTION:** What counsel does society often give where the need for forgiveness is felt, but where it is not possible to obtain that needed forgiveness?
3. RETURN to a main point of the lesson, "cosmic guilt." If there is a supreme being we have great responsibility to him. If people (society) are (is) the creation of God then society is more than a "contract" between people and has been designed to function by rules and standards originating with God. Other persons can forgive our "wrong" against them (horizontal relationships), but who can forgive our vertical relationship when it goes awry? "That is what only God, if there is one, can do."
4. Draw a pyramid triangle on the chalkboard or on a dri-erase whiteboard. Print "God" outside the angle at its peak. Outside the base angles print "My neighbor" at one point and "Society" at the opposite point. Discuss how this illustrates that, if the Creator God exists, we have responsibilities for obedient actions toward God (our vertical responsibility) and toward humankind (our horizontal responsibility). The existence of the Creator God implies responsibility that if not fulfilled generates guilt.
5. Use the example of David, Bathsheba, and Uriah to illustrate how wrongs are both against God and man (use Exod. 20:13–14, 17; 2 Sam. 11:1–27; 12:1–14; Ps. 51, esp. v. 4).
6. Break into small groups and appoint a leader for each. Have each group look up Scriptures and discuss the following: (1) The apostle Paul considered himself "exceedingly righteous" before he met Christ (see Phil. 3:4–6). What was his attitude after he had walked with Christ (see Phil. 3:7–11; 1 Tim. 1:15)? (2) Describe the emotions and desires present when David faced his guilt of murder and adultery (see 2 Sam. 12:13a; Ps. 51:1–12); (3) What do the Scriptures reveal about the one who can "take out the spots" (see Ps. 103:8–10, esp. v. 12; Isa. 1:18; Luke 7:47–48; 1 John 4:19)?

7. Discuss the "complete" forgiveness of God and the mandate that man must forgive in the same manner as does God: (1) Use the parable of the lost sheep in Matthew 18:10–14 (see also Neh. 9:17b; Ps. 103:12; Col. 2:13); (2) Jesus' mandate to forgive (Matt. 6:14–15; 18:21–35, esp. v. 35); (3) Peter is not "ousted" from the fellowship because of a moment of faltering faith (Mark 14:66–72; 16:7; John 21:15–18); and (4) God's forgiveness cancels out any supposed disqualification from the Lord's service (see 1 Cor. 15:9–10; Heb. 8:12).
8. Point out that experiencing God's complete forgiveness should result in love for and service to him (see 2 Cor. 5:13–15; 1 John 4:19).
9. YES, it matters that there is a God. The "spot" of guilt is "washed clean" by the forgiveness of God (see Heb. 9:14).

Chapter 13. So What?

1. The author skillfully likens the decision about whether or not it matters if there is a God to the "wager." Explain the concept of the "wager" in terms of the relationship between choices and their consequences. Give illustrations.
2. **MAKE MUCH OF THE KEY VERSE:** Matthew 16:26. "For what will it profit a man if he gains the whole world and forfeits his soul? Or what shall a man give in return for his soul?" Ask: What are you planning to gain by saying "It does not matter if God exists"; or, "By believing that God exists (and you accept him) what consequences will you avoid?" What are you "betting on"? A living God? No God?
3. Make it clear what it is that a person is "wagering" with regard to the claims of Christ, and ask what risks the class members are willing to take if they do not believe him. Wagering that:
   (1) He is or is not God (see John 3:31; Phil. 2:6; Col. 2:9; Titus 2:13; 1 John 5:20).
   (2) He is or is not the Savior and Lord of the world (see Luke 19:10; John 4:42; 2 Cor. 5:19).
   (3) He is or is not the only pathway to God (see 1 John 2:23).
   (4) He either does or doesn't give everlasting life (see John 3:16).
   (5) He is or isn't head of the church (see Eph. 2:19; 5:23).

(6) He is either an impostor and fraud, or who he said he was.

(7) He is either "God with us," or he is a deranged megalomaniac (see Matt. 1:23).

4. Give a challenge to the skeptic: Pray this prayer: Lord Jesus, if you really exist, and the Bible is your message, please enable me to conquer my unbelief.

5. Read the story of the healing of a boy with an evil spirit in Mark 9:14–26. Stress what the father said when Jesus asked him if he believed (v. 24): ". . . I do believe; help me overcome my unbelief." Use this as an encouragement to class members.

6. **DOES IT MATTER IF GOD EXISTS?** We have learned that God's existence matters for the following reasons:

(1) His existence answers a haunting question in the breasts of honest seekers: Is there any meaning to my existence?

(2) I now have the standard by which to measure all claims to truth. God's truth is the "plumb line."

(3) I need not question nor fear my tomorrows. "I am" means the God who "will be" in my future as well as my present.

(4) Somebody knows my name. God made me in his image.

(5) I know somebody is in charge.

(6) He is sovereign, not me or society.

(7) I have an IDENTITY. I am more than a number.

(8) Death does not "end it all." Life is "forever."

(9) My weaknesses make me dependent on another's strength.

(10) Evil is not going to win.

(11) I am truly free when I am enslaved to the one (God) who leads me toward my full potential.

(12) There is a forgiveness that "gets out the spots."